Microsoft®
Windows®
Shell Script
Programming
for the absolute beginner™

To Alexander, William, Molly, and Mary.

Acknowledgments

A number of individuals deserve credit for their work on this book. I especially want to thank Todd Jensen, who served as the book's acquisitions editor and who has worked with me on numerous other writing projects. I also want to thank the book's project editor and copy editor, Dan Foster, for his guidance and suggestions. Finally, I want to acknowledge the book's technical editor and CD-ROM developer, Keith Davenport, as well as everyone else at Premier Press for all their hard work.

About the Author

Jerry Lee Ford, Jr. is an author, educator, and IT professional with over 15 years of experience in information technology, including roles as an automation analyst, technical manager, technical support analyst, automation engineer, and security analyst. Jerry is a MCSE and has earned Microsoft's MCP and MCP+ Internet certifications. In addition, he has a master's degree in Business Administration from Virginia Commonwealth University in Richmond, Virginia.

Jerry is the author of 12 other books, including *Learn JavaScript in a Weekend*, *Learn VBScript in a Weekend*, *Microsoft Windows Shell Scripting and WSH Administrator's Guide*, *VBScript Professional Projects*, and *Microsoft Windows XP Professional Administrator's Guide*.

He has over 5 years of experience as an adjunct instructor teaching networking courses in Information Technology. Jerry lives in Richmond, Virginia, with his wife, Mary, and their children, William, Alexander, and Molly.

Contents at a Glance

Contents

Windows Shell Scripting Basics 57

CHAPTER 4

Storing and Retrieving Information in Variables 87

CHAPTER 5

Applying Conditional Logic 123

Creating Loops to Process Collections of Data 155

Creating Procedures and Subroutines 201

Debugging and Error Handling 241

APPENDIX

Windows Shell Scripting Administrative Scripts 297

APPENDIX

What's on the CD-ROM? 341

APPENDIX C What Next?   349

Letter from the Series Editor

At some point, you've probably begun to want more control of your computer. You may want to make programs act a little bit differently than the default behavior, automate tedious tasks, or perform certain jobs automatically. Ultimately, such tasks come down to programming. The programming world can be very intimidating, with all the integrated environments, complex languages, and dizzying variety of resources. Programming looks hard, and, frankly, it looks boring.

In this book, Jerry Lee Ford will show you how to control your computer in amazing ways. You'll learn some relatively easy tricks that will profoundly improve the way you work with your computer, and you'll learn the basics of the programming art along the way. Windows shell scripting is not the most complex programming environment, and that's a major part of its charm. This reasonably clean language is ideal for beginners precisely because it is so focused.

While shell scripting is extremely useful, that doesn't mean learning about it has to be dry and boring. Like all the books in this series, this book teaches through simple game programming. Nobody's going to use Windows shell scripting to write the next immersive 3-D action game, but games can be an interesting way to learn about the process of writing more traditional programs. Don't worry, there will be lots of practical examples as you go through this book.

If you're new to programming, you won't find a better place to start than this book. If you're already an experienced programmer, you'll be amazed at how you can use the skills in this book to leverage your abilities. Regardless, you'll learn a lot and have a good time doing it.

Andy Harris

For the Absolute Beginner Series Editor

Introduction

Windows shell scripting is a built-in scripting language found on modern Windows operating systems. It provides the ability to create and run small programs or Windows script files made up of Windows shell script statements and Windows commands. Windows shell scripts are created as plain text files that are saved with .bat or .cmd file extensions and run from the Windows command prompt.

Windows shell scripts are often small files that can be created and tested within minutes. In fact, many good Windows shell scripts are less than 10 or 15 lines long. This makes it a perfect language for quickly automating Windows tasks. This also makes Windows shell scripting a great first language to learn.

Unlike many modern program languages, Windows shell scripting is not object oriented. In addition, it does not require you to first learn how to operate a complex development environment. However, Windows shell scripting does have a complete collection of statements—the elements that make up its programming language. This allows first-time programmers to focus on learning the basics of program design without being burdened with the added requirements imposed by many other programming languages.

Windows shell scripts also provide a way to automate complex tasks, especially those prone to human error. Once created, Windows shell scripts can be shared with other people, allowing you to distribute and share your work. Using Windows shell scripts, you can access and manipulate Windows resources such as the Windows file system and disk and printer resources, and you can even automate the execution of network tasks. In addition, as this book will demonstrate, you can create Windows shell scripts that automate and control the execution of all kinds of things. For example, this book will show you how to create Windows shell scripts that

- Play computer games like Rock, Paper, Scissors and Tic-Tac-Toe.
- Copy and move files and folders.
- Establish connections to network resources such as network disk drives and folders.
- Create text reports and log files.

- Execute Windows utilities such as the Windows Disk Defragmenter.
- Create user accounts and administer group account membership.
- Control third-party applications such as WinZip.

Why Windows Shell Scripting?

Windows shell scripting is a great language for developing small scripts that auto-mate commonly performed tasks. At the same time, you can use it to create some incredibly complex scripts. However, in most cases you will find that most Windows shell scripts are not very large. Often Windows shell scripts are only a fraction of the size of programs written in higher-level languages such as Visual Basic and C++. This reduces complexity and results in shorter development time. It also makes Windows shell scripting a great tool for rapid development, allowing you to quickly create and test scripts and then move on to other work.

Windows shell scripting makes an excellent first programming language. As far as programming languages go, it is straightforward and easy to learn. Yet, using Windows shell scripting you can learn even the most complex programming concepts. All that you need to begin creating Windows shell scripts is a plain text editor such as Windows Notepad.

By learning Windows shell scripting, you will begin to build a foundation for learning other programming languages. Once you have mastered Windows shell scripting you may wish to tackle other scripting languages such as VBScript or JScript, both of which can be used to perform advanced shell scripting on Windows computers. You may also want to use Windows shell scripting as a jumping off point for more advanced object-oriented programming languages like Visual Basic and C++. The bottom line is that learning how to use Windows shell scripts will give you a foundation that will facilitate learning other programming languages.

Who Should Read This Book?

I have designed this book to teach you how to become a programmer using Windows shell scripting. A previous programming background is not required. However, you will need a basic understanding of computers in general and a good overall working knowledge of at least one Microsoft operating system.

So whether you are a first-time programmer looking for a good language to learn as you begin your programming career or you are looking to quickly learn a second programming language, this book can help you. In addition, I think you will find that this book's games-based approach will help to keep things fun as you learn.

What You Need to Begin

To use this book effectively, you will need a number of things. First, you will need a Windows operating system that supports Windows shell scripting. These operating systems include

- Windows NT 4.0
- Windows 2000
- Windows XP
- Windows 2003

You will also need an editor that supports the creation of plain text files. As a starter editor, you can begin working with the Windows Notepad text editor. However, over time you will probably find that Notepad is rather limited, and you will want to use a more advanced editor that supports features like syntax color-coding and advanced search-and-replace features. To help you out, I have included two excellent editors on this book's companion CD-ROM. To learn more about these two editors, check out Appendix B, "What's on the CD-ROM?"

How This Book Is Organized

I wrote this book based on the assumption that you would read it sequentially, from beginning to end. If this is your first programming experience or if you feel that you need a programming refresher, I suggest that you read the book in this manner. If you are a veteran programmer and intend to learn Windows shell scripting as an additional language, you may want to skip around and read topics that are of the most interest to you.

The first part of this book introduces you to Windows shell scripting. It provides an overview of Windows shell scripting and the Windows command prompt.

The second part of this book teaches you the basics of Windows shell script development. It covers how to display script output and how to use comments and variables. It also covers the shell script statements that provide the ability to apply conditional logic and establish loops.

The third part of this book focuses in on a variety of advanced topics. Here I'll show you how to improve the organization of your Windows shell scripts using procedures and subroutines. I'll also go over the steps involved in debugging and handling script errors.

The final part of this book contains the book's appendixes. Here you will find a collection of real-world sample scripts, information about the materials found on the book's CD-ROM, and information about places where you can go to continue your Windows shell scripting education.

A detailed breakdown of the information you will find in this book is outlined below.

- **Chapter 1—Introducing Windows Shell Scripting.** This chapter explains what Windows shell scripting is and why it is an excellent first programming language to learn. This chapter provides a brief history of Windows shell scripting as well as a comparison to Microsoft's other scripting technology, the Windows Script Host, and explains the differences between these two scripting solutions. This chapter closes by teaching you how to write your first Windows shell script by showing you how to develop your first Windows shell script game, the Knock Knock joke.

- **Chapter 2—Interacting with the Windows Shell.** This chapter provides you with a review of the Windows shell and explains how to work with it (e.g., starting a new shell, issuing commands, and closing the shell). The chapter goes on to discuss how to work with the Windows command prompt and explains basic command syntax. Specific commands that affect the appearance of the Windows command console are then reviewed. This will lead into a discussion on command console customization. Finally, the chapter concludes by showing you how to write a script called the Unpredictable Command Prompt.

- **Chapter 3—Windows Shell Scripting Basics.** In this chapter, I will provide you with a review of basic Windows shell scripting techniques, including how to control the display of output and how to format the display using blank lines. I will discuss the importance of creating a documentation template. This chapter will also show you how to control shell input and output and how to redirect command output in order to create report and log files. This chapter will also show you how to create the Fortune Teller game, which answers questions asked of it by the player.

- **Chapter 4—Storing and Retrieving Information in Variables.** This chapter shows you how to write scripts that accept and process argument input at run time. You will also learn how to retrieve information about your computer from system variables. You will then learn about the rules that apply to the creation of variables. This chapter will also demonstrate different ways to manipulate the value of numeric variables as well as how to access all or a portion of text stored in string variables. The chapter will end by teaching you how to create "The Story of Buzz the Wonder Dog" game, which creates a customized story based on information it collects from the user.

- **Chapter 5—Applying Conditional Logic.** In this chapter, you will learn how to apply conditional logic in your scripts. This will enable you to create scripts that can collect and test the value of data and then alter the way the script executes depending on the value of the data. You will also learn how to develop more complicated logic by nesting one logical test within another. This chapter concludes by introducing the Guess a Number game, in which the player is challenged to guess a number between 1 and 32,000 using the fewest possible guesses.

- **Chapter 6—Creating Loops to Process Collections of Data.** This chapter covers the creation of loops as a means of processing large amounts of data. It will demonstrate how to use loops to process string contents, command output, and file and folder contents. This chapter also introduces you to the use of pseudo code as a tool for establishing a high-level script design. This chapter ends by teaching you how to create the Six-Million-Dollar Quiz game. In this game, the player is presented with a series of quiz questions that, once answered, are graded and used to generate a game score card report file.

- **Chapter 7—Creating Procedures and Subroutines.** This chapter introduces you to the use of flowcharts as a design tool. It also shows you how to execute one script from within another script. The chapter also covers the use of procedures and subroutines, which enable you to improve script organization while also reducing complexity. This chapter concludes by covering the development of the Rock, Paper, Scissors game.

- **Chapter 8—Debugging and Error Handling.** In this final chapter, I'll introduce you to a number of different topics. I'll give you tips on how to develop your script in a modular fashion and how to test your scripts one module at a time. You'll also learn how to test intermediate results during script development and testing. Things constantly change on a computer system, and as a result your scripts may break or experience problems over time. To deal with these situations, I'll provide you with some basic debugging techniques and give you advice that will help you to detect and deal with script errors. This chapter will end by stepping you through the development of one final game project called Tic-Tac-Toe.

- **Appendix A—Windows Shell Scripting Administrative Scripts.** This appendix provides you with a collection of practical examples that demonstrate the use of Windows shell scripting in real-world situations. I included this appendix to assist you in making a transition from the book's game-based approach to real-world script development.

- **Appendix B—What's on the CD-ROM?** In this appendix, I'll supply you with information about the sample scripts that you will find on the book's accompanying CD-ROM. I'll also provide you with a freeware copy of the EditPad Lite text editor and a shareware copy of the EditPad Pro text editor along with a brief overview of what these two editors can do.

- **Appendix C—What Next?** In this appendix, I give you advice on how to continue your Windows shell scripting education. I'll include references to other books that I think you will find useful, and I'll also provide you with information about a number of Web sites where you'll find more information, including plenty of free sample scripts that you can download.

- **Glossary.** This unit provides you with a glossary of the key terms used throughout the book.

This book uses computer game development as a means of teaching you how to program using Windows shell scripting. Each game you encounter will be a little more complex than the one before it. In the first few chapters, you'll see scripts that will include elements not yet covered in that point of the book. For these scripts, you'll need to keep reading with the understanding that everything you see will eventually be explained. Meanwhile, I will provide you with as much information as I can without overwhelming you in the early stages of the book.

Conventions Used in This Book

To make it easier for you to read and work with, this book uses a number of conventions. These conventions are described below.

 HINT As you read along, I'll offer suggestions for different or better ways of doing things that will help make you a better and more efficient programmer.

 TRAP I'll also point out places where it's easy to make mistakes, and I'll give you advice for avoiding them.

 TRICK Whenever possible, I'll share shortcuts and techniques that will make things easier for you.

 DEFINITION To aid your understanding, I'll define key terms along the way. (You can also refer to the glossary in this book for additional information.)

IN THE REAL WORLD

Throughout the book, I'll stop along the way to point out how the knowledge and techniques you are learning can be applied to real-world scripting projects.

EXERCISES

At the end of every chapter, I'll include a collection of small project suggestions that you can do to continue building on the skills you've learned.

Introducing Windows Shell Scripting

indows shell scripting is one of two scripting solutions provided by Microsoft for developing small programs, or scripts, that automate a variety of tasks on Windows computers. (The other scripting solution is known as the Microsoft Windows Script Host, or WSH.) Scripts provide a means of developing small utility programs that automate mundane or complex tasks with a minimal investment of time and effort.

Windows shell scripting provides a way to perform tasks on Windows computers without requiring you to wade though the array of windows and dialogs boxes that make up the Windows graphical user interface, or GUI. Scripts help to eliminate typing mistakes or other errors that often occur when you perform a task manually. Therefore, scripts not only help you work faster but more accurately as well, especially when you're working on tasks comprised of a large number of steps. In this chapter, I'll introduce you to Windows shell scripting and provide you with the background information you'll need for the rest of the book. In addition, I'll show you how to develop your first Windows shell script game.

Specifically, you will learn

- **The capabilities of Windows shell scripts**

- **The history of Windows shell scripting**

- **The differences between Windows shell scripts and the Windows Script Host**

- **How to configure the script development and testing environment**

Project Preview: The Knock Knock Joke

This chapter, like all other chapters in this book, concludes by showing you how to develop a computer game using Windows shell scripting. The game you will learn to write in this chapter is called the Knock Knock joke. By going through the steps required to develop this game, you will learn the basic mechanics involved in creating and running Windows shell scripts.

The Knock Knock joke is a simple script as far as game-based Windows shell scripts go. You will run it by opening the Windows command prompt, typing in the name of the script, and pressing the Enter key. The script will respond by displaying the opening Knock Knock message, as shown in Figure 1.1. The user must then type "Who is there?" (including the opening and closing quotation marks) and press Enter. The script will respond by displaying the reply of Orange. The user must then type "Orange Who?" as shown in Figure 1.2.

DEFINITION The Windows *command prompt* appears, by default, in the form of a drive letter followed by a colon, the backslash character, and then the "greater than" symbol (for example, C:\>). The command prompt accepts text input that is passed to the operating system for processing.

Finally, the script displays the joke's punch line as shown in Figure 1.3. If the player makes a typo when entering one of the required responses to the joke, one of the two messages shown in Figure 1.4 and 1.5 will be displayed.

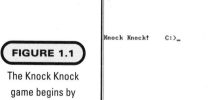

FIGURE 1.1

The Knock Knock game begins by displaying a *Knock Knock* message.

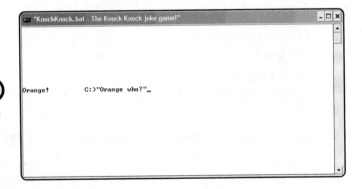

FIGURE 1.2

The game prompts the player to respond to the second part of the joke.

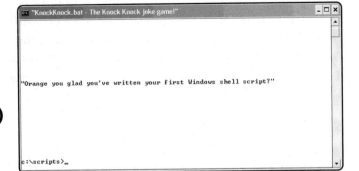

FIGURE 1.3

The game delivers the joke's punch line.

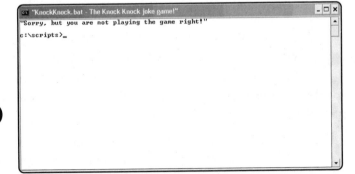

FIGURE 1.4

The game notifies the player of any incorrect input.

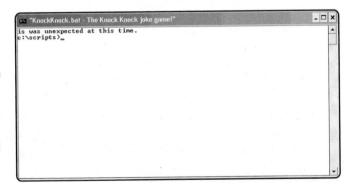

FIGURE 1.5

With incorrect player input, the game may prematurely exit and generate an error message.

Don't worry about trying to understand every line of code that you'll type into the script; you'll learn what everything means as you read through this book. The important thing to learn in this chapter are the steps involved in creating and saving your first script. By completing this script, you will prepare yourself for the more advanced programming concepts introduced in later chapters.

Overview of Windows Shell Scripting

In the very early days of Windows operating systems, there was no point-and-click graphical user interface. Everything was done via the keyboard by typing in commands at the Windows command prompt. This meant that users had to memorize all kinds of commands in order to use their computers. Worse still, most Windows commands could be entered using a number of variations, making it virtually impossible to memorize all possible commands. Naturally, this meant that people spent a lot of time looking up commands. Often users found that they needed to type the same set of commands over and over again. To make this easier and to eliminate typing errors, users and administrators created batch files. A *batch file* is a plain-text file made up of the same Windows commands that you type in at the Windows command prompt. Batch files have a .bat file extension. They are executed by typing in their name at the command prompt and pressing the Enter key. The operating system then executes each command in the batch file, one at a time, starting at the beginning of the file.

In the early 1980s, Microsoft introduced its graphical user interface and most users happily left behind all memory of Windows commands and the command prompt. However, batch files still remained valuable tools for automating the execution of collections of commands and utilities, and were especially useful to power users and administrators.

Batch files remained limited to sequential Windows command execution. The only alternatives available to batch files were manually executing commands at the Windows command prompt, purchasing an application written to perform equivalent set tasks, or writing a custom program using an advanced programming language such as C or C++ to create a new custom application capable of performing the required tasks.

As I'm sure you must be thinking, none of these three options was very practical. They required either too much money or more time than users and administrators were willing to spend. Finally, in the early 1990s, Microsoft introduced Windows NT. This Microsoft operating system featured a built-in scripting language known as Windows shell scripting. Windows shell scripting differed from old-style batch files in that it featured a complete set of programming statements, thus allowing for the development of scripts that included support for conditional logic, iterative logic, and the storage and retrieval of data using computer memory.

The term *conditional logic* refers to a script's ability to examine data and then adjust what it does based on the results of a conditional analysis.

The term *iterative logic* refers to a script's ability to repeatedly execute a series of steps over and over again.

A *statement* is a line of code. Most statements fit on a single line; however, lengthy statements can be spread over multiple lines.

Microsoft has since added support for Windows shell scripting to all Windows operating systems that have been built on Windows NT technology (e.g., Windows 2000, XP, and 2003).

While the collection of programming statements that make up the Windows shell script language has remained essentially the same over the years, a few of the statements have been modified to extend their functionality. Rather than attempt to identify and examine differences in Windows shell scripting statements between each of the different Windows operating systems, this book uses Windows XP as its assumed development platform.

If you plan on writing scripts that will be executed by older Windows operating systems, you should retest the scripts on each operating system to make sure that they work as you expect them to. In addition, you can check any Windows command's syntax to see what syntax it supports on a given operating system by accessing the Windows command prompt and typing the name of the command followed by a space and the word HELP.

Windows shell scripts are saved with a .bat ("batch") or .cmd ("command") file extension. This way, when the operating system is asked to run them, it will know to execute them using the Windows shell.

The *.cmd* file extension is another file extension that Windows associates with Windows shell scripts.

What Can Shell Scripts Do?

Windows shell scripts can accomplish any task that can be completed from the Windows command prompt. Despite continual efforts to improve the Windows graphical user interface and to make things easier for users by providing only a complete point-and-click experience, Microsoft has continued to update and expand the Windows command line functionality (e.g., each new Windows operating system adds new commands and refines existing commands).

Microsoft also adds command line access to many of its utility programs, allowing them to be accessed and controlled by scripts. For example, the Defragmenter utility (which reorganizes files stored on your disk drive for more efficient storage) can be run from the Windows graphical user interface on Windows XP by selecting Start, All Programs, Accessories, System Tools, and then Disk Defragmenter. Alternatively, you can execute this utility program from within a Windows shell script. For example, by typing defrag C: /f you can automate the defragmentation of your computer's C drive using this utility.

Windows shell scripts can be used to automate all of the following categories of tasks:

- **Complicated tasks**. This category of scripted tasks includes any tasks that are highly subject to error when performed manually, such as the administration of system resources like disk drives and printers.
- **Repetitive tasks**. These scripted tasks include any tasks that must be performed over and over again, such as the deletion of certain file types from specific folders on a regular basis.
- **Lengthy tasks**. These scripted tasks include any tasks that take too long to perform manually, such as the creation of a few hundred new user accounts.
- **Scheduled tasks**. These scripted tasks include any tasks that must be run during off hours, at times when users and administrators are not using their computers (such as the Disk Defragmenter utility).

You can develop Windows shell scripts that perform an assortment of different tasks on Windows computers. Once completed, these scripts will help you work faster and be more productive. For example, using Windows shell scripts, you can

- Collect and display information about your computer
- Manage Windows services
- Manage shared folders and drives
- Automate the creation of new user accounts
- Create output files and reports
- Process data stored in input files

- Create and manage scheduled tasks
- Manage local and network printers
- Set up connections to network folders and drives
- Execute Windows commands or command line utilities

Supported Microsoft Operating Systems

As mentioned previously, Windows shell scripting is supported on Windows NT, 2000, XP, and 2003. However, other Microsoft operating systems do not support it. These other operating systems include Windows 95, 98, and Me. Of course, you can still use old-style batch files to automate the execution of small collections of commands on the operating systems, but the ability to add programmatic logic on the level of Windows shell scripts is still missing. If you need to develop scripts for these operating systems, you will need to look at other alternative scripting languages, which I'll cover in the following sections.

Alternatives to Windows Shell Scripting

While Windows shell scripting may be the easiest scripting language to learn, there are plenty of alternative scripting languages available from Microsoft and other third-party software developers. Below, I briefly discuss some of these other scripting languages. However, if you are new to programming, I recommend that you first master Windows shell scripting before you consider moving on and trying to learn the somewhat more complicated scripting languages.

The Windows Script Host

The Windows Script Host, or WSH, provides Microsoft operating systems with an advanced script *execution environment*. Using WSH, you can develop scripts that can execute on any Windows operating systems starting with Windows 95. This means that unlike Windows shell scripts, which run only on Windows NT, 2000, XP, and 2003, WSH scripts can also run on computers that use Windows 95, 98, or Me (provided that WSH is installed on these computers). The WSH runs as an add-on to the Windows operating system and can be enabled or disabled. By default, WSH is installed and enabled on Windows 2000, XP, and 2003.

DEFINITION The term *execution environment* refers to the grouping of resources that scripts require in order to execute, such as a script interpreter that translates script statements into instructions that the computer can execute.

WSH Advantages and Disadvantages

When deciding whether it is better to use Windows shell scripting or the WSH to automate a task, there are a number of criteria to consider. WSH provides a more comprehensive execution environment with direct access to many resources that are not directly accessible to Windows shell scripts. For example, a WSH script can write messages to Windows event logs or read and write to the Windows registry. Therefore, if your scripts will need to access these resources, using the WSH may make more sense. However, a great many tasks never require access to such resources, thus negating these WSH advantages.

 The Windows *application event log* is a log file maintained by the Windows NT, 2000, XP, and 2003 operating systems where application errors and messages are recorded for later audit and review.

 The Windows *registry* is a special built-in database that is a part of all Windows operating systems, starting with Windows 95, where configuration information is stored regarding system, application, hardware, and users settings.

To use the WSH you need to know how to write scripts using at least one scripting language, such as VBScript or JScript. You also have to learn how to work with the WSH execution environment.

Typically, it makes more sense to use the WSH to create scripts when

- You have expertise with another scripting language such as VBScript or JScript and need access to a programming feature provided by these languages only

- You need to run your scripts on Windows operating systems other than Windows NT, 2000, XP, and 2003

IN THE REAL WORLD

If you have access to the Windows Resource Kit for the operating systems for which you are developing scripts, you can often use command line utilities provided by the Resource Kit to indirectly access system resources. For example, using the LOGEVENT command line utility you can write to the Windows application event log from within a Windows shell script. Similarly, using the REG command line utility, you can access and change information stored in the Windows registry. To learn more about Windows Resource Kits, visit www.microsoft.com/windows/reskits/default.asp.

- You cannot find a Windows or Resource Kit command or command line utility that can perform a specific task
- You need to communicate directly with users via graphical pop-up dialogs
- You need to work directly with other applications such as Microsoft Word or Excel
- You need to perform advanced file and folder administration

In contrast, you may want to work with Windows shell scripting when

- You are writing a script that will run on Windows NT, 2000, XP, or 2003
- You know of a command or command line utility that can perform the desired task
- You do not have expertise with a WSH-compatible scripting language
- You want to automate the execution of Windows command or command line utilities
- You want to execute a collection of Windows commands repeatedly

WSH Complexities

In order to write scripts that work with the WSH, you must first learn how to write scripts using a WSH supported scripting language. By default, the WSH provides support for VBScript and JScript. *VBScript* is a scripting language that consists of a subset of the Visual Basic programming language. *JScript* is Microsoft's WSH-compatible version of Netscape's JavaScript scripting language. In addition, you can use third-party WSH-compatible scripting languages that allow the WSH to run scripts written in the Perl, Python, and REXX scripting languages.

Unlike Windows shell scripts, these other scripting languages involve learning how to use language-specific statements and commands, many of which are not very Windows like. Therefore it takes longer to master these languages. In addition to learning how to develop scripts using a different scripting language, you must also learn how to work with the WSH object model in order to develop WSH scripts. The WSH core object model provides access to Windows resources such as printers, drives, files, and folders by representing them as objects that scripts can access and manipulate programmatically. The WSH object model is complex and requires a great deal of time and effort to master. First-time programmers are better off learning how to write Windows shell scripts. The Windows shell scripting language uses familiar Windows commands and does not require mastery of an object model, thus allowing first-time programmers to focus on learning core programming concepts and logic without the requirement of learning advanced concepts. In addition, Windows shell scripting provides an excellent platform for jumping over to other more advanced scripting and programming languages.

Third-Party Scripting Languages

In addition to Windows shell scripting and the WSH, you can also develop scripts on Windows based computers using any of a number of third-party scripting languages. One scripting language that you could use is Perl. *Perl* stands for *Practical Extraction and Reporting Language*. Perl started out as a scripting language for the UNIX operating system where it was originally used to read and extract information from text files and to create new reports.

Compared to Windows shell scripting, Perl is a complicated scripting language to master, especially as a first language. Over the years, support for Perl has been added to most major operating systems. Perl can be used as a WSH-compatible scripting language, allowing you to create Perl scripts that leverage the strengths of the WSH.

Another scripting language with a UNIX heritage that has been ported to Windows is Python. *Python* was named after the comedic troupe Monty Python. Python enjoys enormous support among Linux users and is generally considered easier to learn than Perl. A version of Python is available that is compatible with the WSH. However, compared to Windows shell scripting, it is still a difficult first language to master.

Another scripting language available to Windows users and administrators is REXX. *REXX* stands *for Restructured Extended Extractor language*. REXX was originally developed as a mainframe scripting language. IBM later made it the built-in scripting language on its OS/2 operating system. Today, there are numerous versions of REXX available for Windows.

Understanding the Windows Shell

To become an effective Windows shell script programmer, you must become intimately familiar with the Windows shell. The Windows shell is a text-based interface to the Windows operating system as opposed to the Windows desktop, which is a GUI-based interface. Figure 1.6 depicts the Windows shell and its relationship to the operating system and the user.

The Windows shell is accessed through the Windows command console. The Windows shell accepts user commands and translates them into a format that can be processed by the operating system. It then displays any output returned by the operating system back in the Windows command console.

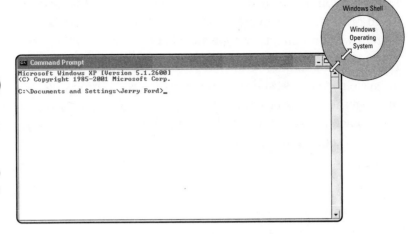

FIGURE 1.6

The Windows shell accepts input from the Windows command console and translates it into a format that can be used by the operating system.

Users type commands at the Windows command prompt. To communicate with the Windows shell, you must open up a Windows command console (as shown in Figure 1.7) by clicking on Start, All Programs, Accessories, and then Command Prompt.

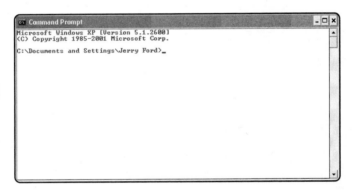

FIGURE 1.7

The Windows console provides access to the Windows command prompt.

HINT

You can also start up a new Windows command console session by clicking on Start, Run, and then typing CMD and clicking on OK.

By default, the Windows command console is set up to display data that is 80 characters wide and 25 lines tall. However, you can modify the height and width of the Windows command console to suit your own preferences. At the top of the console, you'll see a blinking underscore character. This is the command prompt's way of telling you that it is ready to receive input.

HINT

I'll show you how to configure the Windows console in Chapter 2, "Interacting with the Windows Shell." If you can't wait to see how it's done, then jump ahead to Chapter 2 and read "Customizing the Windows Command Console."

To send a command to the Windows shell for processing, type it in at the command prompt and press the Enter key. For example, to display the contents of the current working directory, type DIR and press Enter.

The Windows shell then translates the DIR command into a format that the operating system can understand. The operating system processes the command by putting together a list of the contents of the current working directory, which it then passes back to the Windows shell. The Windows shell displays the listing in the Windows command console. It then redisplays the command prompt in order to allow you to type additional command input as demonstrated below.

```
C:\Documents and Settings\Jerry Ford>dir

 Volume in drive C is IBMDOS_6

 Volume Serial Number is 2B6A-58F8


 Directory of C:\Documents and Settings\Jerry Ford


11/10/2003  01:29 PM    <DIR>          .

11/10/2003  01:29 PM    <DIR>          ..

11/10/2003  01:38 PM    <DIR>          My Documents

11/10/2003  01:38 PM    <DIR>          Favorites

11/10/2003  01:02 PM    <DIR>          Desktop

11/10/2003  01:02 PM    <DIR>          Start Menu

12/03/2003  11:47 PM    <DIR>          WINDOWS

               0 File(s)              0 bytes

               7 Dir(s)     153,255,936 bytes free


C:\Documents and Settings\Jerry Ford> _
```

DEFINITION   **The term *current working directory* refers to the Windows folder that the Windows command console is currently focused on. By default, Windows XP sets the current working directory to the user's own Documents and Settings folder.**

Assembling Your First Windows Shell Script

Now let's examine the steps involved in creating, saving, and executing a Windows shell script. The best way to learn how to do this is by working though an example. The example that I'll show you will only be one line long; however, regardless of the size of your scripts, the same process is used each time to create, save, and run them.

First, begin by opening your editor. For example, to use Windows Notepad you would click on Start, All Programs, Accessories, and then Notepad. Notepad opens and displays an empty file. Type the following line into Notepad (as shown in Figure 1.8).

```
Echo Hello World!
```

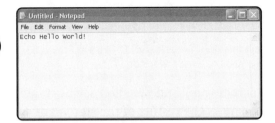

FIGURE 1.8

Using Notepad to create your first Windows shell script.

IN THE REAL WORLD

Unlike many programming languages, Windows shell scripting does not require you to first learn how to use a complicated GUI-based development environment to write scripts. Instead, you can create Windows shell scripts using any editor that can save your files as plain text. However, there are advantages to using GUI-based script editors. These advantages include

- **Statement color-coding of Windows shell script keywords to make code more readable**

- **Line numbering to make locating a specific line easier**

- **Advanced find and replace capabilities**

- **Automatic indenting and outdenting of statements to make code more readable**

- **The ability to manage multiple scripts as a single project**

Fortunately, a number of third-party text and script editors include these advanced features. I have provided two excellent editors on this book's companion CD-ROM. To learn more about them, see Appendix B, "What's on the CD-ROM?"

Next click on File and then Save. The Save As dialog appears. Type Hello.bat in the File name field, set the location where the file is to be saved as C:\ and click Save. You should now have a Windows shell script stored on your computer's hard drive. Now let's run the script and see what happens. First click on Start, All Programs, Accessories, and then Command Prompt. When the Windows console appears, type CD \ and press the Enter key. This command changes your current working directory to the same location where you saved the script. Now type the following command and press Enter.

```
Hello.bat
```

You should see the following output displayed in the Windows console.

```
C:\>Echo Hello World!
Hello World!


C:\>
```

The first line of output shows the Windows shell script statement that is being executed. The second line shows the results of the statement once it has been executed. Finally, the third line shows the Windows command prompt, indicating that the Windows shell is ready for your next command.

If you created and ran this script for yourself and it did not run as described above, then you probably made a typo. Reopen your script file and double-check its contents. Once you have the script running as advertised, you can close the Windows command console like any other Window by clicking on the X icon in the upper right hand corner of the Window or by clicking on the command prompt icon displayed in the upper left hand corner and selecting Close.

 HINT A quick way to close the Windows command prompt is to type EXIT **and press** Enter.

By default, Windows shell script automatically displays each statement in the script just before executing it. The effect of this behavior is that output displayed when the script is run may be intermingled with script statements, resulting in some very unattractive output. You can view this behavior even when running the one-line script above. Fortunately, you have the ability to suppress the display of Windows shell script statements when your scripts execute such that only the script's output is displayed. To accomplish this trick, add the following statement to the beginning of your script on a separate line, and then save and run it again.

```
@Echo off
```

The next effect of adding the statement as the first line in your Windows shell scripts is a much cleaner output. For example, if you run the `Hello.bat` script after making the change, you should see the following output:

```
C:\>hello

Hello World!


C:\>
```

 TRICK **You may have noticed that I ran the** `hello.bat` **script by simply typing** `hello` **and not** `hello.bat`. **This works because when you type in a file name without specifying its file extension, the Windows shell automatically looks for an executable file with that same file name and executes the first one that it finds. I'll go over how the Windows shell knows which files are executable in Chapter 2, "Interacting with the Windows Shell."**

As you can see, the script displayed only its output. As your scripts grow in size, you will appreciate the ability to prevent the display of script statements in this manner.

Creating a Scripting Environment

In the previous script example, you saved your first Windows shell script in C:\>. As a general rule, you should avoid storing any files, including scripts, in this location. Instead, I recommend that you create a folder specifically for storing your scripts. For example, when I was developing the scripts for this book, I wanted to store all my Windows shell scripts in a convenient place for easy execution. So I created a folder called C:\Scripts and stored all my scripts in it. You should create the same folder on your computer before you work through the following example.

To further simplify the execution of Windows shell scripts, I added a shortcut to my Windows desktop for the Windows command prompt. I accomplished this task as follows.

1. Right-click on an open area of the Windows XP desktop and select New followed by Shortcut.
2. The Create Shortcut wizard opens. Type `cmd.exe` in the `Type the location of the item` field and click on Next.
3. Type `Command Prompt` in the `Type a name for this shortcut` field and then click on Finish.

You should now see a shortcut on your desktop called Command Prompt. Double-click on it to open a new Windows console and access the Windows command prompt. By default, the working directory will be the Windows folder. Type CD and press Enter, and then type CD Scripts to switch over to the C:\Scripts folder. At this point you can execute any script that you save in this folder by simply typing its name at the command prompt.

You can make things a little easier by configuring your new shortcut to automatically switch to C:\Scripts as it opens a new Windows console. The following procedure outlines the steps involved in performing this task.

1. Right-click on the new shortcut you just created and select Properties. The cmd.exe Properties dialog appears.

2. Type c:\scripts in the Start In field, as shown in Figure 1.9.

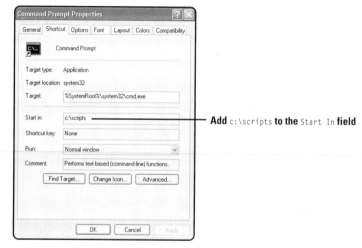

Add c:\scripts to the Start In field

FIGURE 1.9

Configuring the shortcut to make the C:\Scripts folder the default starting location.

3. Click on OK.

Now when you double-click on the shortcut, the Windows console that opens will automatically set its focus to c:\scripts (Figure 1.10).

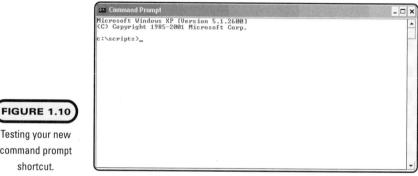

FIGURE 1.10

Testing your new command prompt shortcut.

Back to the Knock Knock Joke

Now let's turn our attention back to the chapter's main project, the Knock Knock joke. Through the development of this script, you will learn how to create a script that interacts with the player by displaying messages, collecting player responses, and displaying additional information based on the player's responses. This basic interaction forms the basis of all Windows shell scripts games.

Designing the Game

The first step in computer game development is to outline the game's design. The Knock Knock joke game is relatively simple, so a lot of up-front design is not required. Just like a regular Knock Knock joke, the game will begin by displaying the message Knock Knock! in the Windows console. It will then wait for the player to respond by typing "Who is there?" The player must type the response exactly as shown, including the quotation marks and question mark character. Once the player types the required response and presses the Enter key, the game will display the message Orange! and wait for the player to type "Orange who?" Once the player types in the second response correctly, the game will display its punch line and terminate, redisplaying the Windows command prompt.

This project will be completed in six steps, as outlined below.

1. Create an initial blank script file and name it KnockKnock.bat
2. Configure the Windows command console's title bar and color scheme
3. Format the display with blank lines
4. Collect player responses
5. Confirm that the player provided valid input
6. Display the joke's final punch line

Starting the Script Development Process

The first step in creating the Knock Knock game is to create an empty file named KnockKnock.bat and save it in the C:\Scripts folder. The following procedure outlines the steps involved in performing this task using the Windows Notepad text editor.

1. Click on Start, All Programs, Accessories, and then Notepad. The Notepad text editor appears.
2. Click on File and then Save. The Save As dialog appears. Type KnockKnock.bat into the File name field and specify c:\scripts as the location where the file should be saved.
3. Click on Save.

Configuring the Execution Environment

At this point you should be looking at an empty Notepad file. Type in the following text.

```
@ECHO off


TITLE "KnockKnock.bat - The KnockKnock joke game!"


COLOR 0E
```

The first statement prevents the display of script statements during execution, making the script's output more presentable. The second statement uses the Windows `Title` command to display the text `KnockKnock.bat - The Knock Knock joke game!` in the Windows console's title bar when the script is executed. The last statement uses the Windows `COLOR` command to display all text in yellow when the script is run. At this point, don't worry about the specifics of any of these commands or their syntax. I'll go over them in detail in Chapter 2. Just accept my somewhat high-level explanations of how things work and keep writing the script while focusing on the overall process you are going through.

Formatting the Display

The default behavior of the Windows command console is to display each line of output immediately after the command that generated it. For example, if you entered two commands, the Windows console would display the first command and then its output, followed by the second command and its output. This can make for a very cluttered display. To format your script's output and make it easier to interact with, you can do a couple of things. First, you can use the `CLS` command to clear the Windows command console, thus displaying a blank display. You can then use the `ECHO` statement to display blank lines to the Windows command console and control the location where text will be displayed. For example, the following statements clear the Windows command console and then display 10 blank lines. This way, the next line of text displayed will appear in the middle of the Windows command console. Note that the period following the `ECHO` command must be included exactly as shown.

```
CLS

ECHO.
ECHO.
ECHO.
ECHO.
ECHO.
ECHO.
ECHO.
ECHO.
ECHO.
ECHO.
```

Collecting Player Responses

The script now needs to display the Knock Knock! message and collect the player's response. This is accomplished by adding the following line of code to the script:

```
SET /p reply="Knock Knock!    C:>"
```

This statement uses the Windows SET command to display the Knock Knock! message followed by the characters C:>, which are supposed to simulate the Windows prompt and make the player feel like he is still interacting with the command prompt when in fact he is communicating with your script. The SET command's /p option tells the command to assign whatever text the user types to a variable called reply.

 DEFINITION A *variable* is a reference to a location in the computer memory where the script stores a value. Variables provide scripts with the ability to store and retrieve data that they collect while they execute.

Validating Player Input

Next, add the following statements to the script:

```
CLS

IF NOT %reply% == "Who is there?" (

  ECHO "Sorry, but you are not playing the game right!"
```

```
      GOTO :EOF )


ECHO.

ECHO.

ECHO.

ECHO.

ECHO.

ECHO.

ECHO.

ECHO.

ECHO.

ECHO.
```

The first statement clears the Windows console. The next three statements check the value assigned to the reply variable to determine if the player properly typed in "Who is there?" If the player provided an incorrect response, the script displays an error message and terminates the script's execution. However, if the player entered the correct response, the script continues executing and writes ten blank lines to the Windows console.

Now add the following statements to your script:

```
SET /p reply="Orange!          C:>"


CLS


IF NOT %reply% == "Orange who?" (

  ECHO "Sorry, but you are not playing the game right!"

  GOTO :EOF )
```

The first statement displays the message Orange! and waits for the player to type in a response, which again is assigned to a variable called reply. The second statement clears the Windows command console. If the player fails to enter "Orange who?", the third statement displays an error message and terminates the script's execution. Otherwise, the script keeps going.

Displaying the Punch Line

Finally, add the following statements to the end of your script:

```
ECHO.

ECHO.

ECHO.

ECHO.

ECHO.

ECHO.

ECHO.

ECHO.

ECHO.

ECHO.


ECHO "Orange you glad you've written your first Windows shell script?"


ECHO.

ECHO.

ECHO.

ECHO.

ECHO.

ECHO.

ECHO.

ECHO.

ECHO.

ECHO.
```

The first collection of ECHO statements displays ten blank lines in the Windows command console. Then the game's punch line is displayed, followed by ten more blank lines. The reason for adding the last ten blank lines was to move the display of the Windows command prompt to the bottom of the Windows command console, so that when the script ends and the Windows shell redisplays the command prompt, its reappearance will not interfere with the presentation of the joke's punch line.

The Final Result

Now look at the fully assembled script as shown below.

```
@ECHO off


TITLE "KnockKnock.bat - The KnockKnock joke game!"


COLOR 0E


CLS


ECHO.
ECHO.
ECHO.
ECHO.
ECHO.
ECHO.
ECHO.
ECHO.
ECHO.
ECHO.


SET /p reply="Knock Knock!    C:>"


CLS


IF NOT %reply% == "Who is there?" (
  ECHO "Sorry, but you are not playing the game right!"
  GOTO :EOF )


ECHO.
ECHO.
ECHO.
ECHO.
```

```
ECHO.

ECHO.

ECHO.

ECHO.

ECHO.

ECHO.


SET /p reply="Orange!        C:>"


CLS


IF NOT %reply% == "Orange who?" (

   ECHO "Sorry, but you are not playing the game right!"

   GOTO :EOF )


ECHO.

ECHO.

ECHO.

ECHO.

ECHO.

ECHO.

ECHO.

ECHO.

ECHO.

ECHO.


ECHO "Orange you glad you've written your first Windows shell script?"


ECHO.

ECHO.

ECHO.

ECHO.

ECHO.
```

```
ECHO.

ECHO.

ECHO.

ECHO.

ECHO.
```

As you can see the script is not very complicated, and if you remove the ECHO. statements, you are really only left with a handful of lines of code. Each time the script writes something to the Windows console, it first executes the CLS command to clear the screen and add focus to the new line of displayed text. Don't worry about the rest of the statements that make up this script; they will be fully covered in Chapter 2, "Interacting with the Windows Shell."

Once you have typed and saved this script, run it. If it does not work as expected, reopen the script and double-check your typing. Once you have everything working, move on to the next chapter where you will learn how to configure the Windows command console.

Summary

You have covered a lot of ground in this chapter. You learned what the Windows shell is and how it provides you with a text-based interface to the Windows operating system. You also learned about other scripting options available for Windows operating systems. You created, saved, and ran your first Windows shell script. Finally, you created your first Windows shell script computer game, the Knock Knock joke.

EXERCISES

1. As computer games go, the Knock Knock game is very simple. Its main purpose was to introduce you to the mechanics of script creation and execution. Try enhancing the scripts by adding additional Knock Knock jokes.

2. Experiment with the TITLE statement by changing the message the script displays in the Windows command console's title bar.

3. Modify the text that is displayed when the player fails to respond correctly to the joke's prompts. Try to make the message more clear and understandable.

CHAPTER 2

Interacting with the Windows Shell

In this chapter, you will learn how to work with and control the Windows shell environment. In doing so you will also learn how to configure the appearance and behavior of the Windows command console and the Windows command prompt. You will also learn about the commands internally defined by the Windows shell. These commands include all of the programming statements that make up the Windows shell scripting language.

This chapter will also explain how the Windows shell works with external commands and utility programs, including how it locates and executes these commands and utilities. The chapter will conclude by demonstrating how to develop the Unpredictable Command Prompt script. This script provides a fun demonstration of how to automate the configuration of the Windows shell environment.

Specifically, you will learn

- **The basics of Windows command syntax**

- **Different ways of starting Windows command consoles and configuring the Windows shell environment**

- **The differences between internal Windows shell script commands and external Windows commands and utilities**

- **How to manually customize the Windows command console from the Windows desktop**

Project Preview:
The Unpredictable Command Prompt

This chapter's main project is called the Unpredictable Command Prompt. It demonstrates how to randomly alter the appearance of the Windows command console. Among the Windows command console features customized by the script are the foreground and background colors of the Windows command console, the text displayed in the title bar, the format of the Windows command prompt, and the message that is initially displayed when the Windows command console first appears.

The Unpredictable Command Prompt script randomly configures one of three different sets of configuration settings each time it is executed. For example, as Figure 2.1 shows, in one scenario the user may be greeted by name and told to Code well and Prosper. The text displayed in the Windows command console appears in green on a black background.

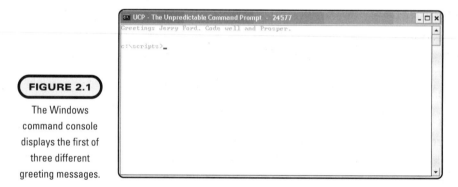

FIGURE 2.1

The Windows command console displays the first of three different greeting messages.

Figure 2.2 shows a second view that the user may see. In this case, the user is greeted by the message, "Hello. It is good to be working with you today!" In addition, the color of the foreground text is changed to yellow and the Windows command prompt now displays both the day of the week and the date.

Figure 2.3 shows the final view the user will see. In this case, the text message, "Boo! Did I scare you?" is displayed and the text appears as black characters on a yellow background.

This script also gives you a sneak peak of several other important Windows shell scripting techniques, which are explored further later in the book. These techniques include the storage of data in variables, the use of conditional logic to control script execution, and the ability to perform numeric comparisons.

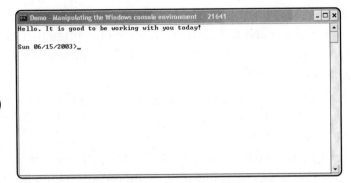

FIGURE 2.2

The Windows
command console's
title bar message is
also changed.

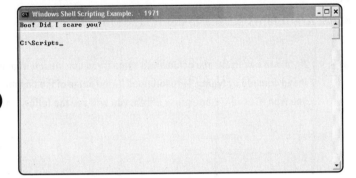

FIGURE 2.3

Foreground and
background colors
are changed
as well.

Command Shell Command Syntax

The Windows shell provides an interface for working with text-based commands and utilities. In addition, you will use it to run your Windows shell scripts. Integrated into the Windows shell is the Windows shell scripting language. This scripting language includes a large number of statements.

Each Windows command has its own unique syntax that must be followed strictly for the command to work. However, all Windows commands follow a common format. Figure 2.4 breaks down this format.

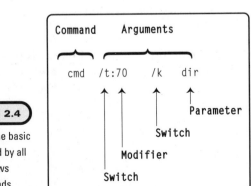

FIGURE 2.4

Examining the basic
format used by all
Windows
commands.

To execute Windows commands from the Windows command prompt, you type the name of the command followed by one or more optional arguments that tell the command what you want it to do. Command arguments can consist of several different elements, including

- **Switches.** Modify the way in which a command is processed. Switches consist of a forward slash followed by one or more characters. Each Windows command has its own unique set of switches.
- **Modifiers.** Change the behavior of a switch. Modifiers consist of a colon followed by one or more characters. Each Windows command has its own set of modifiers.
- **Parameters.** Arguments passed to commands for processing.

HINT If you are uncertain of a command's syntax, you can view it from the Windows command console by typing Help followed by the name of the command. For example, if you type HELP DATE and press Enter, you will see the following:

```
C:\>HELP DATE

Displays or sets the date.


DATE [/T | date]


Type DATE without parameters to display the current date setting and a prompt
for a new one.  Press ENTER to keep the same date.


If Command Extensions are enabled the DATE command supports the /T switch
which tells the command to just output the current date, without prompting
for a new date.


C:\>
```

A good way to gain an understanding of Windows command syntax is by looking at an example. The following example shows the command syntax of the CMD command.

```
CMD [/A | /U] [/Q] [/D] [/E:ON | /E:OFF] [/F:ON | /F:OFF] [/V:ON | /V:OFF]
    [[/S] [/C | /K] string]
```

As you can see, the syntax of the CMD command consists of its name, a collection of switches, some of which have modifiers, and a string which would consist of any data that you wanted the CMD command to process (such as the name of a Windows shell script).

You must follow a number of formatting rules when working with Windows commands. These rules are outlined below.

- Spaces must be used to separate each component of the command
- Arguments shown inside brackets are optional
- Arguments inside brackets that are not shown in italics must be typed exactly as shown
- Arguments in italics represent values that you must supply
- Arguments inside brackets and separated by a | sign are mutually exclusive
- Arguments that contain spaces must be enclosed within a matching pair of double quotes

DEFINITION   When referring to Windows commands, the term *mutually exclusive* means that only one of a collection of options can be selected. For example, when executing the CMD command you have the option of specifying the E:/ON or E:/OFF, but you cannot specify both options at the same time.

In this book I have chosen to display Windows commands in upper case. However, Windows commands are not case-sensitive, which means that you can type them using upper case, lower case, or a combination of upper and lower case and achieve the same results. For example, as far as the Windows shell is concerned, all of the following commands are equivalent:

- `ECHO Greetings`
- `echo Greetings`
- `Echo Greetings`
- `EcHo Greetings`

Starting Windows Shell Sessions

You can use one of two commands to open Windows shell sessions. These commands are CMD and START. When executed from the Windows Run dialog (click on Start, Run, type CMD, and click on OK), CMD opens a new Windows command console.

However, when executed within an open Windows command console, the CMD command opens a new Windows shell session within the current console. In contrast, the START command (which works only from within an already open Windows command console) starts a new Windows shell session by opening a new Windows command console each time.

Working with the CMD Command

Most often, you will use the CMD command to initiate a Windows shell session. The syntax of the CMD command is shown below. Table 2.1 defines each of its switches. Don't worry if you see some terms mentioned in the table that you have not yet learned. They will be explained as they are used throughout the rest of the book.

```
CMD [/A | /U] [/Q] [/D] [/E:ON | /E:OFF] [/F:ON | /F:OFF] [/V:ON | /V:OFF]
    [[/S] [/C | /K] string]
```

TABLE 2.1 CMD.exe COMMAND SWITCHES

Switch	Function
/C	Executes the command and closes the Windows shell
/K	Executes the command but does not close the Windows shell
/S	Changes the handling of the string after the /C or /K switch
/Q	Disables echo
/D	Prevents the execution of AutoRun commands specified in the registry
/A	Formats command output in ANSI format
/U	Formats command output in Unicode format
/T:FG	Sets the Windows command console's foreground and background colors
/E:ON	Enables extensions to the Windows shell required by certain commands
/E:OFF	Disables extensions to the Windows shell (required by certain commands)
/F:ON	Enables file and folder name completion
/F:OFF	Disables file and folder name completion
/V:ON	Allows for the delayed expansion of environment variables
/V:OFF	Prevents the delayed expansion of environment variables

TRAP Command line extensions are improvements made to Windows commands in later versions of Windows operating systems. By default, command line extensions are enabled. The only reason you might want to disable them is to allow an old script that uses the old version of a Windows command that does not support the execution of command line extensions. Many Windows commands support these extensions, including ASSOC, CALL, CD, COLOR, DEL, ENDLOCAL, FOR, FTYPE, GOTO, IF, MD, POPD, PROMPT, PUSHD, SET, SETLOCAL, SHIFT, **and** START.

Let's look at a few examples of how to work with CMD. First, click on Start, Run, and then type CMD and click on OK to start a new Windows shell session. This opens a new Windows command console with which you can begin working with the Windows command prompt.

If you want, you can start a new Windows shell session and pass it a command to execute at the same time by clicking on Start, Run, and then typing CMD followed by a command as shown below.

```
CMD /K TITLE Welcome
```

In this example, a new Windows command console will open and display the text message of Welcome in its title bar. Sometimes you may want to simply start a new Windows shell session, pass it a command, have the command execute, and then automatically close the Windows command console. You can do this as follows.

```
CMD /C DEL C:\Temp\*.txt
```

The CMD command's /K and /C switches are examples of mutually exclusive parameters. /K specifies that the Windows command console should remain open after executing the command whereas /C specifies that the Windows command console should close after the command completes processing.

The next example demonstrates how to use a modifier to control the execution of the CMD command. In this example, the /T switch, which sets foreground and background colors, is used to invert the Windows color scheme from white on black to black on white.

```
CMD /T:F0
```

In this example, the switch is /T. It has a modifier, which is preceded by the colon character. The first character in the modifier sets the Windows command console's foreground color (e.g., the color of text) and the second character of the modifier sets the background color. You can specify a range of different foreground and background colors in the Windows command console, as shown in Table 2.2.

TABLE 2.2 COLORS FOR THE WINDOWS COMMAND CONSOLE

Color	Value
Black	0
Blue	1
Green	2
Aqua	3
Red	4
Purple	5
Greenish Yellow	6
Light Gray	7
Gray	8
Light Blue	9
Light Green	A
Light Aqua	B
Light Red	C
Light Purple	D
Light Yellow	E
Bright White	F

Working with the START Command

The START command provides an alternative way of opening a Windows command console and starting a new Windows shell session. The START command automatically opens a new Windows command console each time it is executed. This provides a handy way to open and work with multiple Windows command consoles at the same time. The START command also provides more control over new Windows shell sessions. The START command's syntax is shown below.

```
START ["TITLE"] [/Dpath] [/I] [/MIN] [/MAX] [/SEPARATE | /SHARED]

  [/LOW | /NORMAL | /HIGH | /REALTIME | /ABOVENORMAL | /BELOWNORMAL]

  [/WAIT] [/B] [Program/Command] [Parameters]
```

As you can see, the START command accepts a large number of parameters, which are explained in Table 2.3. Again, don't worry if you see some terms mentioned in the table that you have not yet learned. They will be explained further as they are used throughout the rest of the book.

Now look at an example of the START command in action. In this example, the START command opens a new Windows command console in a maximized state with above normal priority.

START /MAX /ABOVENORMAL

To test this command, open a Windows command console, type in the command at the command prompt, and press the Enter key.

TABLE 2.3 START COMMAND PARAMETERS

Parameter	Description
"title"	Text to be displayed in the Windows command console's title bar
/d Path	Specifies the startup folder
B	Starts a script without opening a new Windows command console
I	Resets the execution environment to the original state of the parent environment
MIN	Opens a new Windows command console in a minimized state
MAX	Opens a new Windows command console in a maximized state
SEPARATE	Starts a 16-bit program in its own memory space
SHARED	Starts a 16-bit program in a shared memory space
LOW	Starts an application using the low priority
NORMAL	Starts an application using the normal priority
HIGH	Starts an application using the high priority
REALTIME	Starts an application using the real-time priority
ABOVENORMAL	Starts an application using the above normal priority
BELOWNORMAL	Starts an application using the below normal priority
WAIT	Starts an application and waits for it to end
Program/Command	An optional program or command to be processed by the Windows shell
Parameters	One or more arguments to be passed to the program or command

Internal vs. External Commands

The Windows shell works with two different types of commands: internal and external. Internal commands are built into the Windows shell, whereas external commands exist as separate executable files stored on the computer's hard drive. Most Windows commands are found in \Winnt\System32. Both internal and external commands follow the same basic syntax rules. Table 2.4 provides a listing of the Windows shell's internal commands.

TABLE 2.4 BUILT-IN WINDOWS SHELL COMMANDS

Command	Overview
ASSOC	Displays or modifies file name extension associations
CALL	Calls one script from another without stopping the calling or parent script. Also provides the ability to switch processing control to labels specified within a script
CD (CHDIR)	Changes the current directory
CLS	Clears the Windows command console screen
COLOR	Sets Windows command console foreground and background colors
COPY	Copies one or more files from one location to another
DATE	Displays or modifies the system date
DEL	Removes one or more files
DIR	Displays a list of files and folders located in the specified directory
ECHO	Displays text messages in the Windows command console
ENDLOCAL	Terminates variable localization by restoring variables to their values as they existed before the preceding SETLOCAL command was executed
ERASE	Removes one or more files
EXIT	Closes the Windows command console and ends a command shell session
FOR	Executes a command for each file in a collection of files
FTYPE	Displays and modifies file types that are associated with file name extensions
GOTO	Alters processing flow in a script by transferring it to a line containing a specified label
IF	Performs conditional processing and alters the execution flow within the script based on tested results

TABLE 2.4   BUILT-IN WINDOWS SHELL COMMANDS *(CONTINUED)*

Command	Overview
MD (MKDIR)	Creates a new directory or subdirectory
MOVE	Moves one or more files from one location to another
PATH	Configures the search path used by Windows to locate executable files
PAUSE	Halts script execution until the user presses a key
POPD	Changes the current folder to the folder stored by a corresponding PUSHD command
PROMPT	Changes the display of the Windows command prompt
PUSHD	Changes to a specified folder and stores the previous folder for later reference by the POPD command.
RD (RMDIR)	Removes a specified folder
REM	Provides the ability to add comments to a script
REN (RENAME)	Renames a file or folder
SET	Creates, modifies, and deletes variables
SETLOCAL	Records the current value assigned to environment variables in the Windows shell, allowing them to be restored later by the ENDLOCAL command
SHIFT	Alters the position of script parameters
START	Starts a new Windows shell session and executes specified commands
TIME	Displays and modifies the system time
TITLE	Modifies the text displayed in the Windows command console title bar
TYPE	Displays the contents of a text file in the Windows command console
VER	Displays the Windows version number

The number of external commands and command line utilities are too numerous and varied to attempt to cover here. You learn more about them as you work your way through this book. These commands consist of any executable file provided by the operating system and any applications that you may have installed on your computer.

How Windows Locates Commands

To work efficiently with the Windows shell, it helps to understand how it locates the commands that you want it to execute. The following series of steps outlines the process that the Windows shell goes through in order to try to execute the commands you specify.

1. If you supply the command's complete path name, the Windows shell looks in the specified folder and executes the command. If the command is not found, an error is generated.

2. If you specify a command without its path, the Windows shell first checks to see if the command is one of its internal commands and executes the command if it is.

3. Next, the Windows shell looks for the command in the current working directory and executes the command if it is found.

4. If the command is not found at this point, the Windows shell begins looking through each of the folders specified in the path variable (in the order in which they are listed). If a matching command is found, it is executed and the search stops. If the command is not found, an error is generated.

Using the PATH Command

Windows stores information about the location of commands in a variable called path. This variable stores a list of folders that the Windows shell will search when it needs to locate an external Windows command. You can view and modify the contents of this variable using the PATH command, which has the following syntax.

```
PATH [[drive:]path[;...]] [%path%]
```

To view the list of folders stored in the path variable, open the Windows command prompt and type PATH. The output displayed by the command will resemble the following output.

```
C:\>path

PATH=C:\WINNT\system32;C:\WINNT;C:\WINNT\system32\WBEM


C:\>
```

The output displayed in this example shows that the Windows shell will search three folders when looking for a command to execute. The folders are searched in the order presented, from left to right. Therefore C:\Winnt\system32 will be searched first and if the command is not found, C:\Winnt will be searched second followed by C:\Winnt\system32\wbem.

If you want, you can add additional folders to the search list stored in the path variable. For example, you might want to add the folder where you store all your Windows shell scripts to the path variable so that the Windows shell can always find them.

The following example demonstrates how to add a folder named C:\Scripts to the beginning of the list of folders stored in the path variable.

```
PATH C:\scripts;%path%
```

As you can see, the structure of this command is PATH followed by the name and path of the folder to be added, a semicolon character, and then %path%.

TRICK Placing a folder at the beginning of the path variable's search list ensures that it will be the first folder checked. This way, if you give a script a name that happens to match a Windows command, your script will be executed in place of the Windows command. Remember, the Windows shell stops looking for commands as soon as it finds the first match.

TRAP I have not yet covered the use of variables in this book, but they are such a fundamental part of scripting that it's almost impossible to do anything without using them. For now, just note that to reference them from within a script you must enclose the variable's name inside a pair of percentage characters. Keep reading along and I will explain how to work with variables in detail in Chapter 4, "Storing and Retrieving Information in Variables."

You can just as easily add a folder to the end of the search list, as shown below.

```
PATH C:\scripts;%path%
```

TRAP Don't forget to always add the %path% variable to either the beginning or the end of the PATH command when modifying the command's search path. Otherwise, the list of folders that made up the original search path will be deleted and replaced by your new addition, which is not what you'll want to do.

Any changes that you make to the path variable by modifying it from a Windows shell script are just temporary. In other words, the changes you make are lost when you close the Windows command console and terminate your Windows shell session.

PATHEXT

When you type an external command, you must specify its name. Optionally, you can specify an external command's file extension. Normally, all that you'll need is the name of the command itself. When you type in a command's name without its file extension, the Windows shell uses the list of file extensions stored in the pathext variable to search for a matching command. The pathext variable lists all of the file extensions that Windows associates as being executable files.

When you type a command without its file extension, the Windows shell uses the collection of file extensions stored in pathext to search for a matching file. It does this by substituting each file extension listed in pathext as the command's file extension until it finds a match. The first match that is found ends the search. The Windows shell then executes this command.

By default, the pathext variable lists the following file extensions in the following order.

- .COM
- .EXE
- .BAT
- .CMD

You can display the contents of the pathext variable by typing the following command at the Windows command prompt.

```
ECHO %pathext%
```

The output you get back should look something like this:

```
C:\>ECHO %pathext%

.COM;.EXE;.BAT;.CMD
```

However, you may see additional file extensions listed depending on what software you have installed on your computer. If you wish, you can add a new file extension to pathext as demonstrated below.

```
SET pathext=%pathext%;.shl
```

In this example, the file extension .SHL is added to the end of the pathext variable using the SET command. You'll find yourself using the SET command a lot when working with variables. I will explain the command in detail in Chapter 4, "Storing and Retrieving Information in Variables."

Other Useful Windows Commands

In addition to the commands that you have seen in this chapter, there are a number of other commands you can use to configure a Windows shell session. These commands include

- TITLE
- PROMPT
- COLOR
- CLS
- ECHO

You'll need to know how to work with these commands to complete this chapter's scripting project, so I'll go over them in the sections that follow.

Using the TITLE Command

The TITLE command provides the ability to display a custom text message in the Windows command console's title bar area. The syntax of the TITLE command is shown below.

```
TITLE [string]
```

To see how the TITLE command works, create a new Widows shell script made up of the following statement.

```
TITLE Greetings!
```

When you run your script, you'll see the message Greetings! in the title bar area, as shown in Figure 2.5.

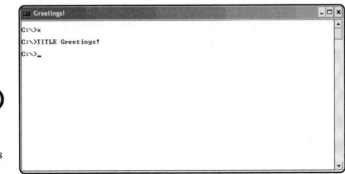

FIGURE 2.5

Posting a message in the Windows command console's title bar.

Working with the PROMPT Command

The PROMPT command is used to modify the display of the Windows command prompt. By default, the Windows command prompt shows the currently selected disk drive and folder in the form of the drive letter followed by a colon, a backward slash, and the "greater than" character as shown below.

```
C:\>
```

However, using the PROMPT command you can display any of the information listed in Table 2.5.

Argument	Displays
$A	& - Ampersand character
$B		- Pipe character
$C	(- Left parenthesis character
$D	The current date
$E	ANSI escape code 27
$F	) - Right parenthesis character
$G	> - Greater-than character (greater-than sign)
$H	Backspace character
$L	< - Less-than character (less-than sign)
$N	The current drive name
$P	The current drive and path names
$Q	= - Equal character (equal sign)
$S	A blank space
$T	Current system time
$V	The Windows version number
$_	Performs a carriage return and linefeed
$$	$ - Dollar character (dollar sign)
$+	A + sign representing the depth of the pushd stack.

TABLE 2.5 COMMAND PROMPT ARGUMENTS

The syntax of the PROMPT command is shown below.

```
PROMPT [text]
```

The value of text represents a combination of one or more of the arguments listed in Table 2.5. For example, to replace the current drive letter with the current time you would type the following:

```
PROMPT $D
```

When executed, the previous command would modify the command prompt as shown below.

```
C:\>PROMPT $D
```

```
Wed 06/18/2003
```

If you prefer a shorter, less intrusive command prompt, then try the following command:

```
PROMPT $G
```

This command turns the command prompt into the > character. If desired, you can combine multiple arguments when modifying the command prompt, as demonstrated below.

```
C:\>PROMPT $D$G
```

```
Wed 06/18/2003>
```

As you can see, the command prompt now display the date followed by the "greater than" character. You can also insert any free-form text that you want as the command prompt, as shown below.

```
C:\>PROMPT Welcome to my PC$G
```

```
Welcome to my PC>
```

Here I changed the command prompt to display a greeting message followed by the "greater than" character. Finally, if you decide that you want to restore the command prompt to its default format, just type PROMPT and hit the Enter key as shown below.

```
Welcome to my PC>PROMPT
```

```
C:\>
```

Changing Colors

By using the COLOR command, you can take control of the foreground and background colors displayed in the Windows command console. The syntax of the COLOR command is outlined below.

COLOR *BF*

The COLOR command requires two arguments. *B* represents a numeric value that specifies the background color to be used, and *F* represents the foreground color (e.g., the color of displayed text). The COLOR command supports the same colors as the CMD command, which were listed earlier in this chapter in Table 2.2.

By default, the Windows command console displays text in white on a black background. Using the COLOR command, you can change these settings as demonstrated below.

COLOR E4

This command modifies the Windows command console so that it displays all text in red on a yellow background. To restore the Windows command console color settings to their default setting, you can type COLOR OF, or, as a shortcut, just type COLOR and the Windows command console default white-on-black color scheme will be restored.

CLS

The Windows command console automatically scrolls text off of the display as its fills up. However, this can make the console look cluttered and difficult to read. If you prefer, you can use the CLS command to clear out all currently displayed text, leaving only the command prompt visible. The CLS command's syntax is outlined below.

CLS

As you can see, the CLS command does not accept any arguments, making it extremely easy to use.

ECHO

The ECHO command gives you the ability to display text messages in the Windows command console. Using the ECHO command you can create scripts that keep the user informed about their execution status and display their results. The syntax of the ECHO command is outlined below.

ECHO [ON | OFF] [*message*]

As you have already seen, the ECHO command's use is very straightforward. For example, create a new Windows shell script consisting of the following text:

```
ECHO This is an example of how to use the ECHO command
```

When executed, the Windows shell displays the following output:

```
C:\>ECHO This is an example of how to use the ECHO command

This is an example of how to use the ECHO command

C:\>
```

As you can see, the original ECHO command and its resulting output are both displayed. To clean up the display, it is generally a good idea to prevent the display of the original command and leave only its output visible. You can accomplish this by adding the @ character to the beginning of the ECHO command, as demonstrated below.

```
@ECHO This is an example of how to use the ECHO command
```

If you make this change to your script and run it again, you'll get the following output.

```
This is an example of how to use the ECHO command

C:\>
```

As you can see, this time only the text message is displayed, followed by the Windows command prompt. Using this same technique, you can suppress the display of any number of ECHO commands, as demonstrated below.

```
@ECHO Once upon a time there was a little boy

@ECHO who lived with his mother in a small

@ECHO cabin out in the woods far away from

@ECHO the big city. Once day a wolf came upon

@ECHO their house and ........
```

Since displaying output is a very common task in Windows shell scripts, a shortcut has been provided to simplify your scripts. To use this shortcut, just type the following statement at the beginning of your Windows shell scripts:

```
@ECHO Off
```

For example, the following statements demonstrate how to rewrite the previous example using the @ECHO Off statement.

```
@ECHO Off

ECHO Once upon a time there was a little boy

ECHO who lived with his mother in a small

ECHO cabin out in the woods far away from

ECHO the big city. Once day a wolf came upon

ECHO their house and ........
```

Customizing the Windows Command Console

The Windows command console provides you with a text-based interface to the Windows shell. By default, it displays text in a Window that is 25 lines long and 80 characters wide. All text is displayed in white and the background color is set to black. Like most Windows features, the Windows command console can be configured from the Windows desktop in a number of different ways.

Customization Options

Windows command console customization is performed from the Command Prompt Properties dialog. You can open this dialog by opening the Windows command console and right-clicking on the Command Prompt icon in the upper-left corner of the console and selecting Properties. This dialog is organized into four property sheets as listed below.

- Options
- Font
- Layout
- Colors

Each of these property sheets configures a different set of properties for the Windows command console as explained in the sections that follow.

Configuring Options Settings

The Windows XP Options property sheet, shown in Figure 2.6, provides access to the following configuration settings:

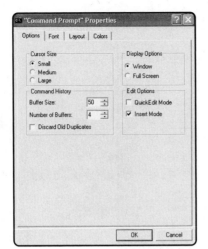

FIGURE 2.6

Use the Options
property sheet to
configure cursor
size and command
history as well as
display and edit
options.

- **Cursor Size**. Sets either a small, medium, or large cursor size.
- **Display Options**. Sets the Windows command console to open either in a window or in full screen mode.
- **Command History**. Sets the number of commands that the Windows command console can recall, the number of available buffers, and controls whether duplicate commands are discarded.
- **Edit Options**. Enables or disables the QuickEdit and Insert modes. QuickEdit allows text to be copied and cut from the Windows command console and pasted, and for text to be pasted to the Windows command prompt. Insert Mode controls whether text is overwritten or inserted when editing command input.

Specifying Font Settings

The Font property sheet, shown in Figure 2.7, provides the ability to configure font size and font type. When you configure font size, you also affect the size of the Windows command console. Any changes you make to font size are immediately reflected in the Window Preview section of the property sheet.

Making changes to font type also has an impact on the size of the Windows command console. Depending on the font type you select, the Bold fonts option (to the right of the selection list) may become enabled. This option can help to make text easier to read. You can preview the effects of your font selection in the Selected Font section.

FIGURE 2.7

Configuring font
type and size for
the Windows
command console.

Setting Up the Windows Command Console Layout

The Layout property sheet, shown in Figure 2.8, allows you to configure the Windows command console's initial size and location on the display where it will open. In addition, you can use it to configure the number of lines that it can display as well as the number of lines that it can scroll back to display previous text. Specifically, you can configure the following settings:

- **Screen Buffer Size**. The Width setting controls the number of characters that can be displayed on a single line. The Height setting determines the number of lines of text the Windows command console will retain in memory (i.e., the lines that you can scroll back and view).

- **Windows Size**. The Width setting specifies initial width of the Windows command console. The Height setting specifies the Windows command console's initial height. However, you can manually resize the Windows command console by right-clicking on one of the console's edges and dragging it to a new location. However, you cannot resize the Windows command console any larger than the height and width setting specified in the Screen Buffer Size section.

- **Windows Position**. These settings allow you to specify the location on the display where you'd like the Windows command console to open. Position is specified in pixels, starting in the upper-left corner.

- **Let System Position Window**. Selecting this option lets the operating system determine where to open the Windows command console on the display.

DEFINITION

The term *pixel* is short for picture element and represents the smallest area that a computer can display or print.

TRICK Set the Screen Buffer Size Height setting to three or four times larger than the height of the Window Size setting. This way you'll be able to scroll back and view previous commands and their output.

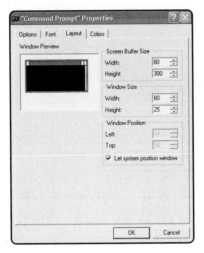

FIGURE 2.8

Configuring screen size and the Windows position of the Windows command console

Specifying Color Settings

You can modify the Windows command console's foreground and background colors from the Colors property sheet, as shown in Figure 2.9. The top portion of this property sheet provides you with the following options:

- **Screen Text**. Select this option and then click on a color from the list of displayed colors to configure the Windows command console's foreground color (e.g., text color).
- **Screen Background**. Select this option and then click on a color from the list of displayed colors to configure the Windows command console's background color.
- **Popup Text**. Select this option and then click on a color from the list of displayed colors to configure the foreground color of the Windows command console's command history dialog box.
- **Popup Background**. Select this option and then click on a color from the list of displayed colors to configure the background color of the Windows command console's command history dialog box.
- **Selected Color Values**. If you prefer, you can select one of the four previous options and then set a custom color for foreground and background colors by specifying various levels of red, green, and blue.

The bottom portion of the Colors property sheet provides a sneak preview of how any changes that you make will affect the Windows command console.

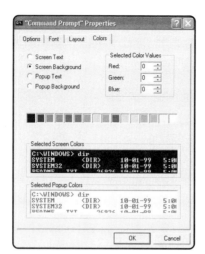

IN THE REAL WORLD

Any true Windows power user or system administrator is, by definition, good at working with the Windows shell. Often working with the Windows shell means typing in the same sets of commands repeatedly. To speed things up and increase their efficiency, power users and administrators learn all kinds of tricks to help them work faster. One technique that many people use is to access command history, which provides a list of previously executed commands that you can quickly access and run again. To access the Windows shell's command history, press the F7 key. Then use the up and down arrows to select a previously executed command and press the Enter key.

Back to the Unpredictable Command Prompt

Now let's turn our attention back to the chapter's main project, the Unpredictable Command Prompt. Through the development of this script, you will learn how to create a script that interacts with the Windows shell environment and the Windows command console. You will also get some more exposure to working with variables and using simple conditional logic.

Designing the Game

The Unpredictable Command Prompt is designed to randomly modify the Windows command console environment each time it is executed. In total, three different scenarios may occur, each of which will modify the Windows title bar, command prompt, and foreground and background colors. In addition, a different greeting message will be displayed each time. I'll show you how to complete the Unpredictable Command Prompt script in nine steps, as outlined below.

1. Get a random number
2. Clear the Windows command console
3. Post a message in the Windows command console's title bar
4. Modify foreground and background colors
5. Greet the user
6. Modify the appearance of the command prompt
7. Terminate the script
8. Build the second scenario
9. Build the third scenario

As in the previous chapter, I will use a couple of programming techniques in this script that I have not yet covered in this book. Specifically, I will use environment variables and the IF statement to do a little conditional logic. It is hard to write a useful script without using either of these resources. However, I wanted to provide you with some foundation concepts regarding Windows shell scripting and the Windows shell before I delve into specific Windows shell scripting. So for now, just follow along with my high-level explanations of the portions of the script that use these programming techniques as you go through the steps involved in creating the script.

Selecting a Random Number

The first step in creating the Unpredictable Command Prompt script is to create a new script and add the following statements:

```
@ECHO off
```

```
SET TestVariable=%random%
```

The first statement prevents the Windows shell from displaying script statements as it processes them. This will make the script's output less cluttered and present a cleaner and more polished looking output. The second statement uses the SET command to assign a random number to a variable called TestVariable. The random variable is generated automatically by the operating system on Windows 2000, XP, and 2003 computers. Whenever it is referenced, it returns a random number between 1 and 32,767.

The script will reference the random value assigned to this variable to determine which of three possible actions to take. Specifically, it will take one set of actions if the value assigned to the variable is greater than 22,000. It will take a different set of actions if the value is greater than 11,000 but less than 22,000. Finally, a third set of actions is taken if the variable's value is less than 11,000 but greater than zero.

The rest of the script consists of three major sections. The statements that make up each section are very similar, so I'll explain the statements that comprise the first section in detail and then provide a high-level overview of the remaining sections.

Clearing the Windows Command Console

Now check the value stored in the TestVariable to see if it is greater than 22,000. You can do this by adding the three lines of code you see below.

```
IF %TestVariable% GTR 22000 (

  CLS

)
```

The first line can be translated like this: "If the value assigned to TestVariable is greater than 22,000, then perform the following action." The action to be performed is enclosed within parentheses (a pair of () characters). Actually, the opening (character is shown at the end of the first line and the closing) character is on the third line. Nonetheless, the CLS command is still considered enclosed within them. This command clears the Windows command console, giving the script a clear screen onto which to write additional text.

Modifying the Windows Command Console Title Bar

Next, add the statement shown below in bold. This statement uses the TITLE command to post a text message in the Windows command console's title bar. The message consists of two parts. The first part is a text string (e.g., UCP - The Unpredictable Command Prompt -). The second part is a reference to the TestVariable. When referenced in this manner, the randomly assigned numeric value assigned to the variables is displayed in place of %TestVariable%. I added the display of this numeric value to the end of the title bar message to make it easy for you to see the randomly assigned number. This way you can validate that your script is executing the right collection of statements each time it runs.

```
If %TestVariable% GTR 22000 (

  Cls

  TITLE UCP - The Unpredictable Command Prompt  -  %TestVariable%

)
```

Changing Background and Foreground Colors

Now add the statement shown below in bold. This statement uses the COLOR command to change the Windows command console's foreground color to yellow and its background color to black.

```
If %TestVariable% GTR 22000 (

  Cls

  TITLE UCP - The Unpredictable Command Prompt  -  %TestVariable%

  COLOR 02

)
```

Greeting the User

The next step in creating the Unpredictable Command Prompt script is to add the two lines shown below in bold. The first of these two lines displays a personalized greeting to the user by wrapping the username variable inside a text message displayed using the ECHO command. username is an environment variable that Windows creates each time you log on. It stores your username. The second line uses the ECHO command to display a blank line. This will make the script's output a little easier to read when the script ends and redisplays the Windows command prompt.

```
If %TestVariable% GTR 22000 (

  Cls

  TITLE UCP - The Unpredictable Command Prompt  -  %TestVariable%

  COLOR 02

  Echo Greetings %username%. Code well and Prosper.

  Echo.

)
```

Changing the Command Prompt

Now add to your script the statement shown below in bold. When used without any additional arguments, the PROMPT statement resets the Windows command prompt to its default setting.

```
If %TestVariable% GTR 22000 (

  Cls

  TITLE UCP - The Unpredictable Command Prompt  -  %TestVariable%

  COLOR 02
```

```
Echo Greetings %username%. Code well and Prosper.

Echo.

PROMPT

)
```

Terminating Script Execution

Now add the statement shown in bold below. This statement uses the GOTO command to alter the default order of statement execution in the script. In this case, it tells the script to go to :EOF, which is a shortcut way of saying jump to the end of the file (i.e., stop executing). By placing this statement here, you ensure that the script will stop running after executing all of the statements in this section of the script. This way, if the value assigned to TestVariable was greater than 22,000, the script will process only the seven lines of code shown below.

```
If %TestVariable% GTR 22000 (

  Cls

  TITLE UCP - The Unpredictable Command Prompt  -   %TestVariable%

  COLOR 02

  Echo Greetings %username%. Code well and Prosper.

  Echo.

  PROMPT

  GOTO :EOF

)
```

If you were to forget and leave out the GOTO :EOF statement from this section of the script, then any changes made by this portion of the script would always be overridden by changes made in the two sections that follow. This will happen because the script would keep on processing the statements that follow. For example, the third section of this script is set up to process whenever the value assigned to TestVariable is greater than zero. Therefore, if the value assigned to TestVariable happens to be 26,000, then any changes made by this first section of the script will be undone later in the script. By adding the GOTO statement, you prevent this from occurring.

Creating the Second Scenario

OK. The second portion of the script is really just a variation of the first part. I have highlighted the differences between the two sections below. As you can see, this section is set up to run whenever the value assigned to TestVariable is greater than 11,000. In addition, a different message is displayed in the Windows command console's title bar, and different foreground and background colors are established. In addition, the greeting message has been changed. Also, the Windows command prompt was changed to display the system date followed by the "greater than" character.

```
If %TestVariable% GTR 11000 (

  CLS

  TITLE Demo - Manipulating the Windows command console environment  -  %TestVariable%

  COLOR 0E

  ECHO Hello. It good to be working with you today!

  ECHO.

  PROMPT $d$g

  GOTO :EOF

)
```

Setting Up the Third Scenario

The last part of the script defines the third possible execution scenario (i.e., executing only when the value of TestVariable is greater than zero and less than 11,000). I have again highlighted the differences between this section and the first section.

```
If %TestVariable% GTR 0 (

  CLS

  TITLE Windows Shell Scripting Example.  -  %TestVariable%

  COLOR E0

  ECHO Boo! Did I scare you?

  ECHO.

  PROMPT $p

  GOTO :EOF

)
```

The Final Result

Now look at the fully assembled script, as shown below. To run it, open a new Windows command console, type the name of the script at the command prompt, and press Enter.

```
@ECHO off


SET TestVariable=%random%


If %TestVariable% GTR 22000 (

  Cls

  TITLE UCP - The Unpredictable Command Prompt  -  %TestVariable%

  COLOR 02

  Echo Greetings %username%. Code well and Prosper.

  Echo.

  PROMPT

  GOTO :EOF

)


If %TestVariable% GTR 11000 (

  CLS

  TITLE Demo - Manipulating the Windows command console environment  -  %TestVariable%

  COLOR 0E

  ECHO Hello. It good to be working with you today!

  ECHO.

  PROMPT $d$g

  GOTO :EOF

)


If %TestVariable% GTR 0 (

  CLS

  TITLE Windows Shell Scripting Example.  -  %TestVariable%

  COLOR E0

  ECHO Boo! Did I scare you?

  ECHO.

  PROMPT $p

  GOTO :EOF

)
```

Summary

The focus of this chapter was to introduce you to the Windows shell and get you comfortable working with it. This included showing you how to modify the appearance of the Windows command console. Specifically, you learned how to change the color scheme, command prompt, and title bar text. In addition, you learned about the differences between internal and external commands as well as how the Windows shell locates and executes these commands. You then completed the Unpredictable Command Prompt script, which helped tie together many of the concepts presented in this chapter.

EXERCISES

1. Create a new Windows shell initialization script that automatically adds to the `path` variable the name and path of the folder where you plan to store your Windows shell scripts.

2. Create a new Command Prompt shortcut and configure it to automatically execute your new Windows shell initialization script. Hint: Use the /K switch and specify the complete path of the folder where the scripts reside.

Windows Shell Scripting Basics

I n this chapter, I'll explain the importance of adding comments to your Windows shell scripting to make your code self-documenting. I'll also provide you with a Windows shell script template that you can use as the basis for organizing and documenting your scripts. You will learn about a programming technique called *redirection,* and you'll learn how to use it to control script input and output.

This chapter also shows you how to group commands and make the execution of one command dependent on the outcome of another command. Finally, you will learn how to create the Fortune Teller game. This game builds on the programming techniques that have been used in previous games and also demonstrates how to create a script that continues to execute indefinitely by looping back and re-executing previous statements.

Specifically, you will learn

- How to add comments to your Windows shell scripts
- How to place two or more statements on the same line
- How to set up conditional command execution
- How to make the output of one command the input for another command
- How to create report and log files and append data to existing report and log files

Project Preview: The Fortune Teller Game

This chapter's main project is called the Fortune Teller game. It demonstrates the application of a number of programming techniques, including how to collect input from the player, how to evaluate player input, and how to create a script that continues to run until the player decides to quit the game.

The game begins by presenting the player with a welcome screen that helps to define the premise of the game, as shown in Figure 3.1.

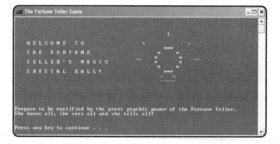

The Fortune Teller game begins by welcoming the player.

The player must press a key for the game to continue, at which point the next screen continues to build upon the game's story line, as shown in Figure 3.2.

FIGURE 3.2

The fortune teller enters the room.

Next, the fortune teller invites the player to ask a question and promises to try and provide an answer, as shown in Figure 3.3.

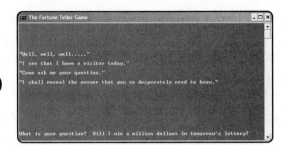

FIGURE 3.3

She invites the
player to ask
a question.

The game then describes the process that the fortune teller goes through as she uses
her psychic powers to come up with an answer. As shown in Figure 3.4, the fortune
teller is not always able to provide the player with a conclusive Yes or No response.

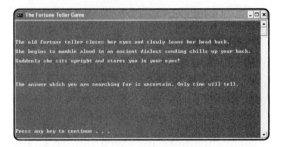

FIGURE 3.4

With as much
drama as she can
create, the fortune
teller answers the
player's question.

After answering the player's first question, the fortune teller continues to allow
additional questions to be asked, as shown in Figure 3.5. The game continues until
the player closes the Windows command console or types the lower case letter e to
end, or exit, the game.

FIGURE 3.5

Players may
continue to ask as
many questions as
they wish.

More Scripting Basics

So far, you have learned how to create, save, and run Windows shell scripts. You
have learned how to display text output, post messages in the Windows command
console's title bar, and perform other tricks like command prompt modification.
Now you should learn a few script housekeeping matters. Specifically, I'll show

you how to add comments to scripts in order to make them self-documenting. In addition, I'll discuss the importance of using comments to create a Windows shell script documentation template that you can use to improve the overall organization and manageability of your scripts.

Documenting Your Scripts with Comments

Adding comments to your Windows shell scripts makes them easier for other people to understand. Comments provide you with the ability to embed documentation with a script so that you can explain how and why you wrote it the way that you did. Adding comments to scripts is a little bit like adding a trail of bread crumbs. They give you something to follow if you find that you need to fix or modify a script sometime down the road.

Comments are added to Windows shell scripts using the REM statement, which has the following syntax:

```
REM Comment
```

Comment is a text string representing the documentation that you wish to embed in the script. REM statements have no impact on the execution of your script. The Windows shell ignores them during script execution. You can use the REM statement in either of two ways. One way to use the REM statement is to include it on a line by itself to describe or document the action of one or more statements that follow, as demonstrated below.

```
@ECHO off


REM Display the Welcome Screen
ECHO.
ECHO.
ECHO W E L C O M E   T O   T H E
ECHO.
ECHO F O R T U N E   T E L L E R   G A M E !
ECHO.
ECHO.
ECHO.


REM Make the player hit a key in order for the game to continue
PAUSE
```

A second way to use the REM statement is to place it at the end of another statement, as demonstrated below.

```
PAUSE      REM Make the player hit a key in order for the game to continue
```

Always begin with the @ECHO off statement as the first script statement. If you forget and leave this statement out of your script, all your script statements (including your comments) will be displayed as the script executes, thus defeating much of the benefit for adding comments to your scripts.

Creating a Script Template

Now that you know how to use the REM statement to add comments to your Windows shell scripts, consider a second application for this highly useful statement. Instead of using the REM statement just to document your script's logic, how about using it to improve your scripts overall organization? Specifically, I am suggesting that you create a Windows shell script template similar to the one I have created below.

```
@ECHO off

REM *************************************************************************

REM

REM Script Name: Xxxxxxxx.bat

REM Author: Xxxx Xxxxx

REM Date: Xxxxx XX, XXXX

REM

REM Description: Xxxxxxxxxxxxxxxxxxxxxxxxxxxxxxxxxxxxxxxxxxxxxxx

REM

REM *************************************************************************


REM Script Initialization Section


REM Main Processing Section


REM Subroutine and Procedure Section
```

In this example, the template begins with the @ECHO off statement and then uses the REM statement to format a script header in which you can document information about the script, including its name, author, creation date, and a description. Three additional statements have been added to the bottom of the template and can be used to organize your scripts into three major sections. In the Initialization section, you would add statements that perform functions such as setting foreground and background colors or posting the name of the script in the Windows command console's title bar.

The Main Processing section is where you would type the core logical portions of your script. Later, in Chapter 7, "Creating Procedures and Subroutines," I'll go over how to isolate portions of your code into discreet subroutines and procedures, which you would then locate in the third section of the template.

By using the template I have provided or by creating one of your own, you lay down a foundation for all future script development with a consistent organizational structure that will be easy to follow and update. For example, the following script demonstrates how to use the template in the creation of a new script.

```
@ECHO off

REM **************************************************************************

REM

REM Script Name: ScriptInit.bat

REM Author: Jerry Ford

REM Date: June 21, 2003

REM

REM Description: Customize a Windows shell scripting work environment

REM

REM **************************************************************************


REM Script Initialization Section


REM Modify the Windows command console title bar

TITLE = Script Environment Configuration


REM Set background color to white and foreground color to black
```

```
COLOR F0


REM Add C:\Scripts to the search path
PATH %path%;C:\Scripts


REM Modify the command prompt to display the greater than sign
PROMPT $g


REM Main Processing Section


REM Clear the screen
CLS


REM Tell the user that everything it set up
ECHO Script environment initialization complete


REM Subroutine and Procedure Section
```

As you can see, anyone who views the script can quickly identify the script's purpose and its author. By looking for the three main script comments, you can also easily locate different sections of the script. By adding additional comments, you can create self-documenting scripts. Note that while this particular example does not have any subroutines or procedures, you might still want to include that section comment in the script as a placeholder for possible future development.

Mastering Command Redirection

So far, all the examples you've seen in this book have demonstrated that script output is, by default, written to the Windows command console. In addition, all input has come directly from the computer's keyboard. However, the Windows shell let's you specify different sources of input, such as

- The keyboard
- A file
- The output generated by another command

In addition, the Windows shell let's you send output to different destinations, such as

- The Windows command console display
- A file
- A printer

Examining Data Input and Output

The Windows shell can work with three different command sources, as outlined below.

- **Standard Input**. The location where the Windows shell looks for command input. By default, this is the computer's keyboard.
- **Standard Output**. The default location where the Windows shell sends all output. By default, this is the Windows command console.
- **Standard Error**. The default location where the Windows shell sends all error messages. By default, this is the Windows command console.

When you modify the Windows shell's default source for input or output, you perform what is known as *redirection*. Input and output redirection is remarkably easy to set up and can be used to perform a number of useful tasks, including

- Automatically supplying commands with input to process
- Report generation
- Error log file creation

To support input and output redirection, the Windows shell uses a number of special characters. These characters and their function are outlined in Table 3.1.

 TRICK In addition to redirecting output to files, you can also send it to a printer by specifying the appropriate port number, such as **LPT1**.

I'll demonstrate how to work with these redirection operators in the sections that follow.

TABLE 3.1 REDIRECTION OPERATORS

Operator	Example	Description
>	command > file	Sends all output to a file or device
<	command < file	Retrieves input from a file
>>	command >> file	Appends output to a file
2>	command 2> file	Sends all error output to a file or device
2>&1	command 2>&1	Sends all error output to the same location as all normal output
|	command1 | command2	Uses the output from one command as the input for another command

Using One Command's Output as Another Command's Input

The | redirection operator enables you to feed, or *pipe*, the output of one command to another command as input. The best way I can explain this is by showing you an example. First, let's say that you created a text file called TestFile.txt, and then added the following lines to it:

```
Strawberry

Apple

Grape

Blue Berry

Orange
```

One way to view the contents of this file from the Windows command console would be with the TYPE command, as demonstrated below.

```
c:\scripts>TYPE TestFile.txt

Strawberry

Apple

Grape

Blue Berry

Orange
```

DEFINITION The TYPE **command displays the contents of files by sending its output to standard output. By default, this is the Windows command console.**

As you can see, the TYPE command displays the contents of the TestFile.txt file exactly as they are stored. However, suppose that you wanted to sort the entries in the file before displaying them. One way to accomplish this is to redirect the output of the TYPE command and use it as input for the SORT command, as demonstrated below.

```
c:\scripts>TYPE TestFile.txt | SORT

Apple

Blue Berry

Grape

Orange

Strawberry
```

DEFINITION The SORT **command sorts data as input and sends the result to standard output.**

Generating Reports

The > redirection operator enables you to send command output to a destination other than standard output. It provides an easy way to generate report and log files. In addition, the >> operators provide the ability to append data to the end of existing report and log files. Look at an example of these two redirection operators in action.

```
@ECHO off

REM *******************************************************************************

REM

REM Script Name: Reporter.bat

REM Author: Jerry Ford

REM Date: June 28, 2003

REM

REM Description: A report generation example

REM

REM *******************************************************************************


REM Script Initialization Section


REM Specify folder where report is to be saved
```

```
SET dest=C:\Scripts\LogFiles\Sample.txt


REM Display report data

ECHO Sample Windows shell script report > %dest%

ECHO. >> %dest%

ECHO Date: %date% >> %dest%

ECHO. >> %dest%

ECHO Created by %username% >> %dest%

ECHO. >> %dest%

ECHO. >> %dest%

ECHO Scripts residing in C:\SCRIPTS: >> %dest%

ECHO ----------------------------------------------------------- >> %dest%

ECHO. >> %dest%


DIR *.bat >> %dest%


REM Notify user that the report is now ready

ECHO Sample.txt report has been created in %dest%
```

DEFINITION The DIR command provides a list of all files and folders stored in the specified folder or directory.

In this example, a variable called dest is established using the SET command. It is assigned the name and path of a report that the script will create. The report is actually created when the first ECHO statement is executed and has its output redirected to the folder specified by the dest variable. Once the file is created, the script continues to write to the file by redirecting the output of ECHO statements using the >> (append) operator.

TRAP This script will fail unless the complete path to the target folder already exists. Before you run this script, make sure that you create a subfolder called LogFiles within your C:\Script folder.

Windows Shell Script Programming for the Absolute Beginner

TRAP Be sure you remember to switch from the > operator to the >> operator after the first redirection operation in the script. Otherwise, instead of appending additional data to the end of the report, your script will continue to overwrite the text stored in the report, leaving only the last line of output in the report.

Figure 3.6 shows an example of the report created by this script.

```
Sample.txt - Notepad                                    _ □ X
File  Edit  Format  View  Help
Sample Windows shell script report

Date: Sat 06/28/2003

Created by Jerry Ford


Scripts residing in C:\SCRIPTS:
------------------------------------------------

 Volume in drive C is IBMDOS_6
 Volume Serial Number is 2B6A-58F8

 Directory of c:\scripts

06/08/2003  12:54 PM                 766 KnockKnock.bat
06/15/2003  01:57 PM                 667 Unpredictable.bat
06/28/2003  10:17 AM               3,932 Fortune.bat
06/26/2003  03:59 PM               1,933 NumberGuess.bat
06/28/2003  09:45 AM               3,095 RockPaperScissors.bat
06/27/2003  03:05 PM                 769 ScriptInit.bat
06/28/2003  01:40 PM                 911 x.bat
               7 File(s)         12,073 bytes
               0 Dir(s)     177,700,864 bytes free
```

FIGURE 3.6

Examining the report created by a Windows shell script using output redirection.

Creating Error Logs

By default, Windows shell scripts send error messages and output to the same location (e.g., the Windows command console). However, if you wish, you can redirect any errors that occur to someplace else. For example, you might want to send all errors to a log file that you can monitor over time to see what's going on with your scripts.

For example, let's say that you created an empty file called Errors.log, located in C:\Scripts in order to have a centralized place to record script error messages as you developed and tested them. Once created, you can write error output from any of your scripts to this file using the 2> redirection operator, as demonstrated below.

```
TYPE C:\Reports\Report.txt 2> C:\Scripts\Errors.log
```

In this example, the TYPE command is used to display the contents of a file called Report.txt located in C:\Reports. If Report.txt exists, then its contents are displayed. If the Report.txt file does not exist, the following error will occur and be written to the C:\Scripts\Errors.log file.

```
The system cannot find the file specified.
```

In addition, since the error shown above was redirected to the log file, it would not have been displayed in the Windows command console when the script executed.

Conditional Command Execution

The Windows shell provides the ability to chain together the execution of multiple commands using a technique referred to as *compound commands.* Compound commands use a collection of reserved characters, shown in Table 3.2, to set up a relationship between two or more commands.

TABLE 3.2 COMPOUND COMMAND OPERATORS		
Operator	**Example**	**Description**
&	command & command	Runs the first command followed by the second command
&&	command && command	Runs the second command if the first command was successful
||	command || command	Runs the second command if the first command had an error
( )	(command || command) || (command & command)	Defines the order in which commands are to be executed

Chaining Two Commands Together

The most straightforward type of compound command is created using the & operator. Using this operator, you can chain together the execution of any two commands, as demonstrated below.

```
MKDIR C:\Scripts\Reports & COPY *.txt C:\Scripts\Reports
```

This compound command begins by executing the MKDIR command, which creates a new directory or subfolder called Reports in the C:\Scripts folder. Once this command completes execution, the second command in the compound command executes. In this example, the COPY command copies all files ending with a .txt extension in the current working directory to C:\Scripts\Reports.

Setting Up Conditional Command Execution

A more advanced compound command is created using the && operator. This operator executes the second command only if the first command was successful. Otherwise, the execution of the second command is omitted. For example, the following statement is set up to display all .log files found in the current working directory and to copy those log files, if any exist, to `C:\Scripts\LogFiles`.

```
DIR *.log && COPY *.Log C:\Scripts\LogFiles
```

The || compound command operator is the exact opposite of the && operator, performing the second command only in the event that the first command fails. For example, the following compound command begins by displaying all .log files in the current working directory. If no .log files are found, then the text of the ECHO statement is redirected to `C:\Scripts\Debug.log`.

```
DIR *.log || ECHO No .log files were found >> C:\Scripts\Debug.log
```

The Windows shell allows you to chain together more than two commands at a time if needed. For example, the following statement chains together three commands:

```
DIR *.log & COPY *.log C:\Tmp & ECHO .LOG files have been copied.
```

Grouping Commands

The Windows shell also enables you to explicitly group commands together to dictate the order in which they are executed. This is accomplished using the () operators. For example, the following statement consists of five different commands:

```
CD C:\Scripts\Reports && (COPY *.txt A:\ & COPY *.bak A:\) && (DEL *.txt & DEL *.bak)
```

The first command changes the current working directory to `C:\Scripts\Reports`. The first && operator ensures that the remaining commands execute only if the first command is successful. The second and third commands have been grouped together to ensure that they both execute before the last two commands are processed, which execute only if the second and third commands are both processed successfully. These two commands copy all .txt and all .bak files to the computer's floppy drive (A:\). Finally, if both of these commands executed successfully, the last two commands execute and delete all .txt and .bak files found in `C:\Scripts\Reports`.

Back to the Fortune Teller Game

Now let's return to the chapter's main project, the Fortune Teller game. Through the development of this script, you will continue to expand on your Windows shell scripting skills. Specifically, you will develop a script that begins by introducing the player to a fictional fortune teller who promises to try to use her psychic powers to answer the player's every question.

The script will answer the player using one of the following three responses:

- No!
- Yes!
- Only time will tell.

The script begins by presenting the player with a series of screens that provide background information for the game, introducing the fortune teller, and having her prompt the player to ask a question. The script will then generate an answer to the player's question by displaying one of three randomly selected responses. The script then continues to allow the player to keep asking questions until the player either closes the Windows command console or types the lower case letter e to end the game.

Designing the Game

The Fortune Teller game will be completed in eight steps, as outlined below

1. Add the script template and establish execution settings
2. Display the initial welcome screen
3. Introduce the fortune teller
4. Collect a question from the player
5. Determine if the player wants to exit the game
6. Randomly select a response
7. Display the fortune teller's answer
8. Prompt the player to ask a new question

As you read the rest of this chapter, I'll break down the programming statements that must be created in each of these steps in detail. By the time you're done, your Fortune Teller game will be ready to begin making predictions, and you'll have something really neat to share with your friends.

Establishing the Execution Environment

The first step in creating the Fortune Teller game is to create a new Windows shell script called Fortune.bat and type the following statements into it:

```
@ECHO off


REM ************************************************************************
REM
```

```
REM Script Name: Fortune.bat

REM Author: Jerry Ford

REM Date: June 22, 2003

REM

REM Description: This Windows shell script game provides random answers to

REM question posed by the player.

REM

REM ***********************************************************************


COLOR 5e

TITLE The Fortune Teller Game


CLS
```

The first statement presents the display of script statements during execution. The next 10 statements provide a place to document the script's name, author, and creation date as well as to provide a brief description. The COLOR statement sets the Windows command console's color scheme to yellow text on a purple background. The TITLE statement then posts the name of the game in the Windows command console's title bar. Finally, the CLS statement clears the display and prepares it for the game's first screen.

Creating a Welcome Screen

The first screen the player will see is a welcome screen that displays a welcome message and a text-based graphic of a crystal ball, as shown below.

```
ECHO.

ECHO.

ECHO.

ECHO                                    ^|

ECHO.

ECHO    W E L C O M E   T O            \           /

ECHO                                        ***

ECHO    T H E   F O R T U N E              *    *

ECHO                                 _    *      *    _

ECHO    T E L L E R ' S   M A G I C        *      *
```

```
ECHO                                           *     *
ECHO      C R Y S T A L   B A L L !          ***
ECHO                                          /   \
ECHO                                          -----
ECHO.
ECHO.
ECHO.
ECHO.
ECHO.
ECHO Prepare to be mystified by the great psychic power of the Fortune Teller.
ECHO She knows all, she sees all and she tells all!
ECHO.
ECHO.


Pause
```

To prevent the above screen from scrolling off of the display as the game executes, thus giving the player a chance to read it, the PAUSE command has been added.

Building the Story Line

Next, another CLS statement clears the display so that the game's second screen can be displayed. The statements that generate this screen are shown below.

```
CLS


ECHO.
ECHO.
ECHO.
ECHO.
ECHO.
ECHO.
ECHO Quiet! Here she comes.......
ECHO.
ECHO The door opens and a small woman with a cane and a limp slowly
ECHO.
```

```
ECHO enters into the room.
ECHO.
ECHO.
ECHO.
ECHO.
ECHO.
ECHO.
ECHO.
ECHO.
ECHO.
ECHO.
ECHO.
ECHO.


PAUSE
```

As you can see, the PAUSE command is again used to ensure that the player has an opportunity to view the information on this screen.

Collecting the Player's Question

Once again, the CLS statement is used to clear the screen—this time, to allow the fortune teller to prompt the player to ask a question. Again, this screen consists mostly of ECHO statements that set up the story line.

```
CLS


ECHO.
ECHO.
ECHO.
ECHO.
ECHO.
ECHO.
ECHO "Well, well, well....."
ECHO.
ECHO "I see that I have a visitor today."
```

```
ECHO.

ECHO "Come ask me your question."

ECHO.

ECHO "I shall reveal the answer that you so desperately need to know."

ECHO.

ECHO.

ECHO.

ECHO.

ECHO.

ECHO.

ECHO.

ECHO.

ECHO.


:QUESTION


ECHO.


SET /p reply="What is your question?  "


SET trigger=%reply:~0,1%
```

Near the end of this section of code, you see a statement that looks like this:

```
:QUESTION
```

This statement represents a label, which is a location in a Windows shell script that can be called upon for execution. Later, you'll see where I add a GOTO statement at the end of the script to create a loop to allow the game to continue to replay over and over again.

 DEFINITION   **A _loop_ is a collection of statements that are executed repeatedly.**

The next statement prompts the player to enter a question for the fortune teller to answer. By placing the :QUESTION label just before the SET statement, I have provided the ability to loop back to this portion of the script and replay the game starting at the point where the fortune teller instructs the player to ask a question.

Next, another SET statement is executed. This statement extracts the first character from the text string entered by the player to see if it is equal to the letter e. If is does equal the letter e, the script assumes that the player is done and wants to end the game.

TRAP

Even though I have not yet covered it in this book, I wanted to use the substring operation presented here to introduce you to a different method of control script termination. Unfortunately, whether it be substring operations, conditional logic, or loops, for your best learning experience I will only formally introduce and explain a limited number of programming concepts at a time. My goal in this book is to introduce and explain basic programming concepts and to continue to build upon them as I go along. However, it's almost impossible to write Windows shell script games without using some advanced scripting techniques. Without some advanced techniques, the game projects in the first two-thirds of this book would have remained very simple while I covered all the concepts that you'll need to write more advanced scripts. But this approach takes away most of the fun and I wanted to present you with game scripts that become increasingly interesting (and therefore difficult) as the book progresses. Whenever I need to use a programming technique that I have not yet formally introduced to you, I'll try to provide a brief explanation of what's going on. I'll then provide a reference to the chapter where the programming technique is more fully explored, and then I'll keep moving on with the script project.

TRICK

I used a substring operation above to provide a quick way for the script to end. When coded in this way, the player could end the game by typing end, exit, or e.

TRAP

Be careful when using a substring operation as shown above because if the player somehow formulates a question using a word that begins with the letter e, the game would end instead of providing the player with an answer. In a game like this one, it's a fairly safe bet that most questions will begin with phrases such as "Will I" and "Should I," so using the letter e is probably safe enough.

IN THE REAL WORLD

The statement SET trigger=%reply:~0,1% is an example of a substring operation. A *substring* is simply a portion of a string found within another string. Extracting or *parsing* out substrings is a very common practice in programming. For example, scripts often have to read and process strings of user input or portions of text files in order to extract specific pieces of data to work with.

Creating an Exit Process

The next few lines in the script perform a test to determine whether the player wants to end or exit the game. If the letter e was typed, then the GOTO :EOF statement is executed, terminating the script's execution. Otherwise, the script continues to run.

```
IF %trigger%==e (

  GOTO :EOF

)
```

Generating Random Answers

The next portion of the script begins by displaying a little more of the story line, as shown below.

```
ECHO.

ECHO.

ECHO.

ECHO.

ECHO The old fortune teller closes her eyes and slowly leans her head back.

ECHO.

ECHO She begins to mumble aloud in an ancient dialect sending chills up your back.

ECHO.

ECHO Suddenly she sits upright and stares you in your eyes!

ECHO.

ECHO.

ECHO.

ECHO.


SET z=%random%


If %z% GTR 22000 (

  SET answer=NO!

  GOTO :Continue

)


  If %z% GTR 11000 (
```

```
  SET answer=YES!

  GOTO :Continue

)


If %z% GTR 0 (

  SET answer=uncertain. Only time will tell.

  GOTO :Continue

)
```

After describing the actions of the fortune teller, a SET statement is used to assign a random number to a variable called z. As in previous script examples, a series of IF statements are then used to assign a value to a variable called answer based on the value of the randomly selected variable. Specifically, if the randomly selected variable is greater than 22,000 the answer returned by the fortune will be NO! and the GOTO statement causes the script to jump down to the label called :Control and continue executing from that point in the script, thus bypassing any remaining validation of the randomly selected value. If the value of the variable is less than 22,000 and greater than 11,000, the answer returned will be YES! Otherwise, the answer will be set to Uncertain. Only time will tell.

Displaying the Fortune Teller's Prediction

The next portion of the script begins with a label called :Continue. This label provides the ability to jump to this location within the script and continue processing. Next, the screen is formatted using a collection of ECHO statements, and the answer selected by the fortune teller is displayed. A PAUSE statement then halts the script's execution and gives the player time to read the answer to his or her question.

```
:Continue


ECHO The answer which you are searching for is %answer%

ECHO.

ECHO.

ECHO.

ECHO.

ECHO.

ECHO.

ECHO.
```

```
ECHO.

ECHO.


PAUSE
```

Replaying the Game

Once the player's question has been answered by the fortune teller, the screen is cleared and a GOTO statement is used to jump back in the script to the :QUESTION label, thus allowing the player to ask the fortune teller a new question.

```
CLS


GOTO :QUESTION
```

The Final Result

Now look at the fully assembled script, as shown below. To help further document the script, I have added comments throughout that help to explain the logical processes that are taking place.

```
@ECHO off
REM ***************************************************************************
REM
REM Script Name: Fortune.bat
REM Author: Jerry Ford
REM Date: June 22, 2003
REM
REM Description: This Windows shell script game provides random answers to
REM questions posed by the player.
REM
REM ***************************************************************************

REM Post the name of the game in the Windows command console title bar
TITLE The Fortune Teller Game


REM Clear the display
```

```
CLS

REM Set the console colors to yellow text on a purple background
COLOR 5e

REM Display the welcome screen
ECHO.
ECHO.
ECHO.
ECHO                                          ^|
ECHO.
ECHO     W E L C O M E   T O              \           /
ECHO                                         ***
ECHO     T H E   F O R T U M E            *     *
ECHO                                  __   *       *   __
ECHO     T E L L E R ' S   M A G I C       *       *
ECHO                                        *     *
ECHO     C R Y S T A L   B A L L !          ***
ECHO                                        /  \
ECHO                                        -----
ECHO.
ECHO.
ECHO.
ECHO.
ECHO.
ECHO Prepare to be mystified by the great psychic power of the Fortune Teller.
ECHO She knows all, she sees all and she tells all!
ECHO.
ECHO.


REM Wait for the player to press a key
```

```
Pause

REM Clear the display
CLS

REM Display additional story text
ECHO.
ECHO.
ECHO.
ECHO.
ECHO.
ECHO.
ECHO Quiet! Here she comes.......
ECHO.
ECHO The door opens and a small woman with a cane and a limp slowly
ECHO.
ECHO enters into the room.
ECHO.
ECHO.
ECHO.
ECHO.
ECHO.
ECHO.
ECHO.
ECHO.
ECHO.
ECHO.
ECHO.
ECHO.

REM Wait for the player to press a key
```

```
PAUSE

REM Clear the display
CLS

REM Display additional story text
ECHO.
ECHO.
ECHO.
ECHO.
ECHO.
ECHO.
ECHO "Well, well, well....."
ECHO.
ECHO "I see that I have a visitor today."
ECHO.
ECHO "Come ask me your question."
ECHO.
ECHO "I shall reveal the answer that you so desperately need to know."
ECHO.
ECHO.
ECHO.
ECHO.
ECHO.
ECHO.
ECHO.
ECHO.

REM This label provides a callable return point in the script
```

```
:QUESTION

ECHO.

REM Prompt the player to type their question
SET /p reply="What is your question?  "

REM Extract the first character of the player's response
SET trigger=%reply:~0,1%

REM If the player typed the letter "e" then it's time to end the game
IF %trigger%==e (
  GOTO :EOF
)

REM Clear the display
CLS

REM Display the text that precedes the fortune teller's answer
ECHO.
ECHO.
ECHO.
ECHO.
ECHO The old fortune teller closes her eyes and slowly leans her head back.
ECHO.
ECHO She begins to mumble aloud in an ancient dialect, sending chills up
ECHO.
ECHO your back. Suddenly she sits upright and stares you in your eyes!
ECHO.
ECHO.
ECHO.
```

```
ECHO.


REM get a random number
SET z=%random%


REM If the random number is greater than 22,000 the answer is NO!
If %z% GTR 22000 (

  SET answer=NO!

  GOTO :Continue

)


REM If the random number is greater than 11,000 the answer is YES!
If %z% GTR 11000 (

  SET answer=YES!

  GOTO :Continue

)


REM If the random number is greater than zero the answer is uncertain.
If %z% GTR 0 (

  SET answer=uncertain. Only time will tell.

  GOTO :Continue

)


REM This label provides a callable return point in the script
:Continue


REM Display the fortune teller's answer
ECHO The answer which you are searching for is %answer%
ECHO.
ECHO.
ECHO.
ECHO.
ECHO.
```

```
ECHO.

ECHO.

ECHO.

ECHO.


REM Wait for the player to press a key
PAUSE


REM Clear the display
CLS


REM Loop back and let the player ask the fortune teller another question
GOTO :QUESTION
```

Summary

In this chapter, you learned how to add comments to your Windows shell scripts in order to document your scripting logic and to create a documentation template. You also learned how to take control of input and output. This included setting up the output of one command to provide another command's input. This also included learning how to create reports and error log files. This chapter also showed you how to combine more than one command to create a compound command as well as how to make the execution of one command conditional on the success of another command. Finally, you had some fun by creating the Fortune Teller game.

EXERCISES

1. The Fortune Teller game's story line is very basic. Add additional story text that helps to better describe what is occurring as the game plays out.

2. The Fortune Teller game currently makes a random selection from one of only three possible answers. Expand the range of available answers to six and then to nine.

3. Currently, the Fortune Teller game ends when the player types the letter e instead of a question. Add instructions to the game that explicitly inform the player of this capability. In addition, experiment with other possible ways to end the game such as requiring that the player enter the word Bye, at which time the Fortune Teller could invite the player to return again later to ask more questions.

CHAPTER 4

Storing and Retrieving Information in Variables

This chapter begins by showing you how to pass data to scripts at execution time and how to write scripts that can accept and process this data. In addition, you will get a formal education on the use of variables within Windows shell scripts. You will learn about environment variables that are created and maintained by the operating system as well as how to create and modify your own script variables.

You will also learn how to replace portions of the contents of string variables and to perform mathematical operations on variables containing numeric data. The chapter will then conclude by showing you how to build a Mad lib-style story called "Buzz the Wonder Dog," in which the reader helps to write the story by supplying key story elements collected from questions presented at the beginning of the script's execution.

Specifically, you will learn

- How to pass data to scripts in the form of arguments

- How to access system information using system environment variables

- How to access user information using user environment variables

- How to create, modify, and delete script variables

- How to limit access to variables within scripts

Project Preview:
"The Story of Buzz the Wonder Dog"

This chapter's main project is "The Story of Buzz the Wonder Dog." This Mad lib-style story collects input from the reader, stores it in variables, and then uses variable substitution to tell a story using the reader's input. The story will begin by displaying an initial welcome screen that introduces the story, as shown in Figure 4.1.

FIGURE 4.1

The story begins by displaying its title screen.

The reader is then informed that in order for the story to be told, he will need to participate, as shown in Figure 4.2.

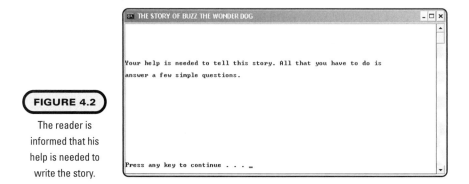

FIGURE 4.2

The reader is informed that his help is needed to write the story.

The reader will be asked a series of five questions, as shown in Figure 4.3. These questions will be asked without providing any context as to their ultimate use. This will help to ensure that the story is both unpredictable and humorous.

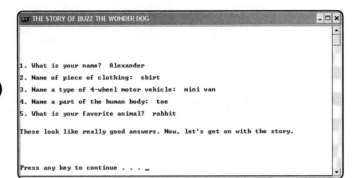

FIGURE 4.3

The answers
collected from five
questions are
substituted into
the story.

Once the reader's input has been collected and assigned to variables within the
Windows shell script, the story is told, as shown in Figure 4.4. As the story unfolds,
the input collected from the reader is woven into the story line.

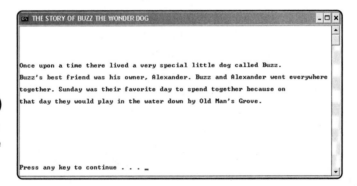

FIGURE 4.4

The story begins by
introducing Buzz the
Wonder Dog and
his friend.

After the entire story has been presented, the script will end and the Windows
command prompt will be displayed, as shown in Figure 4.5.

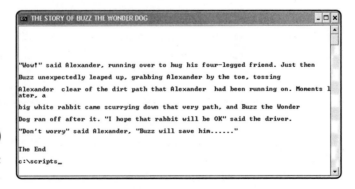

FIGURE 4.5

The story ends. Buzz
saves the day again.

By completing this project, you will reinforce your understanding of how to use variables within Windows shell scripts and lay some foundation for developing more advanced scripts.

Passing Data to Scripts at Execution Time

Often you can write completely self-contained scripts, meaning that they do not require any additional information in order to execute and perform a useful function. However, many scripts, especially games, require interaction with the user in order to execute. Earlier in this book, you have seen several sneak previews of the use of variables as a means of collecting input from the user. This chapter will explain in detail how to work with and control variables.

But before I go over this material, I want to take a little time to go over another option for passing data to scripts. Using this option, you pass data or *arguments* to the script when you run it. Arguments are passed to scripts by typing the name of the script followed by a space and then one or more arguments, each of which is separated by a space as demonstrated below. The space serves as a *delimiter* between each argument passed to the script.

```
ScriptName argument1 argument2 ......
```

DEFINITION An *argument* is a piece of data passed to a command or script when it executes.

DEFINITION A *delimiter* is a marker that identifies the boundaries of individual pieces of data passed to a script or command.

TRICK Don't be fooled if you see that someone else has used commas, tabs, equal signs, or semicolons as delimiters within Windows shell scripts. While most programmers use blank spaces to separate arguments, the Windows shell will allow any of these characters to serve as delimiters.

IN THE REAL WORLD

As you continue to create Windows shell scripts, you may find that you sometimes need to create more than one script to tackle certain tasks. In these situations, you'll probably want to start one script and then have it trigger the execution of the next script. In this scenario, you'll probably need to have the first script pass arguments to the second script in order for the second script to know what to do.

A Windows shell script processes arguments by assigning them to parameters. The Windows shell allows you to access up to eleven different script input parameters at a time, as listed in Table 4.1.

TABLE 4.1 WINDOWS SHELL SCRIPT PARAMETERS

Parameter	Description
%*	Lists all the arguments that have been passed to the script
%0	Stores the name of the script
%1	Stores the first argument passed to the script
%2	Stores the second argument passed to the script
%3	Stores the third argument passed to the script
%4	Stores the fourth argument passed to the script
%5	Stores the fifth argument passed to the script
%6	Stores the sixth argument passed to the script
%7	Stores the seventh argument passed to the script
%8	Stores the eighth argument passed to the script
%9	Stores the ninth argument passed to the script

Look at an example of how to write a Windows shell script that processes a pair of arguments passed to it at execution time.

```
@ECHO off

ECHO %1

ECHO %2
```

This script should be easy to understand. It simply displays the arguments that have been passed to it. Go ahead and create and save this script as Test.bat. Then run it by typing its name followed by two arguments, as demonstrated below.

```
Test.bat C:\Temp C:\Scripts
```

Once executed, you should see the following results displayed in the Windows command console:

```
C:\Temp

C:\Scripts
```

Handling Large Numbers of Arguments

Using the information just presented, you should be able to create Windows shell scripts that can accept and process up to nine arguments at execution time. While this will certainly accommodate most situations, at some time you may find a need to create a script that can accept and process more than nine arguments at run time.

When you think of script parameters, think of them as being lined up in a row with the first argument passed to the script lined up on the far left and the last argument passed to the script lined up on the far right. At most, the Windows shell allows you to access nine parameters at a time, as shown below.

```
%1 %2 %3 %4 %5 %6 %7 %8 %9
```

However, the Windows shell allows you to pass as many arguments as you want to your scripts. For example, the following list defines a collection of 12 arguments that you might want to pass to a script.

```
arg1 arg2 arg3 arg4 arg5 arg6 arg7 arg8 arg9 arg10 arg11 arg12
```

The Windows shell automatically associates each argument with its corresponding parameter. For example, the first argument passed to the script would represent the script's first parameter, as represented by %1.

While the Windows shell won't let you directly access more than nine arguments at a time, it does allow you to pass as many arguments as you need. To access any arguments passed to the script beyond the ninth one, you must learn how to use the SHIFT command. This command allows you to move to the left by one all parameters representing arguments passed to your script. For example, the following command moves all of the parameters to the left by one.

```
SHIFT
```

The net effect of the previous command is that the value stored in %2 becomes %1 and the value stored in %3 becomes %2, and so on. As a result, the script's ninth parameter (e.g., %9) frees up and is then automatically assigned the value passed to the script by the tenth argument. Therefore, by executing the SHIFT command repeatedly, you can create a script that can access every argument passed to it.

TRICK If you wish, you can specify the parameter position at which you begin shifting arguments. For example, typing SHIFT /3 leaves the contents stored in %1 and %2 unaltered but shifts the values stored in the rest of the script's input parameters. Thus the values of the arguments stored in %3 - %9 would all be shifted to the left by one.

Handling Arguments That Include Blank Spaces

Sometimes a single argument may consist of more than a single word. In other words, it may include blank spaces. Unless you take special steps to mark the beginning and end of the argument, the Windows shell will treat each word in the argument as a separate argument, producing undesirable effects within your Windows shell scripts.

To prevent this from occurring, make sure you remember to enclose all multi-word arguments within a pair of matching double quotation marks before passing it to a script. For example, suppose you had a script to which you wanted to pass the following files as arguments:

```
C:\Temp\Rough Outline.txt
```

```
C:\Temp\Sample Report.doc
```

Since both of these files have file names that include blank spaces, you would need to surround both file names with double quotes before passing them to your script, as demonstrated below.

```
Test.bat "C:\Temp\Rough Outline.txt" "C:\Temp\Sample Report.doc"
```

The script, `Test.bat`, would then be able to reference these two file names at `%1` and `%2`, respectively.

Working with Variables

Now let's turn our attention to understanding and working with variables. A *variable* is a reference to a location in the computer's memory where your scripts can store and retrieve data. There are two primary types of variables that you will work with in Windows shell scripts, environment variables, and script variables. An *environment variable* is created and maintained by the operating system. Your scripts can access and use the values stored in environment variables. The other type of variable that you'll use are script variables. A *script variable* is created during the execution of a script and then deleted when the script stops running.

The Windows shell provides the SET command as your primary means for displaying, modifying, and deleting variables. The SET command supports several different variations of syntax, as shown below.

```
SET [Variable=[Value]]
```

```
SET /A Expression
```

```
SET /P Variable=[MessagePrompt]
```

When used in its first form, the SET command displays, creates, modifies, and deletes variables. *Variable* specifies the name of the variable to be displayed, created, modified, or deleted. *Value* specifies an optional data assignment.

The second form of the SET command defines numeric variables. /A designates that the value stored in the variable is to be treated as a number and *Expression* specifies the value assigned to the variable.

The final format of the SET command allows you to interactively prompt the user to type input, which is then assigned to a variable. /P specifies that the SET command should prompt for user input. *Variable* defines the name of the variable to which the user's input is assigned, and MessagePrompt is an optional text string that you can use to present the user with instructions on what you want him to enter.

Accessing Environment Variables

Windows operating systems collect and store information about the computer and its users in a special database known as the Windows registry. The information stored in the registry is collected from a number of sources. Some of the registry's information is made available to you in the form of environment variables. There are two types of environment variables:

- **User environment variables** provide information specific to the individual users.
- **System environment variables** provide information specific to the computer and its execution environment.

Viewing Environment Variables

On Windows XP, a number of environment variables can be accessed from the System Properties dialog using the following procedure:

1. Click on Start, right-click on My Computer, and select Properties from the menu that appears. The System Properties dialog appears.
2. Select the Advanced property sheet.
3. Click on the Environment Variables button located at the bottom on the dialog. The Environment Variables dialog appears, as shown in Figure 4.6.

User variables associated with the currently logged-on user are displayed at the top of the dialog. In this example, two user environment variables are shown, both of which specify the location of different temporary folders.

FIGURE 4.6

On Windows XP, both user and system environment variables can be viewed and modified from the `Environment Variables` dialog.

System environment variables are displayed at the bottom of the dialog. You'll usually find a number of different system environment variables listed here, including

- **COMSPEC**. Specifies the location of the Windows shell (e.g., CMD.EXE).
- **OS**. Identifies the currently running Windows operating system.
- **PATH**. Specifies the default search path.
- **PATHEXT**. Lists file extensions that represent executable programs.
- **Prompt**. Specifies the default command prompt format.
- **TEMP**. Specifies the location of a folder where the system may store temporary files.
- **WINDIR**. Identifies the folder where system files are located.

Modifying Environment Variables

While you can view and access environment variables from within your Windows shell scripts, you cannot permanently change them. You can, however, make permanent changes to user and system environment variables from the `Environment Variables` dialog provided that you have administrative rights for the computer on which you're working.

By clicking on the `New`, `Edit`, or `Delete` buttons associated with either the user or system environment variables, you can create, change, or delete environment variables. For example, to create a new system variable, click on the `New` button located at the bottom of the `Environment Variables` dialog. The `New System Variable` dialog will appear, as shown in Figure 4.7. To create the new variable, type its name in the `Variable name` field and its value in the `Variable value` field and click on `OK`.

FIGURE 4.7

Defining a new
system environment
variable.

TRICK

For any changes you make to user environment variables to take effect, you must log off the computer and log back in again. For any changes you make to system variables to take effect, you must restart the computer.

Some environment variables cannot be viewed from the Environment Variables dialog. However, the Windows shell will let you view and reference them using the SET command. For example, to view a list of all environment variables accessible by your scripts, type SET at the Windows command prompt and hit the Enter key. You should see output displayed similar to the following:

```
C:\>SET

ALLUSERSPROFILE=C:\Documents and Settings\All Users

APPDATA=C:\Documents and Settings\Jerry Ford\Application Data

CommonProgramFiles=C:\Program Files\Common Files

COMPUTERNAME=WRKSTN0001

ComSpec=C:\WINDOWS\system32\cmd.exe

HOMEDRIVE=C:

HOMEPATH=\Documents and Settings\Jerry Ford

LOGONSERVER=\\WRKSTN0001

NUMBER_OF_PROCESSORS=1

OS=Windows_NT

Path=C:\WINDOWS\system32;C:\WINDOWS;C:\WINDOWS\COMMAND;C:\DOS;C:\WINDOWS\system3
2\WBEM

PATHEXT=.COM;.EXE;.BAT;.CMD;.VBS;.VBE;.JS;.JSE;.WSF;.WSH

PROCESSOR_ARCHITECTURE=x86

PROCESSOR_IDENTIFIER=x86 Family 6 Model 6 Stepping 0, GenuineIntel

PROCESSOR_LEVEL=6

PROCESSOR_REVISION=0600

ProgramFiles=C:\Program Files
```

```
PROMPT=$p$g

SESSIONNAME=Console

SystemDrive=C:

SystemRoot=C:\WINDOWS

TEMP=C:\DOCUME~1\JERRYF~1\LOCALS~1\Temp

TMP=C:\DOCUME~1\JERRYF~1\LOCALS~1\Temp

USERDOMAIN=WRKSTN0001

USERNAME=Jerry Ford

USERPROFILE=C:\Documents and Settings\Jerry Ford

windir=C:\WINDOWS

C:\>
```

 TRICK **While you cannot make permanent changes to environment variables from within your Windows shell scripts, you can create variables that have the same name as environment variables and modify their values. These variables will then temporarily override the values of the environment variables for your script.**

Although you cannot see them using any of the previously mentioned procedures, Windows 2000 and XP also provide access to a small collection of dynamically created environment variables. These variables are listed in Table 4.2.

TABLE 4.2 DYNAMIC ENVIRONMENT VARIABLES

Variable	Description
CD	Stores a string representing the current working directory
DATE	Stores a string representing the current system date
Time	Stores a string representing the current system time
RANDOM	Retrieves a random number between 0 and 32,767
ERRORLEVEL	Retrieves the exit code of the previously executed command
CMDEXTVERSION	Stores a string identifying the Windows shell version number
CMDCMDLINE	Stores a string showing the command that was used to start the current Windows shell session

Creating, Modifying, and Deleting Script Variables

While you are limited as to what you can do within a script with environment variables, you have complete control over your script variables. For example, to create a script variable called gamename and assign it a value of WonderDog, you would use the SET command to define the variable, as shown below.

```
SET gamename=Wonderdog
```

Note that there are no blank spaces between either the variable name and the equals sign or between the equals sign and the assigned value. If a blank space were added before the equals sign, the Windows shell would interpret that to mean that the blank space was part of the variable's name. If a blank space were inserted between the equals sign and the assigned value, the Windows shell would interpret the blank space as part of the assigned text.

To change the value assigned to the variable, you would again use the SET command, as demonstrated below.

```
SET gamename=BuzzTheWonderDog
```

When used this way, the SET command simply replaces the value assigned to the specified variable. You can also use the SET command to delete a variable by setting the variable equal to nothing, as demonstrated below.

```
SET gamename=
```

Naming Variables

While the Windows shell is very flexible when it comes to working with variables, there are still a few rules that you must follow to avoid errors. These rules are outlined below.

- If you include quotation marks as part of the variable's assigned value, the Windows shell will treat the quotation marks as part of the value assignment.
- You may not include reserved characters in a variable's value assignment unless you enclose them within double quotation marks.
- Blank spaces included before the equals sign are considered part of the variable's name.
- Blank spaces included after the equals sign are considered part of the variable's assigned value.

In addition to these rules, I have some additional friendly advice that you should keep in mind when working with variables.

- Make variable names as descriptive of their contents as possible.
- While there is no practical limit to the length of a variable name, I recommend keeping them less than 20 characters long to help make them easy to read and manage.
- Variable names are not case-sensitive. However, I recommend that you be consistent in whatever naming convention you choose to adopt. In other words, don't mix things up.

Determining the Limits of Variable Access

By default, access to variables is global throughout a script, meaning that variables can be accessed from any location within the script. However, if you wish to exercise strict control over variables in your scripts, you can localize accessibility to variables by restricting the location within a script where they can be referenced. To perform this trick you'll need to learn how to work with the SETLOCAL and ENDLOCAL commands.

You use the SETLOCAL and ENDLOCAL commands together to define a starting and ending location within a script where a variable and its value can be referenced. For example, consider the following script:

```
@ECHO off


SETLOCAL
   SET x=true
   ECHO x = %x%
ENDLOCAL


ECHO x = %x%
```

This script begins by using the SETLOCAL command to localize the value of a variable called x. It then assigns a value of true to x and displays its value. The ENDLOCAL command is then used to terminate the scope of the x variable, effectively deleting it. Therefore, when the script attempts to reference it a second time, no value is displayed. The following output shows what you will see if you create and run this script.

```
x = true

x =
```

The SETLOCAL and ENDLOCAL commands can also be used to localize changes made to an existing variable, with the result that any changes made to the variable within the localized scope are discarded when the scope terminates. For example, consider the following example.

```
@ECHO off


SET x=true
ECHO x = %x%


SETLOCAL
  SET x=false
  ECHO x = %x%
ENDLOCAL


ECHO = %x%
```

In this example, the script begins by defining a variable called x and assigning it a value of true. It then displays this value. Next, the SETLOCAL and ENDLOCAL commands set up a temporary localized scope in which the value of x is changed to false and then displayed. However, as soon as the localized scope terminates, the previous value assigned to x is restored. Thus when the value of x is displayed again, its value is equal to true again, as shown below.

```
x = true
x = false
x = true
```

 TRICK The SETLOCAL and ENDLOCAL **commands are often used in combination with subroutines and procedures, which are covered later in Chapter 7, "Creating Procedures and Subroutines."**

Working with Mathematical Variables

As mentioned earlier, when the /A switch is used with the SET command, the Windows shell knows that it needs to treat any data assigned to the defined variable as numeric. By labeling a value as numeric, you enable the ability to manipulate it using mathematical expressions. The Windows shell can manipulate numbers within the range of −2,147,483,648 to 2,147,483,647. Any attempt to work with a number smaller or larger than this range will result in an error. However, I doubt that this limitation will ever affect your scripts.

The following statement demonstrates how to assign a numeric value to a variable.

```
SET /A x = 1
```

In this example, x has been set to equal 1. You can also use mathematical expressions to assign a numeric value to a variable, as demonstrated below.

```
SET /A x = 1 + 2
```

In addition, you can use values stored in other numeric variables in building expressions, as demonstrated below.

```
SET /A x = 1
SET /A y = 2
SET /A z = x + y + 3
ECHO z
```

If you ran this example, you would see that the value of z is 6. In each of these examples, the = (equals sign) is used to assign numeric values to variables. The Windows shell also provides a number of other arithmetic operators, as listed in Table 4.3, that you can use to assign values to numeric variables.

TABLE 4.3 ASSIGNMENT OPERATORS

Operator	Purpose
+=	Adds two values together and assigns the result
-=	Subtracts one value from another and assigns the result
*=	Multiplies two values and assigns the result
/=	Divides one value into another and assigns the result
%=	Assigns the remaining portion of a division operation (e.g., the modulus)

For example, the following statement sets the value of x equal to the current value of x plus 1.

```
SET /A x += 1
```

Likewise, the following example sets x equal to x plus 5.

```
SET /A x += 5
```

In addition to the assignment operators listed in Table 4.3, you may use any of the arithmetic operators shown in Table 4.4 when manipulating the contents of numeric variables.

Operator	Purpose
TABLE 4.4 ARITHMETIC OPERATORS	
+	Adds numeric values together
-	Subtracts one value from another
*	Multiples two values together
/	Divides one value into another
%	Determines the quotient when dividing two numbers (also referred to as the modulus)

For example, the following statements define a variable called x, assign it an initial value of 2 and then multiplies the result by 5 before subtracting 3.

```
SET /A x = 2
SET /A x = x * 5 - 3
```

The end result is that x is equal to 7.

TRICK I don't know if you have noticed yet or not, but when you use the /A switch with the SET command, you can add blank spaces before and after the arithmetic operator and the Window shell automatically ignores them. This allows you to make your scripts more readable.

TRAP The Windows shell follows a strict set of rules whenever it performs a mathematical operation. First, it resolves quotient values (i.e., the modulus). Then it performs multiplication and division from left to right. Finally, it does any remaining addition and subtraction, again working from left to right.

Variable String Manipulation

The Windows shell also provides you with tools for manipulating the contents of variables containing text strings. The first programming technique is known as *string substitution* and involves the search for and replacement of a portion of text within a string. The second technique is to perform a substring operation. A *substring operation* is one in which you extract a portion of text from a text string.

Replacing a Portion of a String

Using string substitution, you can replace all or part of one string with another string. You might find substring operations useful in situations where you need your script to edit arguments passed to the script or to edit input provided by the user. For example, you might create a script that prompts the user to reply by entering the letter Y in order to continue running. However, some users may instead respond by typing in Yes instead. By performing a substring operation on the input provided by the user, you could replace the Yes string with a Y string.

The syntax you must follow when performing string substitution operations is outlined below.

```
%VariableName:ReplacementString=OriginalString%
```

%*VariableName* is the name of a variable to which you want to assign the result of the substring operation. It is immediately followed by the colon character. ReplacementString is a placeholder representing the string to be substituted (e.g., the Y string in the previous example) and OriginalString is a placeholder representing the string in which the replacement is to occur (e.g., the Yes string in the previous example).

Below is an example of string substitution in action. In this example, a variable called x is set equal to a small text phrase. Then, using string substitution, a second variable called z is set equal to the value of x, but only after a substring operation has been completed. In the substring operation, the word blue is substituted for the word gray.

```
@ECHO off


SET x=The sky above was quite gray
SET z=%x:gray=blue%


ECHO %z%
```

If you save and run this script, you'll see the output shown below.

```
The sky above was quite blue
```

You may also use string substitution to delete portions of text from a text string. To accomplish this trick, leave the replacement string blank. For example, to remove the word gray **from the string in the previous example, you would set the value of** z **as shown below.**

```
SET z=%x:gray=%
```

Extracting a Portion of a String

Another string manipulation technique supported by the Windows shell is substring operations, in which a portion of a text string is extracted from the string. You simply specify the starting location of the first character in the string to be extracted and, optionally, the number of characters to be extracted from that point on. What you do with the substring once you have extracted it is up to you. You might assign it as the value of a new variable or reassign it back to the original variable, thus replacing the original string with the substring.

The syntax you must follow when performing a substring operation is outlined below.

```
%VariableName:~StartPosition,Length%
```

First you specify the variable name. Then you add the colon and the tilde character (~) exactly as shown above. Next the StartPosition placeholder is used to specify the position of the first character in the substring. Length is optional. If Length is omitted, the substring will consist of all characters starting at StartPosition all the way to the end of the string. When Length is specified, the substring will consist of all the characters beginning at StartPosition plus the number of specified characters to the right of the starting position. To see how substring operations work, look at the following example:

```
@ECHO off


SET x=The sky above was quite gray
SET z=%x:~0,7%


ECHO %z%
```

In this example, the second SET statement extracts a substring from a text string stored in the x variable. It then assigns the substring text to a variable called z.

The substring operation begins at character position zero (e.g., the first letter of the first word of the text string) and consists of 7 characters. If you were to run this script, you would see the that the substring that is extracted and assigned to z is The sky.

Back to "The Story of Buzz the Wonder Dog"

The purpose behind "The Story of Buzz the Wonder Dog" is to provide reinforcement of your understanding of how to create and reference variables within Windows shell scripts. Using a Mad lib-style format, you will write a script that prompts the reader for input that the script will then use to help tell the story. The trick, however, is that readers won't know in advance how their input will be used within the story. As you will see when you run the completed script, this can lead to some surprising and unusual twists and turns.

Designing the Game

"The Story of Buzz the Wonder Dog" will be completed in five steps, as outlined below.

1. Initialize the scripting environment
2. Display the welcome screen
3. Notify the reader that their help is required
4. Prompt for reader input
5. Display the story

In the sections that follow, I'll explain just what you need to do to complete the script development of each of these steps.

Configuring the Windows Command Console

As with previous Windows shell script projects, this one begins by disabling the display of statements within the scripts at execution time, as shown below. In addition, the foreground text color is modified to display as yellow. Next, the screen is cleared and the title of the story is posted in the Windows command console's title bar.

```
@ECHO off
```

```
COLOR EC
```

```
CLS
```

```
TITLE = THE STORY OF BUZZ THE WONDER DOG
```

Building the Welcome Screen

The initial screen welcomes the reader to the story. It consists of a series of ECHO statements as shown below.

```
ECHO.
ECHO.
ECHO.
ECHO.
ECHO.
ECHO.
ECHO WELCOME TO THE ..........
ECHO.
ECHO.
ECHO.
ECHO.
ECHO.
ECHO STORY OF BUZZ THE WONDER DOG!
ECHO.
ECHO.
ECHO.
ECHO.
ECHO.
ECHO.
ECHO.
ECHO.
ECHO.

PAUSE
```

The last statement in this section uses the PAUSE command to ensure that the reader has the chance to read and ponder the story that is about to be told.

Providing the Reader with Instructions

The second screen that readers will see informs them that their participation is required in order to tell the story and explains that all they need to do is provide answers to a few simple questions.

```
CLS


ECHO.
ECHO.
ECHO.
ECHO.
ECHO.
ECHO.
ECHO Your help is needed to tell this story. All that you have to do is
ECHO.
ECHO answer a few simple questions.
ECHO.
ECHO.
ECHO.
ECHO.
ECHO.
ECHO.
ECHO.
ECHO.
ECHO.
ECHO.
ECHO.
ECHO.
ECHO.
ECHO.


PAUSE
```

This section, like all sections that follow, begins by clearing the screen before displaying any text and ends by executing the PAUSE command.

Collecting Key Story Elements from the Reader

To tell the story, the script needs to collect information from the reader that will then be assigned to the following script variables:

- player. The name of the person reading the story (a.k.a. the name of Buzz's fictional owner)
- clothes. The piece of clothing that Buzz grabs onto when saving his owner for the first time.
- vehicle. The type of motor vehicle that almost runs over Buzz's owner at the beginning of the story.
- bodypart. The part of his owner's body that Buzz grabs onto when saving his owner for the second time.
- animal. The type of animal that almost runs over Buzz's owner at the end of the story.

These pieces of information are collected and assigned to variables using the SET command with the /P switch, as shown below.

```
CLS


ECHO.

ECHO.

ECHO.

ECHO.

ECHO.

ECHO.


SET /p player=1. What is your name?


ECHO.


SET /p clothes=2. Name of piece of clothing:


ECHO.


SET /p vehicle=3. Name a type of 4-wheel motor vehicle:
```

```
ECHO.


SET /p bodypart=4. Name a part of the human body:


ECHO.


SET /p animal=5. What is your favorite animal?


ECHO.

ECHO.

ECHO These look like really good answers. Now, let's get on with the story.

ECHO.

ECHO.

ECHO.

ECHO.

ECHO.


PAUSE
```

Using Variable Substitution to Write the Story

From this point on, the script consists of statements that display a portion of the story, clear the screen, and pause the display. Rather than break out each screen the reader will see in this section, I'll provide you with the rest of the story (shown below) and let you determine how to format the display of these screens.

```
Once upon a time, there lived a very special little dog called Buzz.

Buzz's best friend was his owner, %player%. Buzz and %player% went everywhere

together. Sunday was their favorite day to spend together because on

that day they would play in the water down by Old Man's Grove.


On one particularly hot summer Sunday, Buzz and %player% were walking down

the side of an old dirt road on their way to Old Man's Grove when

suddenly Buzz stopped and spun around, grabbing %player%'s %clothes%,

dragging %player% off the road down into the ditch. A split second later,
```

a big red %vehicle% came tearing by out of control, running right over the
stretch of the road where Buzz and %player% had been walking.

"Good boy," said %player%. "You really saved me that time Buzz. But what
about the man in that %vehicle%? If he doesn't slow down quickly, he'll never
make the turn at Old Man's Grove!" %player% stared as the %vehicle% barreled
down the road. When %player% looked back to see Buzz, the four-legged friend
was gone.

Moments later, as the %vehicle% was about to crash into the grove, Buzz
leaped off of the top of a large bolder and onto the top of the
%vehicle%. He then squeezed his way through an opening in the back of the
%vehicle% and found that the driver was unconscious.

Thinking quickly, Buzz pulled the driver out of the way and took over
at the wheel, quickly applying the brakes and stopping the %vehicle%
just inches before it reached the edge of the grove. The quick-
thinking Buzz saw that the man was not breathing and began pulling
him out of the %vehicle%.

By the time %player% arrived a few minutes later, the man had
revived and was sitting upright on the ground, petting Buzz as the
dog licked his face. "This here your dog?" the driver asked. "Yes sir,"
said %player% with a great big smile. "Well, it looks like I owe you a lot.
Your dog just saved my life. Had he not given me CPR, I think I'd have
been a goner for sure!" said the driver.

"Wow!" said %player%, running over to hug his four-legged friend. Just then
Buzz unexpectedly leaped up, grabbing %player% by the %bodypart%, tossing %player%
clear of the dirt path that %player% had been running on. Moments later, a
big white %animal% came scurrying down that very path, and Buzz the Wonder
Dog ran off after it. "I hope that %animal% will be OK" said the driver.
"Don't worry" said %player%, "Buzz will save him......"
The End

I suggest that you attempt to complete the development of this story before I show you how I finished it in the next section. However, if you are not sure how to finish it up or don't have the time to do so right now, then by all means, please keep reading.

The Final Result

Now look at the completely assembled script. To help document the script and make it easier to follow along, I added comments throughout that explain the logical processes that are taking place.

```
@ECHO off


REM *************************************************************************
REM
REM Script Name: WonderDog.bat
REM Author: Jerry Ford
REM Date: July 1, 2003
REM
REM Description: This Windows shell script tells the story of "Buzz the Wonder
REM Dog" using input provided by the reader.
REM
REM *************************************************************************


REM Set the Windows command console to display yellow on black
COLOR OE


REM Clear the display
CLS


REM Write the name of the story to the Windows command console's title bar
TITLE = THE STORY OF BUZZ THE WONDER DOG


REM Display the welcome screen
ECHO.
ECHO.
```

```
ECHO.

ECHO.

ECHO.

ECHO.

ECHO W E L C O M E   T O   T H E ...........

ECHO.

ECHO.

ECHO.

ECHO.

ECHO.

ECHO.

ECHO S T O R Y   O F   B U Z Z   T H E   W O N D E R   D O G !

ECHO.

ECHO.

ECHO.

ECHO.

ECHO.

ECHO.

ECHO.

ECHO.

ECHO.

ECHO.


REM Pause until the reader presses a key

PAUSE


REM Clear the display

CLS


REM Let readers know that their help is required to write the story

ECHO.

ECHO.

ECHO.
```

```
ECHO.

ECHO.

ECHO.

ECHO Your help is needed to tell this story. All that you have to do is

ECHO.

ECHO answer a few simple questions.

ECHO.

ECHO.

ECHO.

ECHO.

ECHO.

ECHO.

ECHO.

ECHO.

ECHO.

ECHO.

ECHO.

ECHO.

ECHO.


REM Pause until the reader presses a key

PAUSE


REM Clear the display

CLS


REM Start collecting input from the reader

ECHO.

ECHO.

ECHO.

ECHO.
```

```
ECHO.
ECHO.


REM Collect the name of Buzz's owner.
SET /p player=1. What is your name?


ECHO.


REM Determine the piece of clothing that Buzz grabs onto when saving
REM his owner for the first time
SET /p clothes=2. Name of piece of clothing:


ECHO.


REM Determine what type of vehicle almost runs over Buzz and his owner
SET /p vehicle=3. Name a type of 4-wheel motor vehicle:


ECHO.


REM Determine the body part Buzz grabs onto when saving his owner for
REM the second time
SET /p bodypart=4. Name a part of the human body:


ECHO.


REM Determine what type of animal almost runs over Buzz's owner the
REM second time
SET /p animal=5. What is your favorite animal?


ECHO.
ECHO.
ECHO These look like really good answers. Now, let's get on with the story.
```

```
ECHO.

ECHO.

ECHO.

ECHO.

ECHO.


REM Pause until the reader presses a key

Pause


REM Clear the display

CLS


REM Tell the first part of the story

ECHO.

ECHO.

ECHO.

ECHO.

ECHO.

ECHO.

ECHO Once upon a time there lived a very special little dog called Buzz.

ECHO.

ECHO Buzz's best friend was his owner, %player%. Buzz and %player% went everywhere

ECHO.

ECHO together. Sunday was their favorite day to spend together because on

ECHO.

ECHO that day they would play in the water down by Old Man's Grove.

ECHO.

ECHO.

ECHO.

ECHO.

ECHO.

ECHO.
```

```
ECHO.

ECHO.

ECHO.

ECHO.


REM Pause until the reader presses a key

PAUSE


REM Clear the display

CLS


REM Tell the second part of the story

ECHO.

ECHO.

ECHO.

ECHO.

ECHO.

ECHO.

ECHO On one particularly hot summer Sunday, Buzz and %player% were walking down

ECHO.

ECHO the side of an old dirt road on their way to Old Man's Grove when

ECHO.

ECHO suddenly Buzz stopped and spun around, grabbing %player%'s %clothes%,

ECHO.

ECHO dragging %player% off the road down into the ditch. A split second later

ECHO.

ECHO a big red %vehicle% came tearing by out of control, running right over the

ECHO.

ECHO stretch of road where Buzz and %player% had been walking.

ECHO.

ECHO.

ECHO.
```

```
ECHO.

ECHO.

ECHO.


REM Pause until the reader presses a key
PAUSE


REM Clear the display
CLS


REM Tell the third part of the story
ECHO.

ECHO.

ECHO.

ECHO.

ECHO.

ECHO.

ECHO "Good boy," said %player%. "You really saved me that time Buzz. But what

ECHO.

ECHO about the man in that %vehicle%? If he doesn't slow down fast he'll never

ECHO.

ECHO make the turn at Old Man's Grove!" %player% stared as the %vehicle%

ECHO.

ECHO barreled down the road. When he looked back to see Buzz, his four-legged

ECHO.

ECHO friend was gone.

ECHO.

ECHO.

ECHO.

ECHO.

ECHO.

ECHO.
```

```
ECHO.
ECHO.


REM Pause until the reader presses a key
PAUSE


REM Clear the display
CLS


REM Tell the fourth part of the story
ECHO.
ECHO.
ECHO.
ECHO.
ECHO.
ECHO.
ECHO Moments later, as the %vehicle% was about to crash into the grove, Buzz
ECHO.
ECHO leaped off of the top of a large bolder onto the top of the
ECHO.
ECHO %vehicle%. He then squeezed his way through an opening in the back of the
ECHO.
ECHO %vehicle% and found that the driver was unconscious.
ECHO.
ECHO.
ECHO.
ECHO.
ECHO.
ECHO.
ECHO.
ECHO.
```

```
ECHO.

ECHO.


REM Pause until the reader presses a key

PAUSE


REM Clear the display

CLS


REM Tell the fifth part of the story

ECHO.

ECHO.

ECHO.

ECHO.

ECHO.

ECHO.

ECHO Thinking quickly, Buzz pulled the driver out of the way and took over

ECHO.

ECHO at the wheel, quickly applying the brakes and stopping the %vehicle%

ECHO.

ECHO just inches before it reached the edge of the grove. The quick-

ECHO.

ECHO thinking Buzz saw that the man was not breathing and began pulling

ECHO.

ECHO him out of the %vehicle%.

ECHO.

ECHO.

ECHO.

ECHO.

ECHO.

ECHO.
```

```
ECHO.

ECHO.


REM Pause until the reader presses a key
PAUSE


REM Clear the display
CLS


REM Tell the sixth part of the story
ECHO.

ECHO.

ECHO.

ECHO.

ECHO.

ECHO.

ECHO By the time %player% arrived a few minutes later, the man had

ECHO.

ECHO revived and was sitting upright on the ground, petting Buzz as the

ECHO.

ECHO dog licked his face. "This here your dog?" the driver asked "Yes sir,"

ECHO.

ECHO said %player% with a great big smile. "Well, it looks like I owe you a lot.

ECHO.

ECHO Your dog just saved my life. Had he not given me CPR, I think I'd have

ECHO.

ECHO been a goner for sure!" said the driver.

ECHO.

ECHO.

ECHO.

ECHO.

ECHO.
```

```
ECHO.


REM Pause until the reader presses a key
PAUSE


REM Clear the display
CLS


REM Tell the final part of the story
ECHO.

ECHO.

ECHO.

ECHO.

ECHO.

ECHO.

ECHO "Wow!" said %player%, running over to hug his four-legged friend. Just then

ECHO.

ECHO Buzz unexpectedly leaped up, grabbing %player% by the %bodypart%, tossing

ECHO.

ECHO %player%  clear of the dirt path that %player%  had been running on. Moments later, a

ECHO.

ECHO big white %animal% came scurrying down that very path, and Buzz the Wonder

ECHO.

ECHO Dog ran off after it. "I hope that %animal% will be OK" said the driver.

ECHO.

ECHO "Don't worry" said %player%, "Buzz will save him......"

ECHO.

ECHO.

ECHO The End
```

Now that the script is complete, run it a number of different times, making sure to feed it different input each time. If any errors occur, go back and check your typing to make sure that you did not mistype any of the script's statements. Once you have everything working properly, pass your game on to a friend, and see what they think.

Summary

In this chapter, you learned how to write scripts that could accept and process input passed to them at execution time. You also learned the ins and outs of working with environment and script variables. This included how to create, modify, and delete variables from within your Windows shell scripts, as well as how to access and permanently modify environment variables. In addition, you learned how to manipulate and extract portions of variables that contained text strings and how to perform mathematical operations on variables containing numeric data.

EXERCISES

1. **Further expand on "The Story of Buzz the Wonder Dog" by adding a few more paragraphs of story line.**

2. **Try removing the** CLS **statements from the story portion of the script. This will result in a scrolling effect each time the reader presses a key to un-pause the story.**

   Hint: You will have to adjust the number of ECHO. **statements to make the effect look right.**

3. **Make the story's outcome even more unpredictable by reviewing the story and looking for keywords that you can replace with variables and then prompt the reader to supply input for these new variables.**

CHAPTER

5

Applying Conditional Logic

You've already seen examples of conditional logic presented in many of the chapter projects presented earlier in this book. That's because conditional logic is such a core programming concept that it is all but impossible to write a useful script of any complexity without using some form of conditional logic.

In Chapter 3, "Windows Shell Scripting Basics," you learned how to perform conditional logic using compound commands in which the execution of one command was made dependent on the success or failure of another command. In this chapter, you will learn how to use the IF statement to implement conditional logic that goes far beyond the capabilities of simple compound commands. You'll also learn how to create multi-line IF statements that allow you to execute numerous commands based on the results of a single conditional test. In addition, you'll learn how to nest, or embed, one IF statement within another to produce powerfully intricate logic.

Specifically, you will learn

- To work with each of the various forms of the IF statement

- How to determine whether variables have been defined

- How to determine whether errors have occurred when executing commands

- How to determine what version of the Windows shell is being used to run your scripts

- How to determine whether files or folders exist before you attempt to access them

Project Preview:
The Guess a Number Game

This chapter's main programming project is called the Guess a Number game. It is designed to give you further experience in working with conditional logic. To complete the game, you will create a Windows shell script that prompts the player for a number and then compares that number to a randomly generated number to see if it is less than, equal to, or higher than the player's chosen number. The game will give the player hints that identify whether the player's guess is high or low and will keep a count of the number of guesses that the player ultimately makes before correctly guessing the randomly selected mystery number.

Figure 5.1 shows the game's opening screen, which greets the player, displays the name of the game, and waits for the player to press a key before continuing.

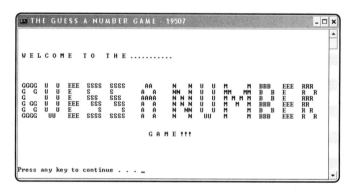

FIGURE 5.1

The opening screen for the Guess a Number game.

Figure 5.2 shows the game prompting the player to make their first guess. As you can see, the player types in a guess on the same line as the prompt and presses the Enter key to submit it.

Figure 5.3 shows the kind of feedback that players receive when their guess is too low. The game will continue to prompt the player to enter guesses until the player correctly guesses the mystery number.

Likewise, Figure 5.4 shows the message that the game displays when the player's guess is too high.

When the player finally guesses the mystery number, the screen shown in Figure 5.5 is displayed, informing the player that the number has been guessed correctly. In addition, the total number of guesses made by the player is also displayed.

FIGURE 5.2

The player is prompted to enter a guess.

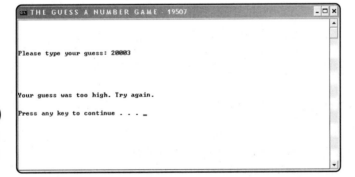

FIGURE 5.3

Players are notified when their guesses are too low.

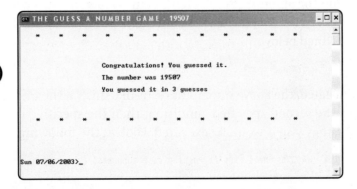

FIGURE 5.4

Players are notified when their guesses are too high.

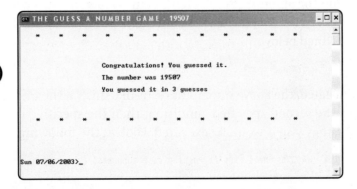

FIGURE 5.5

When the game ends, the player is told how many guesses it took to finally guess the mystery number.

Applying Conditional Logic to Control Script Execution

While you can always use compound commands to apply limited conditional logic when developing Windows shell scripts, the IF statement provides a significantly more flexible and powerful alternative that is capable of performing conditional tests on a wide range of different situations. The IF statement comes in many different flavors, as outlined in Table 5.1.

TABLE 5.1 TYPES OF IF STATEMENTS

Type	Function
IF	Performs a true/false test to determine whether one or more commands should be executed
IF...ELSE	Executes either of two sets of commands based on the outcome of a conditional test
IF DEFINED	Determines whether a variable already exists
IF ERRORLEVEL	Checks the exit code of the previously executed command
IF CMDEXTVERSION	Retrieves a numeric value indicating the current version of the Windows shell
IF EXIST	Determines whether a file or folder exists
IF NOT	Performs a conditional test and takes an action based on a negative result

Working with the IF Statement

The IF command performs a conditional test and executes a command if the result of the test proves to be true. People perform this same type of test all the time. For example, when I go to lunch today I'll probably decide whether or not I want to eat steak based on the amount of cash I have in my wallet. If I have $10, then I'll order the steak. Otherwise, I won't. The IF statement works in much the same way. Its syntax is outlined below.

```
IF condition1 == condition2 command
```

Loosely translated, the above statement reads like this: "If the first specified condition equals the second specified condition, then the specified command will be executed." Otherwise it won't be executed. Look at the following example:

```
IF %OS% == Windows_NT ECHO The script is running on a supported operating system
```

Chapter 5 Applying Conditional Logic

In this example, the value assigned to an environment variable called `OS` is compared to a text string that consists of `Windows_NT`. If `OS` has a value of `Windows_NT`, then the result of the test will be `true` and the `ECHO` command that follows the test will execute automatically. Otherwise, the `ECHO` command will be skipped.

 TRICK **The `%OS%` variable identifies the type of operating system currently running. This variable will be set equal to `Windows_NT` on any computer running a Windows NT, 2000, XP, or 2003 operating system.**

Note that in the previous example blank spaces were included both before and after the double equals sign. Although not required, adding blank spaces in this manner helps make things easier to read. Now look at another example. In this example, the statement is set up to compare the value stored in the first argument passed to the script against a text string of `PLAY`. If the results of the test are `true`, then the `ECHO` command that follows will be executed.

```
@ECHO off

IF %1% == Play ECHO Ready to begin play.....
```

Save this example as a script and run it by entering the name of the script followed by a blank space and then the word `Play`. You should see the following output displayed:

```
Ready to begin play.....
```

Now, run the script again and either pass it an argument other than the word `Play` or just don't enter anything at all. As you'll see, the following error will appear:

```
ECHO was unexpected at this time.
```

This error occurred because the value of `%1%` was not set and the Windows shell ended up with a logical statement that looked like the one shown below. Since this statement is syntactically incorrect, the error occurred.

```
IF == Play ECHO Ready to begin play.....
```

There may be times when you want your scripts to keep on running even when they are started without any arguments. For example, you could perform a test to see if an argument was supplied, and if it wasn't, you could instead use a default value that you hard coded into your script. To prevent the above error from appearing, you should enclose both of the conditionals tested by the `IF` statement within a pair of matching double quotation marks, as shown below.

```
IF "%1%" == "Play" ECHO Ready to begin play.....
```

Using double quotation marks in this manner does not affect the results of the test when both conditions are equal. They still remain equal even with the addition of the double quotation marks. However, in the case where the argument is missing, formatting your IF statement in this manner prevents an error because the Windows shell would interpret the command as shown below. Syntactically, this passes the muster and allows the script to continue executing without an error.

```
IF "" == "Play" ECHO Ready to begin play.....
```

There are other times when you will want to enclose your variables within double quotation marks. For example, there may be a time when you write a script that prompts the user for input. However, you may have no way of knowing in advance whether users will include one or more blank spaces in their response. To ensure that the blank spaces are properly interpreted, you should enclose the variable within double quotes. You may remember from Chapter 1, "Introducing Windows Shell Scripting," that when you created the Knock Knock joke game you had to make the player responsible for enclosing his response inside double quotation marks. Using this new technique, you can rewrite the script and unburden the player from that responsibility.

In the previous example, you compared a variable's value against a hard-coded text string. However, you can just as easily compare the values stored in two variables, as demonstrated below.

```
SET hisname=Alexander

SET hername=Molly

IF %hisname% == %hername% ECHO We have a match!
```

When comparing text string values against one another, the Windows shell examines not only the text of both strings but also their case. Therefore, for example, it would interpret X and x as not being equal. However, if you wish, you can override this case-sensitivity requirement and perform a case-insensitive comparison by using the /I switch, as demonstrated below.

```
SET hisname=CHRIS

SET hername=Chris

IF /I %hisname% == %hername% ECHO We have two people named Chris with us today.
```

In addition to determining whether two strings are equal, the IF statement provides the ability to perform a host of mathematical comparisons. For example, the following statements demonstrate how to compare the values stored in two numeric variables.

```
SET /A totalcount = 10

SET /A currentcount = 10

IF %totalcount% == %currentcount% ECHO Both values are the same
```

Providing for an Alternative Course of Action

By itself, the IF statement provides the ability to test two conditions and take an action when the result of the test is true. But what if you want to take one action if the result is true and a different action if the result of the comparison is false? The solution to this dilemma is to append the ELSE keyword to the IF statement. This version of the IF statement has the following syntax:

```
IF condition1 == condition2 (command1) ELSE (command2)
```

If both conditions are equal, then command1 is executed; otherwise, command2 is executed. You must place both commands inside parentheses for the Windows shell to recognize the ELSE portion of the statement. The following statement demonstrates one particularly good use of the IF...Else statement:

```
IF "%OS%" == "Windows_NT" (ECHO Script now executing) ELSE (GOTO :EOF)
```

In this example, the IF statement begins by checking to see if the script is executing on a computer running Windows NT, 2000, XP, or 2003. If the result of the comparison is true, then a message announces that the script will now begin executing. Otherwise, if the comparison results in a value of false, the ELSE portion of the statement executes, in which case a GOTO :EOF causes the script to terminate its own execution.

 TRICK By including a check of the OS variables at the beginning of your Windows shell scripts, you can prevent their accidental execution on unsupported operating systems such as Windows 95, 98, or Me. These operating systems lack a robust scripting environment, and while your scripts will try to run on them, they probably won't run for long before an error occurs.

Determining Whether a Variable Already Exists

Errors occur when your Windows shell scripts run into something unexpected. One example of something unexpected would be a missing environment variable. For example, suppose you created a script that accesses an environment variable called ScriptFolder, which you had created some time ago to store the location of the folder where you keep your Windows shell script files. If you were to run this script on any other computer; without first remembering to create a new instance of the environment variable on the other computer, your script would probably fail when it tried to reference a variable that was not defined. This is because the Windows shell returns an empty value any time it is unable to locate a variable.

Depending on how you wrote your script, what it was designed to do, and at what point in the script the variable reference occurred, the results could be unpredictable. As a result, your script may have done nothing, or it may have had the opportunity to complete a portion of its task, leaving you to manually figure out what was and was not done and potentially having a mess to clean up.

However, you could avoid this problem by adding code to the beginning of your script that would prevent it from running in the event that it could not find your custom environment variable. This is accomplished using the IF DEFINED statement, which has the following syntax:

```
IF DEFINED variable command
```

For example, the following statement demonstrates how to determine whether an environment variable named ScriptFolder has been defined:

```
IF DEFINED ScriptFolder SET sourcefolder=%ScriptFolder%
```

In this example, a check is made to determine whether the ScriptFolder variable has been defined. If it has been defined, then script variable is defined and set equal to the value stored in ScriptFolder. Otherwise, the script variable is not defined.

In certain cases you may be able to provide your scripts with default settings that it can use in the event that they are unable to locate needed environment variables. For example, by adding the ELSE keyword to the previous example, you could specify a default folder to be substituted when necessary.

```
IF DEFINED ScriptFolder (SET sourcefolder=%ScriptFolder%) ELSE (SET sourcefolder=C:\Scripts)
```

Keeping an Eye Out for Errors

You've probably already experienced more than one error as you have followed along with this book and tried to duplicate the scripts that you have seen. Sometimes errors are your fault. For example, you might use the wrong syntax when working with a command. This is referred to as a syntax error. You might also create an error by trying to tell your scripts to do something they cannot do, such as trying to multiply a number and a text string together. We call these logical errors. Another category of errors is run-time errors, which occur when a script is executing and runs into a problem that is not the result of a syntax or logical problem. For example, a run-time error would occur if a script tried to delete a file that did not exist. It might be that the application that creates this file every night wasn't run like it was supposed to be on a given night. Perhaps someone renamed the file. There could be any number of reasons why a run-time error might occur.

You can prevent many syntax errors by double-checking your code before running your scripts. You can prevent many logical errors by taking the time to properly design your script before you begin working on it and by carefully testing it as you develop it.

TRAP Even the best programmers run into syntax and logical errors, so don't be shocked when they happen to you. To help you work your way through these types of situations, I'll give you some basic debugging tips in Chapter 8, "Debugging and Error Handling."

One way to deal with run-time errors is to try to anticipate places within your scripts where errors are likely to occur, and then test to see if they occurred. You can do this using the IF ERRORLEVEL statement, which checks the exit code of the previously issued command.

DEFINITION An *exit code* (or *return code*) is a numeric value returned by commands that indicates whether they ran successfully or experienced an error.

IN THE REAL WORLD

Almost every Windows command and utility program provides information in the form of a numeric exit code. This code is returned by the command to the resource that invoked it (e.g., your Windows shell script). The value of the exit code indicates whether the command thought that it ran correctly. Commands that process without any errors will return an exit code of 0. Any value higher that 0 indicates some type of error. Many Windows commands and utilities document their possible range of exit codes and their meanings. You may be able to find information about the possible range of exit codes for a given command or utility by checking the Windows Help system or by searching www.microsoft.com. If you're working with a command or utility provided by a third-party software developer, you can consult both the supplied documentation and the vendor's Web site.

You can use either of two versions of the IF ERRORLEVEL statement when developing your Windows shell scripts. The syntax for the first version of the IF ERRORLEVEL statement is outlined below.

```
IF ERRORLEVEL exitcode command
```

exitcode is a placeholder representing a numeric value that specifies the minimum error level that you are looking for. If the exit code returned by the previously executed command is equal to or greater than the value specified by exitcode, then the specified command is executed. Otherwise the command is not executed and the script continues processing. For example, look at the following statements:

```
COPY c:\Script\TestScript.bat C:\Temp

IF ERRORLEVEL 1 ECHO Copy operation terminated. The specified file was not found.
```

The first statement attempts to copy a file to the C:\Temp folder. The second statement checks to see if an error occurred when the first statement executed and displays an error message if an error did occur.

The syntax for the second version of the IF ERRORLEVEL statement is outlined below.

```
IF ERRORLEVEL == exitcode
```

This time exitcode specifies a specific error code that must be exactly matched in order to trigger the execution of the specified command. In other words, if you set exitcode equal to 2, as demonstrated below, and an exitcode of 1 is returned, the execution of the specified command is skipped.

```
IF "%ERRORLEVEL%" == "2" ECHO Fatal error occurred & GOTO :EOF
```

In the above example, the IF ERRORLEVEL statement checks to see if the previous command returned an exit code of 2, and if it did, an error message is displayed and the script's execution terminates.

Checking the Windows Shell Version

Microsoft has continued to steadily improve and enhance its operating systems over the years. This includes enhancements to the Windows shell. Windows shell scripting was first introduced with Windows NT 4. It was later enhanced in Windows 2000 with the addition of new command extensions. If you find that you need to work with Windows NT 4, some functionality might be missing that you have come to expect from Windows 2000, XP, or 2003. For example, Windows NT 4 does not support the SET command's /P switch that allows the command to prompt the user for input.

In addition to scanning your scripts and looking for statements that might not be supported on earlier versions of Windows operating systems, you can use the IF CMDEXTVERSION statement to check to see what version of the Windows shell is being used. Windows NT 4 runs version 1. Windows 2000, XP, and 2003 all run version 2. This means that while your scripts might run into trouble on Windows NT, they will probably work just fine on these other Windows operating systems.

> **IN THE REAL WORLD**
>
> As mentioned in Chapter 2, "Interacting with the Windows Shell," numerous commands have been enhanced to support new command extensions. A list of these commands includes ASSOC, CALL, CD, COLOR, DEL, ENDLOCAL, FOR, FTYPE, GOTO, IF, MD, POPD, PROMPT, PUSHD, SET, SETLOCAL, SHIFT, and START. **If you create Windows shell scripts that take advantage of features provided by the new command extensions on these commands and then try to run your scripts on a computer running a version of Windows that does not support the command extensions, your scripts will run into errors. Therefore, you must test your Windows shell scripts rigorously on all operating systems you intend to support. If, for example, you have a script that needs to run on Windows NT 4 that currently uses the** SET **command's** /P **switch to interact with the user, you will need to rewrite the script to remove the unsupported command switch. In this example, you can instead use the Windows NT 4 Resource Kit's** CHOICE.EXE **command to interactively prompt the user for the information the script requires.**

By using the IF CMDEXTVERSION statement to check the value of the CMDEXTVERSION variable, you can enable your scripts to detect which version of the Windows shell is being used to execute them and then to react accordingly. For example, if your scripts make use of command extensions, you might halt script execution, or you might use conditional logic to have your scripts skip certain steps.

The syntax you must follow to use the IF CMDEXTVERION statement is outlined below.

```
IF CMDEXTVERSION VersionNo Command
```

VersionNo is a placeholder that represents the Windows shell version number that you want to test for, and Command is a Windows command that will be executed if the value of CMDEXTVERSION is equal to or less than the value specified by VersionNo. For example, the following script checks to see whether the script is being executed on a computer running Windows NT, 2000, XP, or 2003, and if it isn't, the script terminates its own execution. Using this programming technique, you can prevent your Windows shell scripts from trying to run on other Windows operating systems.

```
@ECHO off

IF CMDEXTVERSION 1 ECHO Unsupported operating system & GOTO :EOF
```

Looking for Files and Folders

A special form of the IF statement allows you to verify whether files or folders exist before your scripts attempt to work with them. For example, if your script is designed to copy or move a particular file from one location to another and that file isn't present when the script executes, an error will occur when the COPY or MOVE command executes. Using the IF EXIST statement you can take steps to prevent these types of errors.

Determining Whether a File Already Exists

The IF EXIST statement has the following syntax:

```
IF EXIST file command
```

file is a placeholder representing the name of the file to be searched for, and *command* specifies a command that will execute if the specified file is found.

Look at a quick example of the IF EXIST statement in action. In this example, shown below, an IF EXIST statement looks for a file called Games.txt in a folder called C:\Scripts. If the file is found, then it is deleted. Otherwise, the DEL command is skipped.

```
IF EXIST C:\Scripts\Games.txt DEL C:\Scripts\Games.txt & ECHO File Deleted
```

In the next example, a Windows shell script begins by determining whether a file called Games.txt exists within a folder called C:\Scripts. If the file exists, then the script says so using an ECHO statement before using a SET statement to display a prompt requesting permission to overwrite the file with a new file. If the user types in a response of n, then the script leaves the existing file alone and terminates its own execution. However, if the user responds by entering a y (or another character other than n), then the script redirects the contents of an ECHO statement using the > character. The effect of this statement is to replace the contents of the file with the text supplied by the ECHO statement.

```
@ECHO off


IF EXIST C:\Scripts\Games.txt ECHO File exists. & SET /P reply=Replace? [y/n]


IF /I %reply% == n (

  ECHO The File was not replaced & GOTO :EOF

) ELSE (

  ECHO > C:\Scripts\Games.txt This report created at %TIME% on %DATE%

)
```

Determining Whether a Folder Currently Exists

It's just as important to check for the existence of folders as it is for files. This way, for instance, if a folder you're looking for does not exist, your script can create it and then continue running without experiencing an error.

Technically, the IF EXIST statement really only works with files, but you can use it to look for a folder and it will provide you with results. However, these results can be misleading in situations where the folder you specify does not exist but a file of the same name exists in the location where you told the IF EXIST statement to look. However, by being a little clever, you can avoid this potential problem. The trick is to look for the presence of a file named . within the folder you're looking for. As demonstrated below, Windows automatically creates a . reference in every subfolder it creates.

```
C:\>cd Scripts


C:\Scripts>dir
 Volume in drive C is jlfhd01
 Volume Serial Number is 23F5-17D7


 Directory of C:\Scripts


07/11/2003  12:10p    <DIR>          .
07/11/2003  12:10p    <DIR>          ..
              0 File(s)          0 bytes
              2 Dir(s)   7,512,241,890 bytes free


C:\Scripts>
```

For example, the following Windows shell script demonstrates how to verify the existence of a folder:

```
@ECHO off


IF EXIST C:\Scripts\. (
  ECHO C:\Scripts folder exists. Creating report.
) ELSE (
  ECHO C:\Scripts folder not found. Creating folder and report. & MKDIR C:\Scripts
)
```

In this example, the script checks to see if the C:\Scripts folder exists by looking for `C:\Scripts\`. It the folder exists, a message is displayed. However, if the folder does not exist, the `ELSE` part of the `IF EXIST` statement is executed and, as a result, the C:\Script folder is created using the `MKDIR` command.

Reversing the Logic of Conditional Tests

Sometimes it makes sense to test for the inverse of a particular condition. For example, to me it makes more sense to check to see if the previous command did not return an exit code of 0 rather than to see if it returned an exit code greater than 0. In the end, I suppose deciding whether inverting a conditional test makes more sense depends on the way you think.

The Windows shell lets you append the `NOT` keyword to each of the supported forms of the `IF` statement. In the sections that follow, I'll show you examples of how to use the `NOT` keyword to invert the conditional logic for each of the different types of `IF` statements that you've seen in this chapter.

IF NOT

By adding the `NOT` keyword to the `IF` statement, you can test for the opposite of any condition that you might want to check. The syntax for this form of the `IF` statement is outlined below.

```
IF NOT condition1 == condition2 command
```

For example, you might want to use the `IF NOT` statement when working with variables. The following example demonstrates how to set up an `IF NOT` statement that checks to see if a variable called `Scripts` has been set equal to `C:\Scipts`, and if it has not, its value is changed.

```
IF NOT "%Scripts%" == "C:\Scripts" SET Scripts=C:\Scripts
```

I recommend that you use the `IF NOT` statement in every Windows shell script you create (especially if you share them with other people) and that you set it up to prevent the script's accidental execution on unsupported Windows operating systems (e.g., Windows 95, 98, and Me). This can be easily accomplished by making the statement a part of your standard Windows shell template as demonstrated below.

```
@ECHO off

REM ***************************************************************************

REM

REM Script Name: Xxxxxxxx.bat
```

```
REM Author: Xxxx Xxxxx

REM Date: Xxxxx XX, XXXX

REM

REM Description: Xxxxxxxxxxxxxxxxxxxxxxxxxxxxxxxxxxxxxxxxxxxxxxx

REM

REM *************************************************************************


REM Script Initialization Section


IF NOT "%OS%" == "Windows_NT" ECHO Unsupported operating system & GOTO :EOF



REM Main Processing Section



REM Subroutine and Procedure Section
```

This way, if someone attempts to run the scripts on an unsupported operating system, you can supply an explanation of why the script cannot run and then terminate the script's execution.

IF NOT DEFINED

The NOT keyword seems especially suited to working with the IF DEFINED statement, providing an easy means of checking to see if a variable does not exist. The syntax for this form of the IF statement is outlined below.

```
IF NOT DEFINED variable command
```

For example, the following IF NOT DEFINED statement checks to make sure that an environment variable called Scripts does not already exist before defining a script variable of the same name. Using this technique, you can set up your Windows shell scripts to look for environment variables that control their execution, but still fall back and use hard-coded default values in the event that the environment variables are not present.

```
IF NOT DEFINED %Scripts% SET Scripts=C:\Scripts
```

Refer to Chapter 4, "Storing and Retrieving Information in Variables," for information on how to manually define and assign values to environment variables.

IF NOT ERRORLEVEL

You may also invert the IF ERRORLEVEL statement with the NOT keyword by using the following syntax:

```
IF NOT ERRORLEVEL exitcode command
```

For example, when executed the following script tries to copy a file named TestScript.bat from the C:\Scripts folder to the C:\Temp folder. The script then uses the IF NOT ERRORLEVEL statement to determine whether the copy operation succeeded. If an error occurred when copying the file, the script clears the screen, displays an error message, and then terminates its own execution.

```
@ECHO off


COPY C:\Scripts\TestScript.bat C:\Temp


IF NOT %ERRORLEVEL% == 0 CLS & ECHO Fatal error occurred & GOTO :EOF
```

IF NOT CMDEXTVERSION

The IF NOT CMDEXTVERSION statement is used to validate that the version of the Windows shell being used to process the script is not lower than a specified value. The syntax for this form of the IF statement is outlined below.

```
IF NOT CMDEXTVERSION VersionNo Command
```

For example, the following Windows shell script terminates its own execution in the event it discovers that it is not running on a Windows 2000, XP, or 2003 operating system:

```
@ECHO off


IF NOT CMDEXTVERSION 2 ECHO Unsupported operating system & GOTO :EOF
```

Likewise, the following script terminates the script's execution if it has not been started on a Windows NT, 2000, XP, or 2003 operating system.

```
@ECHO off


IF NOT CMDEXTVERSION 1 ECHO Unsupported operating system & GOTO :EOF
```

IF NOT EXIST

The final form of the IF statement that supports the NOT keyword is the IF NOT EXIST statement, which has the following syntax:

```
IF NOT EXIST file command
```

Using this statement, you can determine whether a file or folder exists before trying to work with it. For example, the following Windows shell script checks to see if the C:\Scripts folder exists and then creates the folder if it doesn't exist.

```
@ECHO off


IF NOT EXIST C:\Scripts\. (

  ECHO C:\Scripts folder not found. Creating folder and report. & MKDIR C:\Scripts

) ELSE (

  ECHO C:\Scripts folder exists. Creating report.

)
```

Building Multi-Line IF Statements

So far, in all the examples you've seen in this chapter, I have managed to accomplish everything I needed to do within single-line IF statements (unless, of course, I used the ELSE keyword to provide an alternative execution path).

For example, the following statement checks the exit code of the previously executed command and then, using compound commands, performs three different tasks:

```
IF NOT %ERRORLEVEL% == 0 CLS & ECHO Fatal error occurred & GOTO :EOF
```

While certainly effective, there is a limit to the usefulness of compound commands. For one thing, bunching together too many commands on a single-line statement can make scripts more difficult to read. Generally speaking, you'll be better off spreading a statement such as the one shown above across multiple lines. I think you'll find that it makes scripts easier to read and easier to write.

To break up complex IF statements into separate lines, use the following syntax:

```
if condition1 == condition2 command  (

  ...

  ...

  ...

)
```

As you can see, using this form of the IF statement, you must enclose all of the statements that you want the IF statement to execute inside a pair of matching parentheses. For example, you could rewrite the previous compound command example using a multi-line IF statement, as shown below.

```
IF NOT %ERRORLEVEL% == 0 (

  CLS

  ECHO Fatal error occurred

  GOTO :EOF

)
```

As you can see, even with this small example, the multi-line form of the IF statement makes things a lot easier to read.

Creating Advanced Conditional Logic Tests

It won't take long before you find yourself wanting to create Windows shell scripts that require the use of some pretty complicated logic. For example, you may want to test a condition and then, based on the results of the test, perform one or more additional tests. To facilitate this type of logical thinking, the Windows shell allows you to embed IF statements inside one another to create nested IF statements.

To see how this works, look at the following example:

```
@ECHO off


SET /A MysteryNumber = %random%


REM Check to see if the correct number was guessed
IF NOT "%1" == "%MysteryNumber%" (


  ECHO A match did not occur!


  REM If the correct number was not guessed, check to make sure it is in bounds
  IF %1 LSS 0 ECHO Your guess is out of bounds! & GOTO :HELP
  IF %1 GTR 32767 ECHO Your guess is out of bounds! & GOTO :HELP


  REM The guess was in bounds, so check to see if it was low or high
```

```
   IF %1 LSS %MysteryNumber% GOTO :GuessAgain

   IF %1 GTR %MysteryNumber% GOTO :GuessAgain


)
```

In this example, the script set a variable called MysteryNumber equal to a randomly selected number between 0 and 32,767. It then checks the value of an argument passed to it to see if the value of the argument is equal to the value assigned to the MysteryNumber variable. If the two values are equal, nothing happens. But if they are not equal, the IF statements nested within the first IF statement begin to execute in order to determine what the script should do next. If the nested IF statements were moved from inside the first IF statement and placed outside of the statement, as shown below, the script would still work. However, the previously embedded IF statements would be needlessly executed in the event that the argument passed to the script was equal to the randomly generated number.

```
@ECHO off


SET /A MysteryNumber = %random%


REM Check to see if the correct number was guessed

IF NOT "%1" == "%MysteryNumber%" (

  ECHO A match did not occur!

)
REM If the correct number was not guessed, check to make sure it is in bounds

IF %1 LSS 0 ECHO Your guess is out of bounds! & GOTO :HELP

IF %1 GTR 32767 ECHO Your guess is out of bounds! & GOTO :HELP


Rem The guess was in bounds, so check to see if it was low or high

IF %1 LSS %MysteryNumber% GOTO :GuessAgain

IF %1 GTR %MysteryNumber% GOTO :GuessAgain
```

Clearly, there is no point to executing the last four IF statements if the first IF statement did not determine that a match had not occurred. Not only is this second script less efficient, but it is also intuitively more difficult to read and understand than the first script.

Performing Different Kinds of Comparisons

Up to this point in this chapter, you have seen the use of the == characters repeatedly as a means of comparing two conditions to determine whether they are equal. The Windows shell supports a number of other comparison operators, which you can use to perform even more complex comparisons. These comparison operators are listed in Table 5.2.

	TABLE 5.2 COMPARISON OPERATORS	
Operator	**Description**
==	Determines whether two values are equal
EQU	Determines whether two values are equal
LSS	Determines whether one value is less than another
GTR	Determines whether one value is greater than another
LEQ	Determines whether one value is less than or equal to another
GEQ	Determines whether one value is greater than or equal to another
NEQ	Determines if one value is not equal to another

For example, you can compare the value of a variable as shown below.

```
IF NOT "%OS%" == "Windows_NT" GOTO :EOF
```

Alternatively, you could rewrite this same statement using the EQU operator, as shown below.

```
IF NOT "%OS%" EQU "Windows_NT" GOTO :EOF
```

The operators listed in Table 5.2 enable you to make numerous types of numeric comparisons, as demonstrated by the following example:

```
SET /a Counter = 3

IF %Counter% LEQ 5 ECHO Terminating script execution.
```

In this example, the value of a variable is arbitrarily set equal to 3 to facilitate the comparison operation that follows. The next statement checks to see if the value of Counter is less than or equal to 5. Since this is the case, the statement displays a message in the Windows command console.

Back to the Guess a Number Game

OK, now it's time to take your knowledge of the IF statement and put it to the test by creating the Guess a Number game. As with previous projects, I'll begin by discussing the steps involved in designing the game. After that, I'll step you through the details of the specific steps, and then you can run and test the game and fix any typos or other problems that you may run into.

Designing the Game

The Guess a Number game will be completed in five steps, each of which is outlined briefly below.

1. Set up the script's execution environment, define variables used by the script, and establish initial variable values
2. Display a welcome screen that greets the player
3. Prompt the player to make a guess, assign the number provided by the player to a variable, and keep a running count of the number of guesses made
4. Interrogate each guess made by the player to determine if the guess is high, low, or correct, and loop back to allow the player to make another guess if necessary
5. Display the results of the game, including the number of guesses it took for the player to win the game

Configuring the Execution Environment

To begin, create a new script called GuessANumber.bat. Next, copy your script template into the file and then add the following statements:

```
@ECHO off

COLOR 0E

CLS

SET RandomNo=%random%

SET /a NoGuesses = 0

TITLE = T H E   G U E S S   A   N U M B E R   G A M E  -   %RandomNo%
```

The first three statements disable the display of script statements, set the color scheme of the Windows command console to yellow on back, and clear the screen. The next statement uses the environment variable random to retrieve a random number between 0 and 32,767 and assign its value to a variable called RandomNo. Next, a numeric variable called NoGuesses is defined and assigned an initial value of 0. The script will use this variable to keep track of the number of guesses made by the player. The last statement shown above displays the name of the game in the Windows command console's title bar.

TRICK

Notice that I also displayed the value of the randomly generated number in the Windows command console's title bar. I did this to make tracking this value easy while I developed this script. This way, each time that I ran and tested the script, I could easily tell what the mystery number was and determine if the script was performing as expected. Of course, when you are done developing and testing the script, you'll want to remove its display.

Displaying the Welcome Screen

As with previous scripts in this book, the welcome screen consists of a collection of ECHO statements that display the name of the game followed by the PAUSE statement, which requires that the player press a key to continue the game.

```
ECHO.

ECHO.

ECHO.

ECHO.

ECHO  W E L C O M E    T O    T H E . . . . . . . . . . .

ECHO.

ECHO.

ECHO.

ECHO.

ECHO GGGG  U  U  EEE  SSSS  SSSS    AA    N   N  U  U  M     M  BBB   EEE  RRR

ECHO G  G  U  U  E     S     S      A A   NN  N  U  U  MM  MM  B  B   E    R  R

ECHO G      U  U  E    SSS   SSS    AAAA  N N  N  U  U  M M M M  B  B   E    RRR

ECHO G GG  U  U  EEE   SSS   SSS    A A   N N  N  U  U  M   M  M  BBB   EEE  RR
```

```
ECHO G  G  U  U  E        S    S  A   A  N   NN  U   U  M        M  B  B  E      R R
ECHO GGGG   UU   EEE SSSS SSSS  A   A  N   N  UU  M    M BBB   EEE  R  R
ECHO.
ECHO.
ECHO                                  G A M E !!!
ECHO.
ECHO.
ECHO.
ECHO.
ECHO.

PAUSE
```

Collecting Player Input

The next section of the script begins by defining a label called :BEGINLOOP. Placing this label here enables the script to rerun as many times as it takes for the player to correctly guess the game's mystery number. Next, a CLS statement is executed to clear the screen and prepare the display for the execution of the SET statements that follow.

The first SET statement displays the prompt "Please type your guess:" and then waits for the player to type in a number. Each time the script returns to this location and the player makes a new guess, the second SET statement increases the value assigned to the NoGuesses variable by 1. The script will later display the value stored in this variable to tell the player how many guesses it took to finally guess the mystery number.

```
:BEGINLOOP


CLS


ECHO.
ECHO.
ECHO.
ECHO.
```

```
ECHO.


SET /p UserNumber=Please type your guess:


SET /a NoGuesses += 1


ECHO.

ECHO.

ECHO.

ECHO.

ECHO.
```

Determining Whether the Player's Guess is High, Low, or Correct

The real brain-power of the script occurs in this next section. This is where you will use conditional logic to evaluate the number supplied by the player to determine whether his guess is high, low, or correct. To set up this logic, use two IF statements. The first IF statement will test for input that is less than the mystery number. The second IF statement will test for input that is greater than the mystery number.

If either of the IF statements result in a result of true (e.g., the player enters a number that is less than or greater than the mystery number), then the player will be informed that the guess was either high or low and will be given another chance to guess again by jumping to the :BEGINLOOP label (after the player presses a key).

```
IF %UserNumber% LSS %RandomNo% (


    ECHO.

    ECHO Your guess was too low. Try again.

    ECHO.

    ECHO.


    PAUSE


    GOTO :BEGINLOOP
```

```
    )


    IF %UserNumber% GTR %RandomNo% (

      ECHO.

      ECHO Your guess was too high. Try again.

      ECHO.

      ECHO.


      PAUSE


      GOTO :BEGINLOOP


    )
```

TRAP The Guess a Number game assumes up front that the player will always enter a number. However, people can be very unpredictable, especially when they interact with computers. Many programming and scripting languages allow you to test input to determine whether it is numeric, thus allowing you to accept or reject user input based on its data type. Unfortunately, Windows shell script does not provide this capability. You might think that since the script is set up to expect numeric input that an error will occur if the player enters non-numeric input. However, because of the manner in which the Windows shell works, it won't produce an error. Instead, any text input entered by the player will be evaluated as being greater than the mystery number (or any number for that matter).

Displaying Game Results

Eventually, if the player does not close the Windows command console or stop the execution of the Guess a Number script by pressing the CTRL+Z keys, the player should guess the mystery number. When this happens, neither of the preceding IF statements will evaluate to true, so the script will be permitted to continue on to this final section.

The first statement in this section clears the screen in preparation for the display of the final results. Next the yellow on black color scheme is changed to red on yellow. Then a collection of ECHO statements are used to congratulate the player on winning the game and to display the mystery number and the total number of guesses that it took to guess the number. These two pieces of data are presented by embedding the variables that contain this information inside the ECHO statements as shown below in bold.

```
CLS

COLOR E0

ECHO.
ECHO    *    *    *    *    *    *    *    *    *    *    *    *
ECHO.
ECHO.
ECHO.
ECHO.
ECHO                    Congratulations! You guessed it.
ECHO.
ECHO                    The number was %UserNumber%
ECHO.
ECHO                    You guessed it in %NoGuesses% guesses
ECHO.
ECHO.
ECHO.
ECHO.
ECHO    *    *    *    *    *    *    *    *    *    *    *    *
ECHO.
ECHO.
ECHO.
ECHO.
ECHO.

GOTO :EOF
```

TRICK Although it is not required in this situation, I added the GOTO :EOF statement to the end of the script to explicitly demonstrate my intention of ending the game at this point. Had I left this statement out, the script would have ended anyway by virtue of reaching the last line of code. However, any time a Windows shell script jumps around a lot using the GOTO statement, things can get a little confusing, so being as explicit as possible can help alleviate some confusion.

The Final Result

At this point you have seen all of the building blocks required to assemble the Guess a Number game. For your convenience, I have listed the fully assembled script below. In addition, to help make it easier to follow along, I have added the script template and embedded comments throughout the script that describe what is going on.

```
@ECHO off


REM *************************************************************************
REM
REM Script Name: GuessANumber.bat
REM Author: Jerry Ford
REM Date: July 5, 2003
REM
REM Description: This Windows shell script game challenges the play to try to
REM guess a number between 0 & 32,767 in the fewest possible number of guesses
REM
REM *************************************************************************


REM Set foreground and background colors to yellow on black
COLOR 0E


REM Clear the display
CLS


REM Get a random number between 1 and 32,767
```

```
SET RandomNo=%random%


REM Define & initialize a variable to track the player's number of guesses
SET /a NoGuesses = 0


REM Write the name of the game in the Windows command console's title bar.
REM Also display the randomly selected number to the right of the game's name
TITLE = T H E   G U E S S   A   N U M B E R   G A M E  -   %RandomNo%


REM Display the game's welcome screen
ECHO.
ECHO.
ECHO.
ECHO.
ECHO  W E L C O M E   T O   T H E ..........
ECHO.
ECHO.
ECHO.
ECHO.
ECHO GGGG  U  U  EEE  SSSS  SSSS   AA    N   N  U   U  M     M  BBB   EEE  RRR
ECHO G  G  U  U  E    S     S     A  A   NN  N  U   U  MM   MM  B  B  E    R  R
ECHO G     U  U  E    SSS   SSS   AAAA   N N N  U   U  M M M M  B  B  E    RRR
ECHO G GG  U  U  EEE  SSS   SSS   A  A   N N N  U   U  M   M    BBB   EEE  RR
ECHO G  G  U  U  E      S     S   A  A   N  NN  U   U  M     M  B  B  E    R  R
ECHO GGGG   UU   EEE  SSSS  SSSS  A  A   N   N   UU   M     M  BBB   EEE  R  R
ECHO.
ECHO.
ECHO                              G A M E !!!
ECHO.
ECHO.
ECHO.
ECHO.
```

```
ECHO.


REM Wait until the player presses a key to continue
PAUSE


REM This label provides a callable return point in the script
:BEGINLOOP


  REM Clear the display
  CLS


  ECHO.
  ECHO.
  ECHO.
  ECHO.
  ECHO.


  REM Prompt the player to type in a guess
  SET /p UserNumber=Please type your guess:


  REM Add one to the total number of guesses made by the player
  SET /a NoGuesses += 1


  ECHO.
  ECHO.
  ECHO.
  ECHO.
  ECHO.


  REM Steps to perform if the player's guess is too low
  IF %UserNumber% LSS %RandomNo% (


    ECHO.
```

```
    ECHO Your guess was too low. Try again.
    ECHO.
    ECHO.


    REM Wait until the player presses a key to continue
    PAUSE


    REM Loop back so that the player can guess again
    GOTO :BEGINLOOP


 )


REM Steps to perform if the player's guess is too low
IF %UserNumber% GTR %RandomNo% (


    ECHO.
    ECHO Your guess was too high. Try again.
    ECHO.
    ECHO.


    REM Wait until the player presses a key to continue
    PAUSE


    REM Loop back so that the player can guess again
    GOTO :BEGINLOOP


 )


REM Clear the display
CLS


REM Reverse the game's color scheme to black on yellow
```

```
COLOR E0


REM Congratulate the player for guessing the number & provide game statistics

ECHO.

ECHO      *    *    *    *    *    *    *    *    *    *    *    *

ECHO.

ECHO.

ECHO.

ECHO                      Congratulations! You guessed it.

ECHO.

ECHO                      The number was %UserNumber%

ECHO.

ECHO                      You guessed it in %NoGuesses% guesses

ECHO.

ECHO.

ECHO.

ECHO      *    *    *    *    *    *    *    *    *    *    *    *

ECHO.

ECHO.

ECHO.

ECHO.

ECHO.


REM Terminate the script's execution

GOTO :EOF
```

Once you have finished creating the entire script, give it a go and see how it works. If you did not make any typos when keying it in, you should find that it works exactly as advertised. When you test the script, try feeding it a range of different data. For example, start by entering a number between 1 and 32,767. Once that works, try supplying it with a negative number and with a number greater than 32,767. Once you are sure that the script is handling these numbers correctly, try entering a few text characters as input and see what happens then.

Summary

In this chapter, you learned how to work with all of the forms of the IF statement supported by the Windows shell. You learned how to check for the existence of files, folders, and variables. You also learned how to test for errors and figure out what version of the Windows shell is being used to run your scripts. On top of all this, I showed you how to create multi-line IF statements as well as how to nest IF statements within one another to create powerful conditional logic tests. You also learned how to invert conditional tests using the NOT keyword. Finally, I showed you how to create the Guess a Number game, in which you learned how to use conditional logic to create a game that runs until the player successfully guesses a randomly generated number.

EXERCISES

1. To make the game easy to debug, I added the display of the randomly selected mystery number to the title bar. Once you have the game up and running properly, disable the display of this number.

2. Modify the Guess a Number game so that it collects additional statistics beyond the number of guesses attempted. For example, track the number of high guesses and low guesses separately.

3. Modify the Guess a Number game to give players better clues as they begin to get close to the mystery number. For example, as soon as players get within 200 of the mystery number you might tell them that they are getting warm, and when they get within 20 you might tell them that they are getting hot.

4. Modify the Guess a Number game so that it offers to restart itself and let the player play another game.

5. As it is currently designed, the Guess a Number game places no limit on the range of numbers that the player can enter, even though it expects the player to enter a number between 1 and 32,767. Using conditional logic, modify the game so that it notifies players if their guesses are outside of this range.

Creating Loops to Process Collections of Data

I n order to create computer games or really powerful administrative scripts, you need a way of repeating a series of steps in order to effectively process collections of data. For example, in the Guess a Number game that you created in Chapter 5, "Applying Conditional Logic," you needed to set the game up so that it would repeatedly give the user chances to guess the mystery number. This kind of *iterative* or repetitive processing is known as *looping*.

The Windows shell provides the FOR command as your tool for creating loops. Like the IF command, the FOR command comes in many different flavors, allowing you to create Windows shell scripts that loop through collections of files and folders, command output, and text strings, and also to repeatedly execute one or more commands. By creating scripts that iteratively loop through collections of data, you can process enormous amounts of data and perform tasks in seconds that would otherwise take you hours to perform manually, and you can do so without the mistakes that humans often make when performing tedious work.

Specifically, you will learn

- How to process collections of files and folders
- How to execute a collection of statements a predetermined number of times
- How to loop through and process the output produced by the execution of your script commands
- How to process the contents of files

Project Preview:
The Six-Million-Dollar Quiz

In this chapter's main project, you will learn how to create the Six-Million-Dollar Quiz. This quiz will test the player's knowledge of the 1970s TV show, *The Six Million Dollar Man*. By completing this script, you will learn how to create and control a text-based menu as well as how to create Help and About screens for your games. The game will present the player with 10 questions and then grade the answers entered by the player. The results will be displayed on the Windows command console as well as in a text report, which the script will store on the computer's hard drive.

Like all the other games in this book, the game will begin by presenting the player with a welcome screen. However, this welcome screen will serve a dual purpose by also presenting the player with a text menu that controls the game execution, as shown in Figure 6.1.

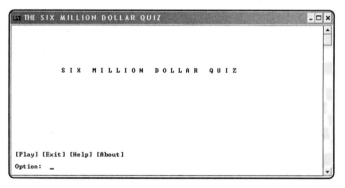

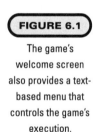

FIGURE 6.1

The game's welcome screen also provides a text-based menu that controls the game's execution.

By typing Help, the player can view information that explains the operation of the game, as shown in Figure 6.2. This help text remains on the screen until the player presses a key, at which time the welcome screen is redisplayed.

By typing About, the player can view information about the game and its author, as shown in Figure 6.3. Again, the player will be returned to the welcome screen after pressing a key.

When the player begins, the game presents a series of 10 questions. Some are "fill in the blank" questions, as demonstrated in Figure 6.4. Others are true/false or yes/no.

FIGURE 6.2

Add a Help screen to provide players with additional instructions and to create a more professional-looking game.

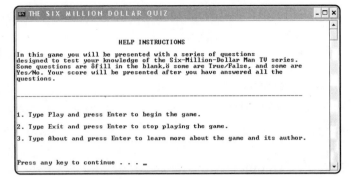

FIGURE 6.3

By creating an About screen, you provide a place to advertise information about yourself and your game.

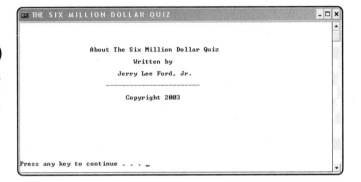

FIGURE 6.4

Each question tests the player's knowledge of *Six Million Dollar Man* trivia.

Once the player has answered all of the questions, the game will grade his answers and present a score card, as demonstrated in Figure 6.5.

Finally, the game creates a text report that provides detailed information about the player's quiz results, as demonstrated in Figure 6.6.

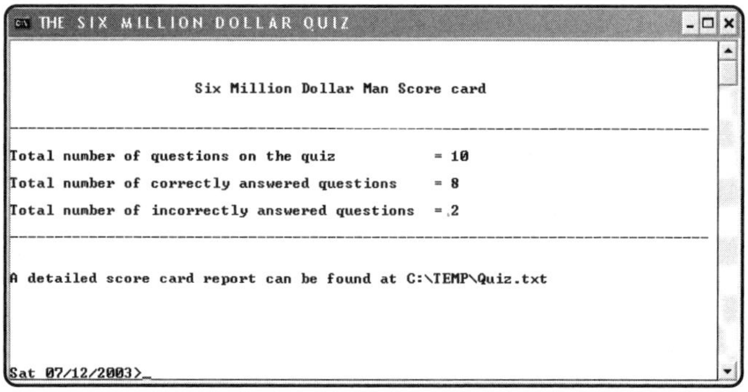

FIGURE 6.5

Viewing the results of the quiz.

FIGURE 6.6

Examining the detailed score card file created by the game.

Creating Loops

You've already seen how to create loops within Windows shell scripts using labels and the GOTO command. This type of loop provides the ability to jump from one point in a script to an earlier point in order to repeat the execution of previous steps, yet this type of loop is generally considered somewhat clumsy. I'll show you a much better way to group statements together for frequent execution in Chapter 7, "Creating Procedures and Subroutines."

The Windows shell provides support for a second type of loop using the FOR command. Loops created with the FOR command are highly specialized. A number of variations of the FOR loop can be established, each of which is designed to process a different type of data. Specifically, you can create FOR loops that can iteratively process any of the following types of resources:

- String contents
- Command output
- Collections of files
- Collections of folders
- Text file contents

In addition, you can set up loops that execute a specified number of times. For example, you could set up a loop that executes exactly 10 times.

While varying slightly, all loops created by the FOR command are based on the following syntax:

```
FOR /switch %%variable IN (collection) DO command
```

The /switch parameter is used to specify the types of data that the loop will process. A list of the switches supported by the FOR command is provided in Table 6.1.

TABLE 6.1 SWITCHES SUPPORTED BY THE FOR COMMAND

Switch	Description
/l	Sets up the loop to process a range of values
/f	Sets up the loop to process all elements stored within a string
/d	Sets up the loop to process all files stored within a specified folder
/r	Sets up the loop to process all subfolders stored within a specified parent folder

The %%variable parameter is a special type of variable referred to as an iterator. The *iterator* variable must be a single letter between A and Z. The FOR command automatically increments the value assigned to the iterator each time the loop repeats itself. The iterator variable is local in scope within the FOR loop, meaning that it cannot be referenced before or after the loop as executed. *Collection* specifies one of the following types of resources:

- A text string
- A list of files
- A list of folders
- A range

Command specifies a command that will be executed each time the loop executes.

TRAP The FOR loops iterator is case-sensitive. This means that I and i are not considered the same. Be careful and make sure that you are consistent when referencing the FOR loops iterator variable so that you don't accidentally mix up the case.

Each of the variations of the FOR command mentioned above are outlined in detail in the sections that follow.

Looping Through String Contents

One of the uses of the FOR command is to set up a loop that can iterate through and parse out the contents of a string. For example, you might want to develop a Windows shell script that deletes a list of files passed to it as arguments. Since %* represents a list of all the arguments passed to the script, you can create a loop that iterates its way through each argument. To set up this type of loop, use the following syntax:

```
FOR /F ["options"] %%variable IN ("string") DO command
```

You can further refine the execution of this type of loop by specifying any of the options listed in Table 6.2.

TABLE 6.2 FOR COMMAND PARSING OPTIONS	
Option	**Function**
DELIMS=x	Changes the characters used to delimit data from the default of a blank space to the specified collection of characters
EOL=c	Specifies an end-of-line character
SKIP=n	Sets a specific number of lines to be skipped at the top of the file
TOKENS=a,b, a-c	Sets the tokens to be used when processing data

DEFINITION A *token* represents a piece of data in a text string.

This particular form of the FOR loop parses out the contents of the specified string and assigns them to tokens. By specifying the TOKENS option when setting up the FOR loop, you can specify which tokens you want your scripts to process.

You can work with tokens in two ways. The first way is to specify specific tokens in the form of a,b, where a and b represent the first and second data elements in the string. The second way is to specify a range of tokens in the form of a-c. Here, the first three tokens in a string are specified.

Below are a couple of examples to help you better understand how to work with this version of the FOR loop. In the first example, I've written a script that uses a FOR loop to parse out and display the first five arguments passed to the script.

```
@ECHO off


FOR /F "DELIMS=, TOKENS=1-5" %%a IN ("%*") DO (


ECHO %%a

ECHO %%b

ECHO %%c

ECHO %%d

ECHO %%e


)
```

By specifying DELIMS=, I have set up the FOR loop to parse out arguments passed to the script and separated by the , character. By specifying TOKENS=1-5, I have configured the FOR loop so that it processes only the first five arguments passed to the script, regardless of how many are actually passed. When executed, this script displays a list of the first five arguments passed to the script. However, you could easily modify the functionality of this script by replacing the ECHO command with a different command. For example, you could change each ECHO command to DEL in order to delete a list of files passed to the script.

Before moving on to the next type of FOR loop, look at one more example. In this example, shown below, a Windows shell script has been set up to process the contents of a string variable. This variable has been assigned a value comprised of five names, each of which is separated, or delineated, by a blank space.

```
@ECHO off

SET UserList=Alexander William Molly Mary Jerry

FOR /F "TOKENS=1-3" %%a IN ("%UserList%") DO (

  ECHO %%a
  ECHO %%b
  ECHO %%c

)
```

Since the default delineator for the FOR command is a blank space, I did not have to specify the DELIMS option this time. In addition, since I only wanted to parse out the first three names stored in the string, I set the TOKENS option equal to 1-3.

Looping Through Command Output

Another variation of the FOR loop enables your scripts to loop through all the output produced by a command. This way, instead of just assuming that a command worked successfully because it did not return a non-zero exit code, you can directly interrogate command results. By iterating through command output, not only can you verify that the command did what you wanted it to, but you can also use the command output as input for script processing.

To use this form of the FOR command, you must use the following syntax:

```
FOR /F ["options"] %%variable IN ('command') DO command
```

The options parameter represents different parsing capabilities for the FOR command, as listed in Table 6.2. Also, take note of the fact that the command whose output is to be parsed must be enclosed inside both a pair of matching single quotation marks as well as a pair of parentheses.

Now look at this form of the FOR statement in action. In this example, I've created a Windows shell script that executes the SET command. When executed without any additional arguments, the SET command displays a listing of environment variables, which can be somewhat hard to read, as demonstrated below.

```
C:\>set

ALLUSERSPROFILE=C:\Documents and Settings\All Users
```

```
APPDATA=C:\Documents and Settings\Jerry Ford\Application Data

CLIENTNAME=Console

CommonProgramFiles=C:\Program Files\Common Files

COMPUTERNAME=WRKSTN0001

ComSpec=C:\WINDOWS\system32\cmd.exe

HOMEDRIVE=C:

HOMEPATH=\Documents and Settings\Jerry Ford

LOGONSERVER=\\WRKSTN0001

NUMBER_OF_PROCESSORS=1

OS=Windows_NT

Path=C:\WINDOWS\system32;C:\WINDOWS;C:\WINDOWS\COMMAND;C:\DOS;C:\WINDOWS\system3

2\WBEM

PATHEXT=.COM;.EXE;.BAT;.CMD;.VBS;.VBE;.JS;.JSE;.WSF;.WSH

PROCESSOR_ARCHITECTURE=x86

PROCESSOR_IDENTIFIER=x86 Family 6 Model 6 Stepping 0, GenuineIntel

PROCESSOR_LEVEL=6

PROCESSOR_REVISION=0600

ProgramFiles=C:\Program Files

PROMPT=$p$g

SESSIONNAME=Console

SystemDrive=C:

SystemRoot=C:\WINDOWS

TEMP=C:\DOCUME~1\JERRYF~1\LOCALS~1\Temp

TEMPDIR=d:\Temp

TMP=C:\DOCUME~1\JERRYF~1\LOCALS~1\Temp

USERDOMAIN=WRKSTN0001

USERNAME=Jerry Ford

USERPROFILE=C:\Documents and Settings\Jerry Ford

winbootdir=C:\WINDOWS

windir=C:\WINDOWS
```

In the next script, below, I have reformatted the SET command's output to help make it easier to read. I accomplished this by specifying the = character as the DELIMS parameter and specifying the TOKENS parameter as 1-2.

```
@ECHO off

FOR /F "DELIMS==, TOKENS=1-2" %%i IN ('SET') DO (

  ECHO Variable Name:  %%i
  ECHO Variable Value: %%j
  ECHO.

)
```

When the script is executed, it issues the SET command and then iterates its way through the command's output, displaying the name of a variable on one line followed by the variable's value on the next line and then a blank line. The results is a much cleaner listing, as demonstrated by the partial output shown below.

```
Variable Name:  USERNAME
Variable Value: Jerry Ford


Variable Name:  USERPROFILE
Variable Value: C:\Documents and Settings\Jerry For


Variable Name:  winbootdir
Variable Value: C:\WINDOWS


Variable Name:  windir
Variable Value: C:\WINDOWS
```

The nice thing about this form of the FOR loop is that it automatically hides the output produced by the command. This way, I can use ECHO statements to choose what output, if any, I want to display.

Processing Collections of Files

One of the many uses of the FOR command is to process all of the files located within a given folder. For example, you may want to create a script that you run at the end of each month that deletes all of the files in your C:\Temp folder in order to help free up disk space. When used to process files in this manner, the FOR command has the following syntax:

```
FOR %%variable IN (collection) DO command
```

collection specifies the location of the folder where the files to be processed reside.

For example, you could use the FOR command to display all Microsoft Word files located in a folder called C:\MyDocs using the following statement:

```
FOR %%i IN (C:\MyDocs\*.doc) DO ECHO %%i
```

Notice that I used the * character to instruct the script to process all files with a .doc file extension. The * character is an example of a *wild card* character. It is used to create matches among files based on a pattern. In the example above, the pattern was set up to match all files ending with the .doc file extension. I could have just as easily looked for all files that begin with the letters Jan and that also end with a .doc file extension by specifying Jan*.doc.

The Windows shell supports a second type of wild card character: the ? character. Unlike the * character, the ? character limits the pattern match to a single character. For example, Jan?.doc would limit matches to files whose file name begins with Jan, and includes a single character between Jan and the .doc file extension, such as Jan7.doc.

You can set up the FOR statement to process more than one file type at a time by separating each file type with a blank space. For example, the following Windows shell script demonstrates how to process all files that begin with either a .bat or .cmd file extension and are located within the same folder as the script.

```
@ECHO off


:DisplayConsole


ECHO.

ECHO --------------------------------------------------------------------------

ECHO.

ECHO                         Windows Shell Script Console

ECHO.

FOR %%I IN (*.bat *.cmd) DO (

  IF NOT %%I == ScriptConsole.bat ECHO      %%I
```

```
)

ECHO.

ECHO ----------------------------------------------------------------------------

ECHO.


SET /P response= Enter script name and any required arguments:


START %response%


CLS

GOTO :DisplayConsole
```

When run, this script will display a screen similar to the one shown in Figure 6.7. At the bottom of the display is a prompt created using the SET command. This prompt allows you to enter the name of a Windows shell script. The script then uses the START command to open a new Windows command console and run the specified script.

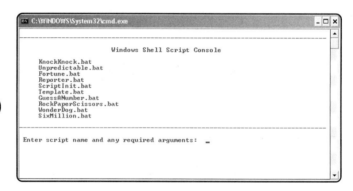

FIGURE 6.7

Using the FOR command to create a menu made up of file names.

Processing Collections of Folders

You can use the FOR command to iterate though a collection of folders just as easily as processing a collection of files. The syntax to perform this task is outlined below.

```
FOR /D %%variable IN (collection) DO command
```

DEFINITION The terms *directory* and *subdirectory* are often used synonymously as terms that refer to Windows folders. However, a subdirectory is actually a directory that is subordinate to whatever parent directory is being referenced.

The /D switch specifies that subfolders (or subdirectories) are to be processed. collection specifies the location of the parent folder in which the subfolders reside. For example, the following script is designed to accept an argument that specifies the name of a folder and then displays a list of all the subfolders located within that folder:

```
@ECHO off


SET /A count = 0
ECHO.
ECHO Folder listing for: %1
ECHO.
ECHO -----------------------------------------
ECHO.
FOR /d %%i IN (%1\*) DO (
  SET /A count += 1
  ECHO %%i
)
ECHO.
ECHO -----------------------------------------
ECHO.
ECHO Total number of folders found is %1 is: %count%
ECHO.
PAUSE
```

Note that to display all of the subfolders, you must add an * character to the end of the parent folder's name. As written, the script expects the user to pass it a folder name such as C:\Games. The script then appends * to the end of the argument to create C:\Games*. When executed, this script will produce results similar to those shown below.

```
Folder listing for: D:\Games


-----------------------------------------


D:\Games\Dos
D:\Games\TextBased
```

```
D:\Games\Windows


------------------------------------------


Total number of folders found is D:\Games is: 3


Press any key to continue . . .
```

You may also use the FOR command to perform a recursive examination of all the subfolders residing within a particular parent folder. To do so, use the following syntax of the FOR command:

```
FOR /R [parentfolder] %%variable IN (.) DO command
```

 DEFINITION When used within the context of displaying folders, the term *recursive* means to iteratively step your way through the Windows file system tree, displaying or processing each successive collection of subfolders.

The /R switch instructs the FOR command to recursively examine all folders residing underneath the specified parent (or top-level) folder. Also note that you must enclose the period character within a matching pair of parentheses exactly as shown above. For example, the following statement demonstrates how to display every subfolder residing under the C:\Games folder:

```
FOR /R C:\Games %%i IN (.) DO ECHO %%i
```

When executed, the output displayed would resemble the following:

```
C:\Games\.

C:\Games\Dos\.

C:\Games\Dos\Old\.

C:\Games\Dos\Old\.

C:\Games\TextBased\.

C:\Games\TextBased\Batch\.

C:\Games\TextBased\Interactive\.

C:\Games\Windows\.
```

Reading Text Files

Another good use of the FOR command is to read and process the contents of text files. This allows you to create scripts that can process files created by other scripts or even other applications such as space-, comma-, or tab-delimited text files created by Microsoft Excel. The syntax for this type of FOR loop is outlined below.

```
FOR /F ["options"] %%variable IN (filenameset) DO command
```

For example, suppose you had the following information stored in a text file called C:\Contact.txt:

```
=========================================================

Personal contact list

=========================================================


name    Internet_Address      Phone_No


Molly   molly@zxyinc.com      550-8888

Williamwilliam@abcd.net       550-9999

X-Man   alexander#xyz.com     050-9876

Mike    michael#ivworld.net   550-1234

Mark    markland@ivworld.net  550-7744

Nick    nick#anyplace.com     666-8912
```

In its current size, this file is small and easy to work with. But as the file grows over time, it may become difficult to work with. By creating a Windows shell script, you can easily read and process some or all of the data stored in this file.

The first six lines in the file consist of headers and two blank lines. Each of the remaining lines in the file contains tab-delimited information about different personal contacts, including their names, e-mail addresses, and phone numbers.

The following script demonstrates how to use a FOR loop to display the first names of all the people listed in the file:

```
FOR /F %%i IN (contacts.txt) DO ECHO %%i
```

In the absence of a TOKENS parameter, the script will default to "TOKENS=1". As a result, this statement processes the file and displays only the information stored in the first token of each line (e.g., the first word in each line). As a result, the statement displays only the following output:

```
===========================================================
Personal
===========================================================

name

Molly

William

X-Man

Mike

Mark

Nick
```

If you want to process all of the information stored in the file, you could rewrite the statement as shown below:

```
FOR /F "TOKENS=*" %%i IN (contacts.txt) DO ECHO %%i
```

As you can see, the TOKENS option has been added to the statement and set equal to *, which means that all tokens should be processed. When executed, this statement would display the following output in the Windows command console:

```
===========================================================
Personal contact list
===========================================================

name      Internet_Address      Phone_No

Molly     molly@zxyinc.com      550-8888

William william@abcd.net        550-9999

X-Man     alexander#xyz.com     050-9876

Mike      michael#ivworld.net   550-1234

Mark      markland@ivworld.net  550-7744

Nick      nick#anyplace.com     666-8912
```

If you wish, you could reformat the previous statement so that it processes only specific tokens. For example, to limit processing to the name and phone number of each individual listed in the file, you would specify TOKENS=1,3. In addition, you can skip the processing of the file's headers by adding the SKIP option and setting it equal to 6 (for the six lines of unwanted text) as demonstrated below.

```
FOR /F "TOKENS=1,3 SKIP=6" %%i IN (contacts.txt) DO (

ECHO Name:  %%i

ECHO Phone: %%j


)
```

In this example, tokens 1 and 3 map out to arguments %%i and %%j. When executed, this statement displays the output shown below.

```
Name:  Molly

Phone: 550-8888

Name:  William

Phone: 550-9999

Name:  X-Man

Phone: 050-9876

Name:  Mike

Phone: 550-1234

Name:  Mark

Phone: 550-7744

Name:  Nick

Phone: 666-8912
```

TRAP Be mindful of using the FOR command to process files that include blank spaces in their file names. Unless you use the following syntax, you'll end up with an error:

```
FOR /F ["options"] %%variable ('TYPE "filename"') command
```

Using this syntax, the filenameset **parameter is replaced with the** TYPE "filename" **parameter.** TYPE **is a required keyword and** filename **is the name of the file. Make sure you include the single and double quotation marks as shown above. For example, the following statement could be used to process all the data stored in a file whose name is** My Contacts.txt.

```
FOR /F "TOKENS=*" %%i IN ('TYPE "My Contacts.txt"') DO ECHO %%i
```

Iterating a Specified Number of Times

The final form of loop supported by the FOR command is one that iterates a prede-termined number of times. In this form of the loop, you must provide the FOR com-mand with a number indicating a starting point, an increment number, and a final number that once reached terminates the loop's execution. The syntax for this form of the FOR loop is outlined below.

```
FOR /L %%variable IN (begin,increment,end) DO command
```

For example, the following statement uses this form of the FOR loop to count to 3. The loop begins at 1, increments by 1 upon each iteration, and stops after the third iteration.

```
FOR /L %%i IN (1,1,3) DO ECHO %%i
```

The output produced by this statement is shown below.

```
1
2
3
```

Now look at a somewhat more useful way to use this form of the FOR loop. In this example, I will use the FOR loop to display the contents of an output screen. As you can see, I was able to create the screen using only four statements (excluding the @ECHO off statement).

```
@ECHO off

FOR /L %%i IN (1,1,11) DO ECHO.
ECHO Welcome to .........
FOR /L %%i IN (1,1,11) DO ECHO.

PAUSE
```

Figure 6.8 shows the screen displayed when this script is executed.

Now compare the number of statements that it took to display this output to the number of statements you've used with previous methods in this book, as shown below.

```
@ECHO off

ECHO.
```

```
ECHO.

ECHO.

ECHO.

ECHO.

ECHO.

ECHO.

ECHO.

ECHO.

ECHO.

ECHO.

ECHO Welcome to ........

ECHO.

ECHO.

ECHO.

ECHO.

ECHO.

ECHO.

ECHO.

ECHO.

ECHO.

ECHO.

ECHO.

ECHO.

PAUSE
```

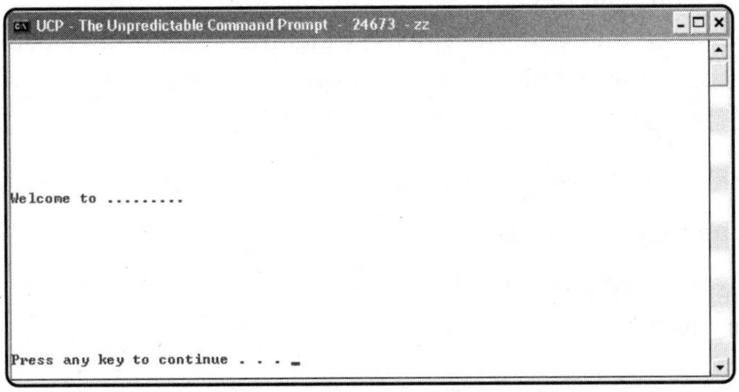

FIGURE 6.8

Using the FOR loop to pad the display screen with blank lines.

Without the FOR loop, it took 24 statements to create the display. Not only does the FOR loop do most of the work for you, but it also can be used to simplify your code and make your scripts smaller and easier to manage.

TRAP **The form of the FOR loop discussed here always checks the value of its begin and end parameters before executing. If you accidentally assign a value to the end parameter that is greater than the begin parameter, your loop will never run. Your script will skip right past it without saying a word, resulting in unexpected results and a problem that may be difficult to track down and fix. So keep an eye on your start, increment, and end values when working with this form of the FOR loop.**

Back to the Six-Million-Dollar Quiz

The Six-Million-Dollar Quiz introduces you to a number of new tricks, including the application of a text-based menu on the game's welcome screen, as well as the addition of Help and About screens. In addition, you'll learn how to create a score card report file that you'll then save on the player's hard drive.

Using Pseudo Code

As your Windows shell scripts grow more and more complicated, you'll find yourself spending more time designing them. One design technique I think you'll find particularly handy is pseudo code.

DEFINITION *Pseudo code* **is a rough, English-like outline of the logic used in all or part of a script.**

Using pseudo code, you can outline a high-level design for particularly complicated sections of your script by simply writing a rough logical outline of the steps involved. For example, one portion of the Six-Million-Dollar Quiz involves the display of a text-based menu on the game's welcome screen. Since you have not worked with text-based menus before, you'll probably find it very helpful to outline its operation using pseudo code, as demonstrated below.

• Display a Welcome menu and set it up to display Play, Exit, Help, and About options.

• Prompt the player to enter an option.

• If the player enters an invalid option, clear the screen and redisplay the Welcome menu.

- If the player presses Enter without entering an option, clear the screen and redisplay the Welcome menu.
- If the player enters Exit, terminate the quiz's execution.
- If the player enters Help, clear the screen and display the Help screen. When the player is done reading the Help screen, clear it and redisplay the Welcome menu.
- If the player enters About, clear the screen and display the About screen. When the player is done reading the About screen, clear it and redisplay the Welcome menu.
- If the player enters Play, clear the screen and begin the game.

With this pseudo outline describing the operation of the script's text-based menu system, you can now work to turn this descriptive outline into code. For example, the first two statements listed above are the English equivalent to the following statements:

```
ECHO  [Play] [Exit] [Help] [About]

SET /p reply= Option:
```

As you will soon see, the rest of the steps outlined in the previous pseudo code example can also be translated directly into code.

Designing the Game

OK. Now take a few moments to outline the steps involved in the development of the Six-Million-Dollar Quiz. As you can see from the list that I have outlined below, I plan to complete the development of the game in 10 steps.

1. Set up the execution environment
2. Display the welcome screen and main menu
3. Process menu selections
4. Set up the Help screen
5. Set up the About screen
6. Control game play
7. Start the score card report
8. Grade quiz results
9. Append quiz statistics
10. Display game results for player review

I'll explain in detail the work involved in completing each of these steps in the sections that follow. When you get to step 3, you can refer back to the pseudo code example shown earlier and see how the pseudo code outline was used to guide the development of the code in that part of the script.

Configuring the Script's Execution Environment

The script begins by disabling the display of statements in the Windows command console. It then sets the console's color scheme to yellow on black. The screen is then cleared, and the name of the game is displayed on the console's title bar. Finally, two variables are defined that are used throughout the script. The first variable is used to keep count of the number of correctly answered quiz questions and the second variable is used to keep track of the number of incorrectly answered questions. Both variables are assigned an initial value of 0.

```
@ECHO off


COLOR 0E


CLS


TITLE = THE   S I X   M I L L I O N   D O L L A R   Q U I Z


SET /A Right = 0
SET /A Wrong = 0
```

Creating a Welcome Screen and Main Menu

The Six-Million-Dollar Quiz's welcome screen looks similar to many of the other welcome screens that you have seen in this book. However, there are several key differences. First, the screen is preceded by a label called :StartGame. This label was placed here to allow the script to redisplay the main menu after the player has visited either the Help or About menus.

```
:StartGame


ECHO.

ECHO.
```

```
ECHO.
ECHO.
ECHO.
ECHO.
ECHO.
ECHO            S I X   M I L L I O N   D O L L A R   Q U I Z
ECHO.
ECHO.
ECHO.
ECHO.
ECHO.
ECHO.
ECHO.
ECHO.
ECHO.
ECHO.
ECHO.
ECHO.
ECHO  [Play] [Exit] [Help] [About]
ECHO.


SET /p reply= Option:
```

Another thing that makes this welcome screen different is the display of a text-based menu at the bottom of the screen. In order to make the menu work, the PAUSE statement that you have seen used here in the past has been replaced by a SET statement that prompts the player to choose one of the listed menu options.

Processing Menu Selections

After designing the Welcome menu, the next step is to set up a process for validating player input and then directing the script along the right logical path. The basic logic that must be followed has already been outlined earlier using pseudo code.

```
IF /I "%reply%" == "" CLS & GOTO :StartGame

IF /I %reply% == Play CLS & GOTO :Play

IF /I %reply% == Exit CLS & GOTO :EOF

IF /I %reply% == Help CLS & GOTO :Help

IF /I %reply% == About CLS & GOTO :About


CLS & GOTO :StartGame
```

As you can see, this section of the script consists of a series of IF statements that determine what to do based on the input typed in by the player. Each possible course of action is implemented using the GOTO command, which switches script execution flow to the specified label.

Creating the Help Screen

Now it's time to set up the game's Help screen. As you can see below, it begins with the :HELP label. This statement is required to allow the use of the GOTO statement to jump to this location in the script when the player enters Help on the welcome screen.

```
:HELP


ECHO.

ECHO.

ECHO.

ECHO                          HELP INSTRUCTIONS

ECHO.

ECHO In this game, you will be presented with a series of questions

ECHO designed to test your knowledge of The Six Million Dollar Man TV series.

ECHO Some questions are "fill in the blank," some are True/False, and some are

ECHO Yes/No. Your score will be presented after you have answered all the

ECHO questions.

ECHO.

ECHO.
```

```
ECHO --------------------------------------------------------
ECHO.
ECHO.
ECHO 1. Type Play and press Enter to begin the game.
ECHO.
ECHO 2. Type Exit and press Enter to stop playing the game.
ECHO.
ECHO 3. Type About and press Enter to learn more about the game and its author.
ECHO.
ECHO.
ECHO.

PAUSE
CLS
GOTO :StartGame
```

In addition to displaying information designed to help the player understand how to complete the quiz, this section ends with a GOTO: StartGame statement that causes the script to dismiss the Help screen and redisplay the welcome screen after the user presses a key.

Creating the About Screen

The About screen is set up exactly the same way as the Help screen and ends with the same GOTO :StartGame statement. The main reason for including this type of screen is to give the player the opportunity to learn more about the quiz. For example, this screen currently displays the name of the script and its author. It also displays copyright information. However, with only a little modification, this screen could also provide an e-mail address or information about a Web site.

```
:About

ECHO.
ECHO.
ECHO.
ECHO.
ECHO                    About The Six-Million-Dollar Quiz
```

```
ECHO.

ECHO                            Written by

ECHO.

ECHO                        Jerry Lee Ford, Jr.

ECHO.

ECHO.                      ------------------------

ECHO.

ECHO                         Copyright 2003

ECHO.

ECHO.

ECHO.

ECHO.

ECHO.

ECHO.

ECHO.

ECHO.

ECHO.


PAUSE

CLS

GOTO :StartGame
```

Managing Game Play

The next section of the script presents the player with 10 questions. Each question is presented one at a time. As soon as the player answers the first question, the screen is cleared and the next question is displayed. The code required to present the first question and collect the player's response is show below.

```
:Play


ECHO.

ECHO.

ECHO.
```

```
ECHO.

ECHO.


SET /p quest1= 1. What was the Six-Million-Dollar Man's first name?


CLS
```

As you can see, the answer given by the player is stored in a variable called quest1. The code required to display and collect the rest of the quiz's questions is the same as that shown above. Rather than reproduce the same set of statements repeatedly, I've listed all of the quiz's questions and their associated answers below.

- What was the Six-Million-Dollar Man's first name? Steve
- Did he have 1 or 2 bionic arms? 1
- Did he have a bionic eye or ear? Eye
- What was his real last name? Majors
- What was the first name of the Six-Million-Dollar Man's real wife? Farrah
- What was the last name of the actress who played the bionic woman? Wagner
- Did the bionic woman have a bionic eye or bionic ear? Ear
- T/F: The bionic woman cost more than the Six-Million-Dollar Man. F
- T/F: The Six-Million-Dollar Man was known as Heath on the "Big Valley." T
- Yes/No: Did the Six-Million-Dollar Man ever marry the bionic woman? Yes

Beginning the Score Card Report

Next, let's begin creating the quiz's score card report. The script is set up to store the report in the C:\Temp folder on the computer's hard drive. Therefore, the first thing you'll want to do is to make sure that this folder exists. If it does not exist, you'll want to create it as done by the first three statements below.

```
IF NOT EXIST C:\TEMP\. (

  MKDIR C:\Scripts

)


ECHO. > C:\TEMP\Quiz.txt

ECHO The Six-Million-Dollar-Man Quiz Score Card Report >> C:\TEMP\Quiz.txt

ECHO. >> C:\TEMP\Quiz.txt

ECHO. >> C:\TEMP\Quiz.txt
```

The last four statements shown above start the creation of a new score card report. The first statement creates the new report using the > redirection character. This redirection character will either create the report if it does not already exist or overwrite it if it already exists. The remaining three statements append the name of the quiz and two blank lines to the report file.

Grading Player Results

Next, the script begins to analyze the player's answers to each of the quiz's 10 questions to see which ones the player got right and which ones he got wrong. Because there is no way of knowing the case in which the player will choose to enter answers, the IF statement includes the /I switch, which results in a case-insensitive comparison. The player's answer is then compared to the correct answer. If the player got the answer right, a series of ECHO statements is redirected to the report file stating so. Otherwise, the ELSE portion of the conditional test executes, redirecting a different set of ECHO statements to the report file. Finally, depending on whether or not the player answered correctly, the value of either the right or wrong variable is increased by one.

```
IF /I %quest1% == Steve (

  ECHO. >> C:\TEMP\Quiz.txt

  ECHO 1. What was the Six-Million-Dollar Man's first name? >> C:\TEMP\Quiz.txt

  ECHO. >> C:\TEMP\Quiz.txt

  ECHO    Your answer was: Steve - Correct! >> C:\TEMP\Quiz.txt

  ECHO. >> C:\TEMP\Quiz.txt

  SET /A right += 1

) ELSE (

  ECHO. >> C:\TEMP\Quiz.txt

  ECHO 1. What was the Six-Million-Dollar Man's first name? >> C:\TEMP\Quiz.txt

  ECHO. >> C:\TEMP\Quiz.txt

  ECHO    Your answer was: %quest1% - Incorrect. >> C:\TEMP\Quiz.txt

  ECHO. >> C:\TEMP\Quiz.txt

  SET /A wrong += 1

)
```

As you might expect, the code required to grade the remaining nine questions is essentially the same as that shown above, so, for the sake of space, I have decided not to list it here. However, you will find it in the fully assembled script at the end of this chapter.

Recording Quiz Results

Next, the script appends a few more blank lines to the score card report, followed by a few lines of information that includes the number of correct and incorrect answers provided by the player, as shown below.

```
ECHO. >> C:\TEMP\Quiz.txt

ECHO. >> C:\TEMP\Quiz.txt

ECHO. >> C:\TEMP\Quiz.txt

ECHO ----------------------------------------------------------------------------- >>
C:\TEMP\Quiz.txt

ECHO. >> C:\TEMP\Quiz.txt

ECHO Score Card: >> C:\TEMP\Quiz.txt

ECHO. >> C:\TEMP\Quiz.txt

ECHO.>> C:\TEMP\Quiz.txt

ECHO Total number of questions on the quiz          = 10 >> C:\TEMP\Quiz.txt

ECHO. >> C:\TEMP\Quiz.txt

ECHO Total number of correctly answered questions   = %right% >> C:\TEMP\Quiz.txt

ECHO. >> C:\TEMP\Quiz.txt

ECHO Total number of incorrectly answered questions = %wrong% >> C:\TEMP\Quiz.txt
```

Displaying Game Results

The final section of the script is shown below. As you can see, it displays the same summary information that the previous section appended to the score card report. In addition, it displays a message informing the player of the existence and location of the score card report.

```
CLS


ECHO.

ECHO.

ECHO.

ECHO                       Six-Million-Dollar-Man Score Card

ECHO.

ECHO.

ECHO -------------------------------------------------------------------------
```

```
ECHO.
ECHO Total number of questions on the quiz           = 10
ECHO.
ECHO Total number of correctly answered questions    = %right%
ECHO.
ECHO Total number of incorrectly answered questions  = %wrong%
ECHO.
ECHO -----------------------------------------------------------------------
ECHO.
ECHO.
ECHO A detailed score card report can be found at C:\TEMP\Quiz.txt
ECHO.
ECHO.
ECHO.
ECHO.
ECHO.


GOTO :EOF
```

Finally, even though its not necessary at this point in the script, the GOTO :EOF statement executes, forcing the termination of the script.

The Final Result

Now you have all the information you need to finish the Six-Million-Dollar Quiz. I recommend that you try to finish it yourself before looking at the fully assembled code that I have provided below. As with previous chapter projects, I have added the script template to the Six-Million-Dollar Quiz and embedded comments throughout to help explain what is going on each step of the way.

```
@ECHO off


REM ***********************************************************************
REM
REM Script Name: SixMillion.bat
```

```
REM Author: Jerry Ford

REM Date: July 12, 2003

REM

REM Description: This Windows shell script game tests the player's knowledge of

REM the 1970's Six-Million-Dollar Man TV show.

REM

REM ***************************************************************************


REM Script Initialization Section


REM Set the color scheme to yellow on black

COLOR 0E


REM Clear the display

CLS


REM Display the name of the game in the Windows command console's title bar

TITLE = THE   S I X   M I L L I O N   D O L L A R   Q U I Z


REM Define and initialize variables that will be used to track the total number

REM of right and wrong answers

SET /A Right = 0

SET /A Wrong = 0


REM Main Processing Section


REM Create a return point

:StartGame


REM Display the initial Welcome screen

ECHO.

ECHO.
```

```
ECHO.
ECHO.
ECHO.
ECHO.
ECHO.
ECHO                SIX  MILLION  DOLLAR  QUIZ
ECHO.
ECHO.
ECHO.
ECHO.
ECHO.
ECHO.
ECHO.
ECHO.
ECHO.
ECHO.
ECHO.
ECHO.
ECHO  [Play] [Exit] [Help] [About]
ECHO.


REM Collect the player's response
SET /p reply= Option:


REM Determine what the player wants to do
IF /I "%reply%" == "" CLS & GOTO :StartGame


IF /I %reply% == Play CLS & GOTO :Play


IF /I %reply% == Exit CLS & GOTO :EOF
```

```
IF /I %reply% == Help CLS & GOTO :Help


IF /I %reply% == About CLS & GOTO :About



REM An incorrect response was provided, so redisplay the Welcome screen

CLS & GOTO :StartGame


REM Set up the Help screen

:HELP


ECHO.

ECHO.

ECHO.

ECHO                              HELP INSTRUCTIONS

ECHO.

ECHO In this game you will be presented with a series of questions

ECHO designed to test your knowledge of the Six-Million-Dollar Man TV series.

ECHO Some questions are "fill in the blank," some are True/False, and some are

ECHO Yes/No. Your score will be presented after you have answered all the

ECHO questions.

ECHO.

ECHO.

ECHO -------------------------------------------------------------------------

ECHO.

ECHO.

ECHO 1. Type Play and press Enter to begin the game.

ECHO.

ECHO 2. Type Exit and press Enter to stop playing the game.

ECHO.

ECHO 3. Type About and press Enter to learn more about the game and its author.

ECHO.

ECHO.
```

```
ECHO.

REM Pause to give the player time to read the screen
PAUSE

REM Clear the display
CLS

REM Return to the Welcome screen
GOTO :StartGame

REM Set up the About screen
:About

ECHO.
ECHO.
ECHO.
ECHO.
ECHO                    About The Six-Million-Dollar Quiz
ECHO.
ECHO                              Written by
ECHO.
ECHO                          Jerry Lee Ford, Jr.
ECHO.
ECHO.                 ------------------------
ECHO.
ECHO                            Copyright 2003
ECHO.
ECHO.
ECHO.
ECHO.
ECHO.
ECHO.
```

```
ECHO.

ECHO.

ECHO.

ECHO.


REM Pause to give the player time to read the screen

PAUSE


REM Clear the display

CLS


REM Return to the Welcome screen

GOTO :StartGame


REM Begin the play of the game

:Play


ECHO.

ECHO.

ECHO.

ECHO.

ECHO.


REM Ask a question

SET /p quest1= 1. What was the Six-Million-Dollar Man's first name?


REM Clear the display

CLS


ECHO.

ECHO.

ECHO.

ECHO.
```

```
ECHO.

REM Ask a question
SET /p quest2= 2. Did he have 1 or 2 bionic arms?

REM Clear the display
CLS

ECHO.
ECHO.
ECHO.
ECHO.
ECHO.

REM Ask a question
SET /p quest3= 3. Did he have a bionic eye or bionic ear?

REM Clear the display
CLS

ECHO.
ECHO.
ECHO.
ECHO.
ECHO.

REM Ask a question
SET /p quest4= 4. What was his real last name?

REM Clear the display
CLS

ECHO.
```

```
ECHO.

ECHO.

ECHO.

ECHO.


REM Ask a question

SET /p quest5= 5. What was the first name of the Six-Million-Dollar Man's real wife?


REM Clear the display

CLS


ECHO.

ECHO.

ECHO.

ECHO.

ECHO.


REM Ask a question

SET /p quest6= 6. What was the last name of the actress who played the bionic woman?


REM Clear the display

CLS


ECHO.

ECHO.

ECHO.

ECHO.

ECHO.


REM Ask a question

SET /p quest7= 7. Did the bionic woman have a bionic eye or bionic ear?


REM Clear the display
```

```
CLS

ECHO.

ECHO.

ECHO.

ECHO.

ECHO.


REM Ask a question

SET /p quest8= 8. T/F: The bionic woman cost more than the Six-Million-Dollar Man.


REM Clear the display

CLS


ECHO.

ECHO.

ECHO.

ECHO.

ECHO.


REM Ask a question

SET /p quest9= 9. T/F: The Six-Million-Dollar Man was known as Heath on the "Big Valley."


REM Clear the display

CLS


ECHO.

ECHO.

ECHO.

ECHO.

ECHO.


REM Ask a question
```

```
SET /p quest10= 10. Yes/No: Did the Six-Million-Dollar Man ever marry the Bionic woman?


REM Clear the display
CLS


REM If the C:\TEMP folder does not exist, then create it
IF NOT EXIST C:\TEMP\. (

  MKDIR C:\Scripts

)


REM Create the Quiz.txt file if it does not exist. Overwrite it if it does exist
ECHO. > C:\TEMP\Quiz.txt


REM Begin appending game results to the report
ECHO The Six-Million-Dollar-Man Quiz Score Card Report >> C:\TEMP\Quiz.txt

ECHO. >> C:\TEMP\Quiz.txt

ECHO. >> C:\TEMP\Quiz.txt


REM Determine whether the right or wrong answer was given and append the
REM the appropriate text for each of the ten questions
IF /I %quest1% == Steve (

  ECHO. >> C:\TEMP\Quiz.txt

  ECHO 1. What was the Six-Million-Dollar Man's first name? >> C:\TEMP\Quiz.txt

  ECHO. >> C:\TEMP\Quiz.txt

  ECHO    Your answer was: Steve - Correct! >> C:\TEMP\Quiz.txt

  ECHO. >> C:\TEMP\Quiz.txt

  SET /A right += 1

) ELSE (

  ECHO. >> C:\TEMP\Quiz.txt

  ECHO 1. What was the Six-Million-Dollar Man's first name? >> C:\TEMP\Quiz.txt

  ECHO. >> C:\TEMP\Quiz.txt

  ECHO    Your answer was: %quest1% - Incorrect. >> C:\TEMP\Quiz.txt

  ECHO. >> C:\TEMP\Quiz.txt
```

```
    SET /A wrong += 1

)


IF /I %quest2% == 1 (

  ECHO. >> C:\TEMP\Quiz.txt

  ECHO 2. Did he have 1 or 2 bionic arms? >> C:\TEMP\Quiz.txt

  ECHO. >> C:\TEMP\Quiz.txt

  ECHO    Your answer was: 1 - Correct! >> C:\TEMP\Quiz.txt

  ECHO. >> C:\TEMP\Quiz.txt

  SET /A right += 1

) ELSE (

  ECHO. >> C:\TEMP\Quiz.txt

  ECHO 2. Did he have 1 or 2 bionic arms? >> C:\TEMP\Quiz.txt

  ECHO. >> C:\TEMP\Quiz.txt

  ECHO    Your answer was: %quest2% - Incorrect. >> C:\TEMP\Quiz.txt

  ECHO. >> C:\TEMP\Quiz.txt

  SET /A wrong += 1

)


IF /I %quest3% == Eye (

  ECHO. >> C:\TEMP\Quiz.txt

  ECHO 3. Did he have a bionic eye or bionic ear? >> C:\TEMP\Quiz.txt

  ECHO. >> C:\TEMP\Quiz.txt

  ECHO    Your answer was: Eye - Correct! >> C:\TEMP\Quiz.txt

  ECHO. >> C:\TEMP\Quiz.txt

  SET /A right += 1

) ELSE (

  ECHO. >> C:\TEMP\Quiz.txt

  ECHO 3. Did he have a bionic eye or bionic ear? >> C:\TEMP\Quiz.txt

  ECHO. >> C:\TEMP\Quiz.txt

  ECHO    Your answer was: %quest3% - Incorrect. >> C:\TEMP\Quiz.txt

  ECHO. >> C:\TEMP\Quiz.txt
```

```
   SET /A wrong += 1

)


IF /I %quest4% == Majors (

  ECHO. >> C:\TEMP\Quiz.txt

  ECHO 4. What was his real last name?  >> C:\TEMP\Quiz.txt

  ECHO. >> C:\TEMP\Quiz.txt

  ECHO    Your answer was: Majors - Correct! >> C:\TEMP\Quiz.txt

  ECHO. >> C:\TEMP\Quiz.txt

  SET /A right += 1

) ELSE (

  ECHO. >> C:\TEMP\Quiz.txt

  ECHO 4. What was his real last name?  >> C:\TEMP\Quiz.txt

  ECHO. >> C:\TEMP\Quiz.txt

  ECHO    Your answer was: %quest4% - Incorrect. >> C:\TEMP\Quiz.txt

  ECHO. >> C:\TEMP\Quiz.txt

  SET /A wrong += 1

)


IF /I %quest5% == Farrah (

  ECHO. >> C:\TEMP\Quiz.txt

  ECHO 5. What was the first name of the Six-Million-Dollar Man's real wife? >> C:\TEMP\Quiz.txt

  ECHO. >> C:\TEMP\Quiz.txt

  ECHO    Your answer was: Farrah - Correct! >> C:\TEMP\Quiz.txt

  ECHO. >> C:\TEMP\Quiz.txt

  SET /A right += 1

) ELSE (

  ECHO. >> C:\TEMP\Quiz.txt

  ECHO 5. What was the first name of the Six-Million-Dollar Man's real wife? >> C:\TEMP\Quiz.txt

  ECHO. >> C:\TEMP\Quiz.txt

  ECHO    Your answer was: %quest5% - Incorrect. >> C:\TEMP\Quiz.txt

  ECHO. >> C:\TEMP\Quiz.txt
```

```
    SET /A wrong += 1

)


IF /I %quest6% == Wagner (

  ECHO. >> C:\TEMP\Quiz.txt

  ECHO 6. What was the last name of the actress who played the bionic woman? >> C:\TEMP\Quiz.txt

  ECHO. >> C:\TEMP\Quiz.txt

  ECHO    Your answer was: Wagner - Correct! >> C:\TEMP\Quiz.txt

  ECHO. >> C:\TEMP\Quiz.txt

  SET /A right += 1

) ELSE (

  ECHO. >> C:\TEMP\Quiz.txt

  ECHO 6. What was the last name of the actress who played the bionic woman? >> C:\TEMP\Quiz.txt

  ECHO. >> C:\TEMP\Quiz.txt

  ECHO    Your answer was: %quest6% - Incorrect. >> C:\TEMP\Quiz.txt

  ECHO. >> C:\TEMP\Quiz.txt

  SET /A wrong += 1

)


IF /I %quest7% == Ear (

  ECHO. >> C:\TEMP\Quiz.txt

  ECHO 7. Did the bionic woman have a bionic eye or bionic ear?  >> C:\TEMP\Quiz.txt

  ECHO. >> C:\TEMP\Quiz.txt

  ECHO    Your answer was: Ear - Correct! >> C:\TEMP\Quiz.txt

  ECHO. >> C:\TEMP\Quiz.txt

  SET /A right += 1

) ELSE (

  ECHO. >> C:\TEMP\Quiz.txt

  ECHO 7. Did the bionic woman have a bionic eye or bionic ear?  >> C:\TEMP\Quiz.txt

  ECHO. >> C:\TEMP\Quiz.txt

  ECHO    Your answer was: %quest7% - Incorrect. >> C:\TEMP\Quiz.txt

  ECHO. >> C:\TEMP\Quiz.txt

  SET /A wrong += 1
```

```
)


IF /I %quest8% == F (

  ECHO. >> C:\TEMP\Quiz.txt

  ECHO 8. True/False: The bionic woman cost more than the Six-Million-Dollar Man. >>
C:\TEMP\Quiz.txt

  ECHO. >> C:\TEMP\Quiz.txt

  ECHO    Your answer was: False - Correct! >> C:\TEMP\Quiz.txt

  ECHO. >> C:\TEMP\Quiz.txt

  SET /A right += 1

) ELSE (

  ECHO. >> C:\TEMP\Quiz.txt

  ECHO 8. True/False: The bionic woman cost more than the Six-Million-Dollar Man. >>
C:\TEMP\Quiz.txt

  ECHO. >> C:\TEMP\Quiz.txt

  ECHO    Your answer was: %quest8% - Incorrect. >> C:\TEMP\Quiz.txt

  ECHO. >> C:\TEMP\Quiz.txt

  SET /A wrong += 1

)


IF /I %quest9% == T (

  ECHO. >> C:\TEMP\Quiz.txt

  ECHO 9. True/False: The Six-Million-Dollar Man was known as Heath on the "Big Valley." >> C:\TEMP\Quiz.txt

  ECHO. >> C:\TEMP\Quiz.txt

  ECHO    Your answer was: True - Correct! >> C:\TEMP\Quiz.txt

  ECHO. >> C:\TEMP\Quiz.txt

  SET /A right += 1

) ELSE (

  ECHO. >> C:\TEMP\Quiz.txt

  ECHO 9. True/False: The Six-Million-Dollar Man was known as Heath on the "Big Valley." >> C:\TEMP\Quiz.txt

  ECHO. >> C:\TEMP\Quiz.txt

  ECHO    Your answer was: %quest9% - Incorrect. >> C:\TEMP\Quiz.txt

  ECHO. >> C:\TEMP\Quiz.txt
```

```
      SET /A wrong += 1

   )


   IF /I %quest10% == Yes (

      ECHO. >> C:\TEMP\Quiz.txt

      ECHO 10. Yes/No: Did the Six-Million-Dollar Man ever marry the Bionic woman?  >> C:\TEMP\Quiz.txt

      ECHO. >> C:\TEMP\Quiz.txt

      ECHO    Your answer was: Yes - Correct! >> C:\TEMP\Quiz.txt

      ECHO. >> C:\TEMP\Quiz.txt

      SET /A right += 1

   ) ELSE (

      ECHO. >> C:\TEMP\Quiz.txt

      ECHO 10. Yes/No: Did the Six-Million-Dollar Man ever marry the Bionic woman?  >> C:\TEMP\Quiz.txt

      ECHO. >> C:\TEMP\Quiz.txt

      ECHO    Your answer was: %quest10% - Incorrect. >> C:\TEMP\Quiz.txt

      ECHO. >> C:\TEMP\Quiz.txt

      SET /A wrong += 1

   )


   REM Append a few blanks lines and then append score card data

   ECHO. >> C:\TEMP\Quiz.txt

   ECHO. >> C:\TEMP\Quiz.txt

   ECHO. >> C:\TEMP\Quiz.txt

   ECHO ------------------------------------------------------------------------------- >>
   C:\TEMP\Quiz.txt

   ECHO. >> C:\TEMP\Quiz.txt

   ECHO Score Card: >> C:\TEMP\Quiz.txt

   ECHO. >> C:\TEMP\Quiz.txt

   ECHO.>> C:\TEMP\Quiz.txt

   ECHO Total number of questions on the quiz           = 10 >> C:\TEMP\Quiz.txt

   ECHO. >> C:\TEMP\Quiz.txt

   ECHO Total number of correctly answered questions    = %right% >> C:\TEMP\Quiz.txt

   ECHO. >> C:\TEMP\Quiz.txt
```

```
ECHO Total number of incorrectly answered questions  = %wrong% >> C:\TEMP\Quiz.txt


REM Clear the display
CLS


REM Display score card data in the Windows command console and inform the player
REM about the availability of the Games.txt file
ECHO.
ECHO.
ECHO.
ECHO                       Six-Million-Dollar-Man Score Card
ECHO.
ECHO.
ECHO -----------------------------------------------------------------------------
ECHO.
ECHO Total number of questions on the quiz         = 10
ECHO.
ECHO Total number of correctly answered questions   = %right%
ECHO.
ECHO Total number of incorrectly answered questions  = %wrong%
ECHO.
ECHO -----------------------------------------------------------------------------
ECHO.
ECHO.
ECHO A detailed score card report can be found at C:\TEMP\Quiz.txt
ECHO.
ECHO.
ECHO.
ECHO.
ECHO.


REM Terminate the script's execution
GOTO :EOF
```

Summary

In this chapter, you learned how to use the FOR statement in numerous different ways in order to iterate through collections of files and folders as well as to process the results returned by commands. You then created the Six-Million-Dollar Quiz where you learned, among other things, how to implement and control a text-based menu system and how to create a report file.

EXERCISES

1. Modify the Six-Million-Dollar Quiz so that it displays the correct answers to any question missed by the player.

2. Modify the Six-Million-Dollar Quiz so that the Score Card Report is not automatically generated. Instead, display a prompt at the end of the game that asks players whether they would like the report to be generated.

3. Each script statement that writes or appends data to the Quiz.txt file has the name and location of the report file hard coded on it. Make the script easier to maintain and modify by defining a variable that specifies the location where the file should be stored and then replace each hard-coded reference with this variable.

4. Add logic to the end of the Six-Million-Dollar Quiz that grades the score the player earned on the quiz. For example, assign A+ if all questions were answered correctly, a B+ if only one question was missed, and so on.

Creating Procedures and Subroutines

The focus of this chapter is to teach you how to improve the overall organization and design of your Windows shell scripts by introducing you to subroutines and procedures. Specific emphasis will be placed on procedures as an organizational tool for enhancing script design. This chapter will also cover two other important topics: the localization of variables and the creation of reusable modules of code.

Specifically, you will learn

- **How to use the** `GOTO` **command to create subroutines**
- **How to use the** `CALL` **command to set up procedures**
- **How to create internal and external procedures**
- **How to localize variables using procedures**
- **How to set up procedures that process arguments**

Project Preview:
The Rock, Paper, Scissors Game

This chapter's main project is called the Rock, Paper, Scissors game. This game is based on the childhood game where two people knock their own hands together in unison three times, and then use one hand to make the shape of a rock, a piece of paper, or a pair of scissors. The game will begin, as shown in Figure 7.1, by displaying a welcome screen. This welcome screen has a dual purpose in that it also displays the rules of the game, just in case the player is not familiar with them.

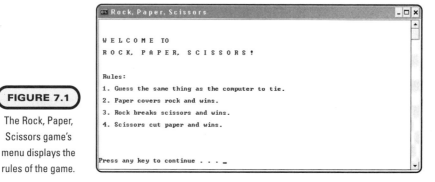

FIGURE 7.1

The Rock, Paper, Scissors game's menu displays the rules of the game.

As Figure 7.2 shows, the player is prompted to type in one of the three game objects.

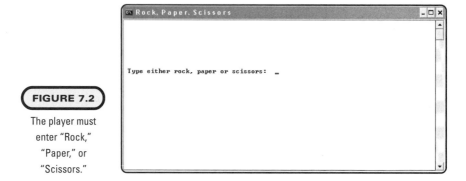

FIGURE 7.2

The player must enter "Rock," "Paper," or "Scissors."

The game then makes its own random selection and compares its selection to that of the player, displaying the results as shown in Figure 7.3.

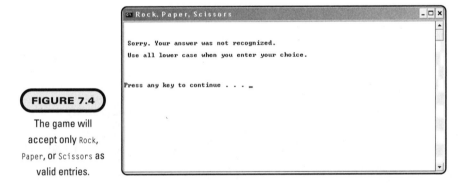

FIGURE 7.3

After each game, the script displays both the player's and the computer's selection and determines the results of the game.

The game will allow players to enter their selections using upper, lower, or mixed case. However, only the words Rock, Paper, or Scissors are valid entries. If the player makes a typo when entering their selection, the error message shown in Figure 7.4 will be displayed.

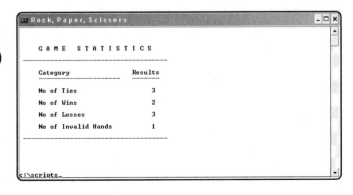

FIGURE 7.4

The game will accept only Rock, Paper, or Scissors as valid entries.

At the end of each game, players are asked whether they would like to play again. Players may play as many games as they wish. When they finally decide to stop playing, then the game screen shown in Figure 7.5 will appear, providing a summary of the number of games won, lost, or tied. In addition, the number of invalid selections (or hands) is also displayed.

FIGURE 7.5

The game allows players to play repeatedly and keeps a running record of the players' wins, losses, and ties.

Reorganizing Your Windows Shell Scripts

As you have now seen many times, Windows shell scripts execute by default from top to bottom. However, you can use the GOTO command along with a LABEL statement to direct scripts to jump from one location to another and resume execution. You have also seen on numerous occasions where I have used the GOTO command and a LABEL statement to set up loops.

The Windows shell provides another use for GOTO command and LABEL statement: creating subroutines. A *subroutine* is created whenever you use the GOTO command and the LABEL statement to switch processing control to a later section of the script (as opposed to a loop, where processing control is passed back to an earlier section of the script).

The Windows shell also allows you to define procedures using the CALL command and the LABEL statement. Using procedures, you switch processing control from one portion of the script to another section and then back again when the procedure finishes executing.

Understanding Labels

Even though you have seen them used many times, I have not yet formally defined labels. *Labels* are markers that you place inside your Windows shell scripts. Labels are used to establish loops, subroutines, and procedures. The syntax for the LABEL statement is shown below.

`:LABEL`

As you can see, a label consists of the colon character followed by the label's name. Label names are not case-sensitive, and you may use any combination of letters and numbers as well as the underscore character when specifying labels.

Defining Subroutines

When you set up a subroutine and then execute it, your script skips the execution of any statements that occur after the GOTO command and before the specified LABEL statement, as depicted in Figure 7.6.

```
@ECHO off

REM **************************************************************
REM
REM Script Name: Xxxxx.bat
REM Author: Jerry Ford
REM Date: Xxxxx XX, XXXX
REM
REM Description: Xxxxxxxxxxxxxxxxxxxxxxxxxxxxxxxx

REM
REM **************************************************************

REM ****** Script Initialization Section ******

.....
.....

REM ****** Main Processing Section ******

.....
.....

GOTO :ProcessFiles
.....
.....

REM ****** Procedure Section ******

:ProcessFiles

.....
.....

GOTO :EOF
```

As you can see in Figure 7.6, a GOTO command executes and calls a subroutine named :ProcessFiles. The arrow shows how the script execution skips over all statements between the GOTO command and the :ProcessFiles label.

Subroutines have complete access to any arguments that may have been passed to the script. In addition, any changes made to variables within a subroutine affect the entire script.

TRICK

The Windows shell provides a built-in function name :EOF (end of file), which you have seen used throughout this book. Windows shell scripts automatically terminate execution at the end of the script file. Therefore, when you use the GOTO command to execute the :EOF subroutine, you are really just telling your script to act as if it has just reached the end of the script file.

Windows Shell Script Programming for the Absolute Beginner

Look at a working example of a script that contains three subroutines, as shown below.

```
@ECHO off

COLOR 0E

TITLE = Subroutine Demo

CLS

FOR /L %%i IN (1,1,4) DO ECHO.
ECHO This script maintains the C:\Temp folder.
FOR /L %%i IN (1,1,16) DO ECHO.
ECHO Options: [Delete] [Rename] [Exit]
ECHO.

SET /P reply=What do you want to do to its contents?

IF /I %reply%==Delete (
  GOTO :DeleteFiles
)

IF /I %reply%==Rename (
  GOTO :RenameFiles
)

IF /I %reply%==Exit (
  GOTO :Exit
)

GOTO :EOF

:DeleteFiles
```

```
   ECHO Deleting all files stored in C:\TEMP

   DEL C:\TEMP\*.*

GOTO :EOF


:RenameFiles

   ECHO Renaming all files stored in C:\Temp

   REN C:\Temp\*.* *.bak

GOTO :EOF


:Exit

   ECHO Terminating script execution

GOTO :EOF
```

 TRAP **Be careful when using wild card characters to identify multiple files. They make it easy to accidentally delete files that you want to keep.**

This script is designed to maintain the C:\Temp folder. It can perform three different sets of actions, each of which is organized into its own function. The first function is called :DeleteFiles, and its job is to delete all the files stored in the folder. The second subroutine is called :RenameFiles, and its job is to rename all files found in the folder using a .bak file extension. The third subroutine is called :Exit. It's job is to terminate the script without performing any other action in the event that the user either ran the script by accident or changed their mind about deleting or renaming the files stored in the C:\Temp folder.

 TRAP **When keying in the previous example, make sure that you include at least one blank space at the end of the text specified as the SET command's message prompt. Otherwise the message prompt and the user's input will run together.**

When executed, the script displays a menu that prompts the user to specify an action. The script then analyzes the user's reply and executes the appropriate subroutine. Since each subroutine ended with a GOTO :EOF statement, each subroutine terminates the script's execution when it executes. Therefore the GOTO :EOF statement not only performs script termination but is also used to define the end of each subroutine.

Improving Script Organization with Procedures

As I have already stated, the CALL command can be used along with the LABEL statement to set up procedures. Unlike subroutines, which switch processing control to another part of the script and then terminate at the end of the file, procedures execute and then return processing control back to the statement that follows the CALL command that executed the procedure in the first place.

The Windows shell supports two different types of procedures, as outlined below.

- **Internal**. A procedure that is defined within the script that when called, executes and then returns control back to the statement that follows the CALL command.
- **External**. A call to another script. The calling script then waits for the called script to execute and terminate at which time the calling script begins executing again.

Setting Up Internal Procedures

Internal procedures are similar to subroutines. However, unlike subroutines they return processing control after they have finished executing, as depicted in Figure 7.7.

Like subroutines, internal procedures start with a LABEL and terminate with the GOTO :EOF statement. Procedures are called and executed by the CALL command, which has the following syntax:

```
CALL :ProcedureName
```

As you can see, the CALL statements begin with the CALL command followed by a space, then a colon, and finally the name of the procedure. The format that must be followed when creating a procedure is outlined below.

```
:ProcedureName

   ...

   ...

   ...

GOTO :EOF
```

The beginning of the procedure is marked by a LABEL called :ProcedureName. The end of the procedure is marked by the GOTO :EOF statement. Everything in between makes up the procedure itself.

```
@ECHO off

REM ***************************************************************
REM
REM Script Name: Xxxxx.bat
REM Author: Jerry Ford
REM Date: Xxxxx XX, XXXX
REM
REM Description: Xxxxxxxxxxxxxxxxxxxxxxxxxxxxxxxx

REM
REM ***************************************************************

REM ****** Script Initialization Section ******

. . . . .
. . . . .

REM ****** Main Processing Section ******

. . . . .
. . . . .

CALL :ProcessFiles
. . . . .
. . . . .

REM ****** Procedure Section ******

:ProfessFiles

. . . . .
. . . . .

GOTO :EOF
```

FIGURE 7.7

Internal procedures are created using the CALL command and a LABEL statement.

TRAP Don't forget to end all your procedures with the GOTO :EOF statement. Otherwise, the Windows shell will treat any statements that follow a procedure as part of that procedure, producing unpredictable results.

Unlike subroutines, which have complete access to all the arguments passed to the script, procedures are expected to accept and process their own arguments. To pass arguments to a script, you simply add the arguments, separated by spaces, to the end of the CALL statement, as outlined below.

```
CALL :ProcedureName arg1 arg2 arg3 ......
```

Procedures can then access these procedure arguments as %1, %2, %3, and so on in the same manner that scripts access script arguments. Since procedures have their own unique set of arguments, they are not permitted to have direct access to script arguments. This is true even if a procedure does not process any procedure-level arguments of its own. However, you can always pass script-level arguments to procedures if need be. For example, to call a procedure named :ProcessFiles and pass it all of the script arguments, you would use the following statement:

```
CALL :ProcessFiles %*
```

OK, now look at how to use procedures as an organizational tool for script development. In this example, the Unpredictable.bat script that was covered in Chapter 2, "Interacting with the Windows Shell," has been redesigned using procedures.

```
@ECHO off


REM ***************************************************************************

REM

REM Script Name: Unpredictable2.bat

REM Author: Jerry Ford

REM Date: July 20, 2003

REM

REM Description: This Windows shell script randomly adjusts the Windows shell

REM working environment

REM

REM ***************************************************************************


REM Script Initialization Section


CLS


REM Main Processing Section


CALL :GetRandomVariable


If %TestVariable% GTR 22000 (

  CALL :FirstConfiguration

  GOTO :EOF
```

```
)


If %TestVariable% GTR 11000 (

  CALL :SecondConfiguration

  GOTO :EOF

)


If %TestVariable% GTR 0 (

  CALL :ThirdConfiguration

  GOTO :EOF

)


REM Procedure Section


:GetRandomVariable

  SET TestVariable=%random%

GOTO :EOF


:FirstConfiguration

  CLS

  TITLE UCP - The Unpredictable Command Prompt  -  %TestVariable%

  COLOR 02

  ECHO Greetings %username%. Code well and Prosper.

  ECHO.

  PROMPT

GOTO :EOF


:SecondConfiguration

  CLS

  TITLE Demo - Manipulating the Windows console environment  -  %TestVariable%

  COLOR 0E

  ECHO Hello. It is good to be working with you today!
```

```
    ECHO.

    PROMPT $d$g

GOTO :EOF


:ThirdConfiguration

  CLS

  TITLE Windows Shell Scripting Example.  -  %TestVariable%

  COLOR E0

  ECHO Boo! Did I scare you?

  ECHO.

  PROMPT $p

GOTO :EOF
```

As you can see, the script's Procedure Section consists of a procedure call and three conditional IF statements which also make procedure calls as appropriate. When reorganized in this manner, the Main Processing Section assumes the job of managing the script's overall execution flow. However, the actual work is performed by a collection of four procedures located in the script's Procedure Section.

Procedures streamline a script's organization and help to create modular code. By modular, I mean that collections of related statements are grouped together. Grouping statements in this manner facilitates your ability to create reusable code. In addition, it makes script maintenance easier by isolating functionality and providing scripts with a predictable structure.

Creating External Procedures

An external procedure is another Windows shell script whose execution you call, or initiate, from within another Windows shell script via the CALL command. But instead of specifying a procedure name, you specify a script name using the following syntax:

```
CALL ScriptName
```

Like internal procedures, you may pass arguments to external procedures. When the called script terminates its execution, the calling script resumes its own execution beginning with the statement following the CALL statement. Figure 7.8 depicts the way that external procedures work.

You may make as many calls to external scripts as you wish. Each external script is executed within the same execution environment as the calling script. Therefore,

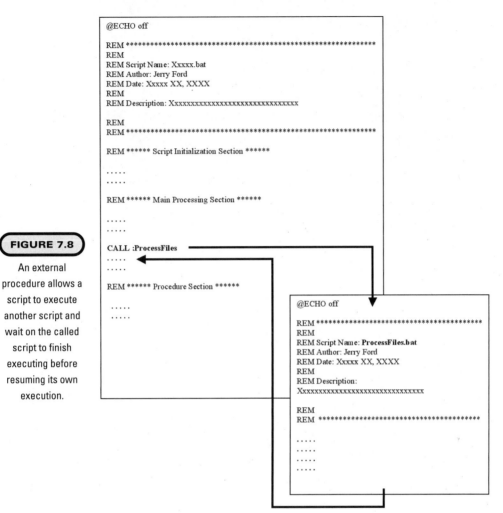

```
@ECHO off

REM ***************************************************************
REM
REM Script Name: Xxxxx.bat
REM Author: Jerry Ford
REM Date: Xxxxx XX, XXXX
REM
REM Description: Xxxxxxxxxxxxxxxxxxxxxxxxxxxxxxx

REM
REM ***************************************************************

REM ****** Script Initialization Section ******

 . . . . .
 . . . . .

REM ****** Main Processing Section ******

 . . . . .
 . . . . .

CALL :ProcessFiles
 . . . . .
 . . . . .

REM ****** Procedure Section ******

 . . . . .
 . . . . .
```

```
@ECHO off

REM *****************************************
REM
REM Script Name: ProcessFiles.bat
REM Author: Jerry Ford
REM Date: Xxxxx XX, XXXX
REM
REM Description:
Xxxxxxxxxxxxxxxxxxxxxxxxxxxxxx

REM
REM *****************************************

 . . . . .
 . . . . .
 . . . . .
 . . . . .
```

FIGURE 7.8

An external procedure allows a script to execute another script and wait on the called script to finish executing before resuming its own execution.

changes made by the called script to script variables originally defined by the calling script will be in effect once the calling script resumes its own execution.

To demonstrate the operation of external procedures, I redesigned the `Unpredictable2.bat` script as shown below. This time I extracted the statements that had made up the script's last three internal procedures and pasted them into three external scripts, which will be called and executed as external procedures. I named the scripts `FirstConfig.bat`, `SecondConfig.bat`, and `ThirdConfig.bat`.

```
@ECHO off


REM ***************************************************************************

REM
```

```
REM Script Name: Unpredictable3.bat

REM Author: Jerry Ford

REM Date: July 20, 2003

REM

REM Description: This Windows shell script randomly adjusts the Windows shell

REM working environment

REM

REM ****************************************************************************


REM Script Initialization Section


CLS


REM Main Processing Section


CALL :GetRandomVariable


If %TestVariable% GTR 22000 (
  CALL FirstConfig.bat
  ECHO Configuration now set.
  GOTO :EOF
)


If %TestVariable% GTR 11000 (
  CALL SecondConfig.bat
  ECHO Configuration now set.
  GOTO :EOF
)


If %TestVariable% GTR 0 (
  CALL ThirdConfig.bat
  ECHO Configuration now set.
```

```
    GOTO :EOF

)


REM Procedure Section


:GetRandomVariable

    SET TestVariable=%random%

GOTO :EOF
```

The following statements show the contents of the new `FirstConfig.bat` script.

```
CLS

TITLE UCP - The Unpredictable Command Prompt  -  %TestVariable%

COLOR 02

ECHO Greetings %username%. Code well and Prosper.

ECHO.

PROMPT
```

The contents of the new `SecondConfig.bat` script are listed below.

```
CLS

TITLE Demo - Manipulating the Windows console environment  -  %TestVariable%

COLOR 0E

ECHO Hello. It is good to be working with you today!

ECHO.

PROMPT $d$g
```

The contents of the new `ThirdConfig.bat` script are listed below.

```
CLS

TITLE Windows Shell Scripting Example.  -  %TestVariable%

COLOR E0

ECHO Boo! Did I scare you?

ECHO.

PROMPT $p
```

When executed, the new `Unpredictable3.bat` script calls each of its external procedures in sequence, producing the same results as the previous version of the script.

TRAP External scripts and the calling script are running within the same instance of the Windows shell. This means that the called script has access to any script variables already defined by the calling script. This also means that any changes made to the script variables by the called script will also be in effect when the calling script begins executing again. So, unless you intend that the calling and called scripts share script variables in this manner, be sure that you use different sets of variables within each script.

One advantage of this redesigned process is that it helps to further isolate the subroutines for debugging purposes. In other words, if I find later that I need to modify the statements stored in just one of the procedures, I can do so without affecting the statements stored in the main script or in the other external procedures. As a result, the effects of a typo are minimized and isolated to just the one procedure instead of an entire script.

TRICK As you begin writing more and more Windows shell scripts, eventually you may find that you begin to rewrite certain common procedures over an over again. For example, you might develop four or five scripts, all of which need to access the contents of a network drive. Using the NET USE command, you can develop an internal procedure that establishes a remote network connection to the network drive. However, rather than duplicate this procedure in each script that needs it, you can save it as a separate script and then call that script as a procedure from any script that needs it. This way, you won't have to keep reinventing the wheel.

Using Procedures to Localize Variable Access

Back in Chapter 4, "Storing and Retrieving Information in Variables," you were introduced to the idea of limiting or localizing access to script variables using the SETLOCAL and ENDLOCAL commands. By combining the use of these commands with procedures, you can lock down the variable access to specific locations within your scripts. This is an especially useful programming technique when you are developing complex and lengthy scripts that perform a lot of variable manipulation. As these types of scripts grow, it can become difficult to keep track of variables, thus opening up the possibility that one part of your script may accidentally alter a variable without you realizing it. By localizing variable access, you can exercise strict control over all your script's variables.

To localize variable access within procedures, make sure that the first statement in each procedure is the SETLOCAL statement and that the last statement is the ENDLOCAL statement, as demonstrated below.

```
:DemoProcedure

  SETLOCAL

  ...

  ...

  ...

  ENDLOCAL

GOTO :EOF
```

Using this format, any variables defined within the procedure are isolated from the rest of the script and are discarded when the procedure terminates.

TRAP When localizing variables within procedures, take extra care to make sure you remember to execute the ENDLOCAL command. Otherwise, your procedure variables will become script variables with potentially damaging effects. One thing you should specifically guard against is the use of GOTO commands within procedures, because that could transfer processing control to a different part of the script without first finishing the procedure. In this case, you can turn the GOTO command into a compound command in order to retain variable localization as demonstrated below.

```
ENDLOCAL & GOTO :ProcedureName
```

Tunneling Data Out of Your Procedures

While there are advantages to localizing variables within procedures via the SETLOCAL and ENDLOCAL commands, it also has one disadvantage. It makes it difficult for your internal procedures to return any results back to the script, which can greatly limit the usefulness of procedures. For example, the following procedure demonstrates this limitation:

```
:DemoProcedure

  SETLOCAL

  SET /A ret = 5

  ENDLOCAL

GOTO :EOF
```

In this procedure, the value of a variable named ret is set equal to 5. However, this variable and its value are not accessible to the rest of the script.

Using a programming technique called *variable tunneling*, you can get around this limitation. Variable tunneling works like this: First you create a variable containing whatever information you wish to pass back to the rest of the script, and then you turn the ENDLOCAL command into a compound command using the following syntax:

```
ENDLOCAL & SET ret=%ret%
```

The result will be a statement that ends the scope of procedure variables while tunneling out, or making accessible, the ret variable, as demonstrated in the following example:

```
:DemoProcedure


  SETLOCAL

  SET /A RET = 5

  ENDLOCAL & SET ret=%ret%
GOTO :EOF
```

Back to the Rock, Paper, Scissors Game

In the Rock, Paper, Scissors game, the player chooses from one of three available selections. The player's selection is then compared to the computer's randomly generated selection, and the results of the comparison are displayed. The criteria used to determine game results are very simple and are outlined in Table 7.1.

Using a Flowchart as a Script Development Tool

As you will see, the Rock, Paper, Scissors game provides an excellent chance to demonstrate the benefits of organizing your Windows shell scripts using procedures. As a preliminary step in designing this game, let's look at a new type of development tool, called flowcharting, which I think you will find vary useful.

DEFINITION A *flowchart* is a graphic outline that provides a high-level overview of the components of a script and shows their relationship to one another.

TABLE 7.1 ROCK, PAPER, SCISSORS RULES		
Player 1 Picks	**Player 2 Picks**	**Results**
Rock	Rock	Tie
Paper	Paper	Tie
Scissors	Scissors	Tie
Rock	Scissors	Rock breaks Scissors: Player 1 wins
Scissors	Rock	Rock breaks Scissors: Player 2 wins
Paper	Rock	Paper covers Rock: Player 1 wins
Rock	Paper	Paper covers Rock: Player 2 wins
Scissors	Paper	Scissors cut paper: Player 1 wins
Paper	Scissors	Scissors cut paper: Player 2 wins

Programmers often begin the development of complex projects by starting with a flowchart design. Flowcharts provide a visual tool for the outline of high-level logic. In addition, they provide the added benefit of serving as an excellent documentation tool.

Figure 7.9 shows the flowchart I developed for this Rock, Paper, Scissors project. As you can see, the flowchart's design is not very complex. I used rectangles to identify discrete modules of code such as procedures. I used a diamond shape to represent major decision points, and I used a circle to identify the logical end of the script. Then, to help show the game's overall flow, I drew arrows showing the logical flow of the game from beginning to end.

Roughly translated, the flowchart reads like this: First the script's Initialization Section processes. Then the script's main menu is displayed and the game starts. Next, the game collects the player's selection and compares it to the computer selection. A check is made to ensure that an invalid selection was not made, and the results of the game are displayed. At this point, the player will be prompted to decide whether to play again. If the player decides to play again, the game restarts. Otherwise, game statistics are displayed and the game ends.

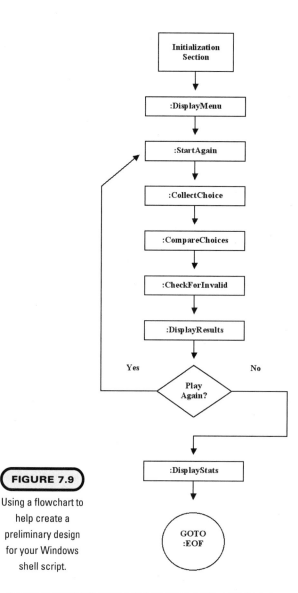

FIGURE 7.9

Using a flowchart to help create a preliminary design for your Windows shell script.

IN THE REAL WORLD

The larger and more complex the project, the more beneficial flowcharting becomes. Programmers use flowcharts to break down projects into discrete tasks. This makes it easier to focus on the development of each individual component of the script by knowing how it relates to other components. Flowcharting also helps programmers who work on teams to break down projects into different parts, each of which may be worked on by a different programmer.

Translating Flowchart Design into Script Requirements

Using the flowchart as a basis for outlining the steps involved in developing the Rock, Paper, Scissors game, I have decided to tackle this project in nine steps, as outlined below.

1. Set up the Initialization Section

2. Set up the Main Processing Section

3. Develop the `:Displaymenu` procedure

4. Develop the `:CollectChoice` procedure

5. Develop the `:GetComputerChoice` procedure

6. Develop the `:CompareChoices` procedure

7. Develop the `:CheckForInvalid` procedure

8. Develop the `:DisplayResults` procedure

9. Develop the `:DisplayStats` procedure

Creating the Initialization Section

The script's Initialization Section, shown below, displays the name of the game in the Windows command console's title bar and sets the color scheme to yellow on black. In addition, four variables that are used throughout the script are defined and assigned initial default values. These variables will be used to track game results and provide the player with information at the end of the game regarding the number of wins, losses, ties, and invalid selections.

```
TITLE = Rock, Paper, Scissors


COLOR 0E


SET /a NoWins = 0

SET /a NoLosses = 0

SET /a NoTies = 0

SET /a NoInvalid = 0
```

Creating the Main Processing Section

The Main Processing Section, shown below, looks a little different than the Main Processing Section of other scripts that you have seen in this book. This Main Processing Section is designed to control the game's overall execution by making calls to the appropriate procedures. In addition to procedure calls, the Main Processing Section includes a label called :StartAgain and an IF...Else statment. By placing the label at the beginning of the Main Processing Section, the IF...Else statement is able to initiate a replay of the game if the player elects to play another round. Otherwise, the :DisplayStatus procedure is called and the script terminates its execution.

```
CALL :DisplayMenu


:StartAgain


CALL :CollectChoice


CALL :GetComputerChoice


CALL :CompareChoices


CALL :CheckForInvalid


CALL :DisplayResults


IF /I "%response:~,1%" EQU "y" (

  GOTO :StartAgain

) ELSE (

    CALL :DisplayStats

    GOTO :EOF

)


GOTO :EOF
```

Developing the :DisplayMenu Procedure

The game's welcome screen is displayed whenever the :DisplayMenu procedure is called. As you can see, this procedure clears the display and then uses FOR and ECHO commands to display the welcome screen.

```
:DisplayMenu

  CLS


  FOR /L %%i IN (1,1,3) DO ECHO.


  ECHO  W E L C O M E  TO
  ECHO.
  ECHO  R O C K ,  P A P E R ,  S C I S S O R S !
  ECHO.
  ECHO.
  ECHO.
  ECHO  Rules:
  ECHO.
  ECHO  1. Guess the same thing as the computer to tie.
  ECHO.
  ECHO  2. Paper covers rock and wins.
  ECHO.
  ECHO  3. Rock breaks scissors and wins.
  ECHO.
  ECHO  4. Scissors cut paper and wins.


  FOR /L %%i IN (1,1,5) DO ECHO.


  PAUSE


GOTO :EOF
```

Like all procedures, this one ends with the GOTO :EOF statement, which returns the processing control of the script back to the statement immediately following the statement that called this procedure.

Developing the :CollectChoice Procedure

The :CollectChoice procedure, shown below, defines several variables and then displays a screen that prompts the player to type his selection.

```
:CollectChoice


  SET answer="No Answer"

  SET response=N

  SET results=None


  CLS


  FOR /L %%i IN (1,1,8) DO ECHO.


  SET /p answer= Type either rock, paper or scissors:


GOTO :EOF
```

Developing the :GetComputerChoice Procedure

The :GetComputerChoice procedure, shown below, obtains a random number between 0 and 32,767 by referencing the random environment variable. If the value of the random number is greater than 22,000, the computer is assigned a selection of rock. If the value of the random number is less than 22,000 and greater than 11,000, the computer is assigned a selection of scissors. Finally, if the value of the random number is less than 11,000, the computer is assigned a selection of paper.

```
:GetComputerChoice


  SET GetRandomNumber=%random%


  If %GetRandomNumber% GTR 22000 (
```

```
   SET CardImage=rock
   GOTO :Continue
)


If %GetRandomNumber% GTR 11000 (
   SET CardImage=scissors
   GOTO :Continue
)


SET CardImage=paper


:Continue


GOTO :EOF
```

Note the inclusion of the :Continue label in this procedure. I added this label to allow the procedure to skip the execution of any remaining statements as soon as the first conditional test proves true. For example, if the randomly generated number is over 22,000, then there is no reason for the procedure to process the other statements outside of those located in its first conditional test.

Developing the :CompareChoices Procedure

The :CompareChoices procedure, shown below, runs through a series of IF statements to determine if the selection entered by the player is equal to rock, paper, or scissors. If the player did enter one of these selections, then a set of three embedded IF statements is executed to determine whether the player won, lost, or tied.

```
:CompareChoices


  IF /I %answer% == rock (
    IF %CardImage% == rock (
      SET results="You Tie"
      SET /a NoTies = NoTies + 1
    )
    IF %CardImage% == scissors (
```

```
      SET results="You Win"

      SET /a NoWins = NoWins + 1

  )

  IF %CardImage% == paper (

    SET results="You Lose"

    SET /a NoLosses = NoLosses + 1

  )

)


IF /I %answer% == scissors (

  IF %CardImage% == rock (

    SET results="You Lose"

    SET /a NoLosses = NoLosses + 1

  )

  IF %CardImage% == scissors (

    SET results="You Tie"

    SET /a NoTies = NoTies + 1

  )

  IF %CardImage% == paper (

    SET results="You Win"

    SET /a NoWins = NoWins + 1

  )

)


IF /I %answer% == paper (

  IF %CardImage% == rock (

    SET results="You Win"

    SET /a NoWins = NoWins + 1

  )

  IF %CardImage% == scissors (

    SET results="You Lose"
```

```
        SET /a NoLosses = NoLosses + 1

    )

    IF %CardImage% == paper (

      SET results="You Tie"

      SET /a NoTies = NoTies + 1

    )

  )


GOTO :EOF
```

The value assigned to the variable called results is a string describing the results of the game. In addition, the values assigned to the NoWins, NoLosses, and NoTies variables are incremented as appropriate.

Developing the :CheckForInvalid Procedure

The :CheckForInvalid procedure, shown below, checks the value of the results variable to make sure that its value was set by the previous procedure. If a value was not set by the previous procedure, then the player did not enter a valid selection, and the variable's default setting will still be set equal to None. If this is the case, the screen is cleared and an error message is displayed.

```
:CheckForInvalid

  IF %results%==None (

    CLS

    SET /a NoInvalid = NoInvalid + 1

    FOR /L %%i IN (1,1,3) DO ECHO.

    ECHO  Sorry. Your answer was not recognized.
    ECHO.
```

```
      ECHO   Use all lower case when you enter your choice.


   FOR /L %%i IN (1,1,4) DO ECHO.


      PAUSE


   )


GOTO :EOF
```

The game continues after the player reads the error message and presses a key.

Developing the :DisplayResults Procedure

At the end of each game, the :DisplayResults procedure, shown below, is executed. Its job is to display the selections made by the player and the computer and to decide who, if anyone, won. This procedure is also responsible for prompting the player to play another game. It assigns the player's reply to a variable called response. When the procedure returns processing control back to the Main Processing Section, this section interrogates the variable's value to determine whether to restart the game.

```
:DisplayResults


   CLS


   FOR /L %%i IN (1,1,3) DO ECHO.


   ECHO        G A M E   R E S U L T S
   ECHO.
   ECHO  -----------------------------------
   ECHO.
   ECHO   You picked:          %answer%
   ECHO.
   ECHO   The computer picked:   %CardImage%
   ECHO.
   ECHO  -----------------------------------
   ECHO.
```

```
ECHO   Results:                  %Results%


FOR /L %%i IN (1,1,9) DO ECHO.


SET /p response=Play another round (y/n)?


GOTO :EOF
```

Developing the :DisplayStats Procedure

The :DisplayStats procedure, show below, is called just before the game terminates its execution. This procedure's job is to display the win, loss, and tie statistics that the game has collected so that players can see how well they faired against the computer. In addition, the number of invalid games (or hands) is displayed.

```
:DisplayStats


  CLS


  FOR /L %%i IN (1,1,3) DO ECHO.


  ECHO      G A M E   S T A T I S T I C S
  ECHO.
  ECHO  -------------------------------------
  ECHO.
  ECHO      Category              Results
  ECHO      --------------------  -------
  ECHO.
  ECHO      No of Ties            %NoTies%
  ECHO.
  ECHO      No of Wins            %NoWins%
  ECHO.
  ECHO      No of Losses          %NoLosses%
  ECHO.
  ECHO      No of Invalid Hands   %NoInvalid%
```

230

```
ECHO.

ECHO ------------------------------------

FOR /L %%i IN (1,1,4) DO ECHO.

GOTO :EOF
```

OK, now you are ready to complete the development of the Rock, Paper, Scissors game. Why don't you try to do so before examining the fully assembled script that I have listed in the next section.

The Final Result

The fully assembled Rock, Paper, Scissors game is shown below. As with previous projects, I have added the shell template and made liberal use of comments to help explain what is going on throughout the script.

```
@ECHO off


REM ***************************************************************************
REM
REM Script Name: RockPaperScissors.bat
REM Author: Jerry Ford
REM Date: July 19, 2003
REM
REM Description: This is a Windows shell script implementation of the popular
REM child's game called "Rock, Paper, Scissors."
REM
REM ***************************************************************************


REM ****** Script Initialization Section ******


REM Display the name of the game in the Windows command console's title bar
TITLE = R o c k ,   P a p e r ,   S c i s s o r s


REM Set the color scheme to yellow on black
```

```
COLOR OE


REM Define globally used variables
SET /a NoWins = 0
SET /a NoLosses = 0
SET /a NoTies = 0
SET /a NoInvalid = 0



REM ****** Main Processing Section ******


REM Call the procedure that displays the main menu
CALL :DisplayMenu


REM This label provides a callable marker for restarting the game
:StartAgain


REM Call the procedure that collect the player's choice
CALL :CollectChoice


REM Call the procedure that randomly determines the computer's choice
CALL :GetComputerChoice


REM Call the procedure that determine if the player won, lost or tied
CALL :CompareChoices


REM Call the procedure that checks for an invalid choice
CALL :CheckForInvalid


REM Call the procedure that displays the results of the game
CALL :DisplayResults


REM Analyze the player's response and either start a new game or display
```

```
REM game statistics (assume an N if response is anything but a Y or y)

IF /I "%response:~,1%" EQU "y" (

  GOTO :StartAgain

) ELSE (

    CALL :DisplayStats

    GOTO :EOF

)


REM Terminate the script's execution

GOTO :EOF



REM ****** Procedure Section ******


REM This procedure displays the game's main menu

:DisplayMenu


  REM Clear the display

  CLS


  REM Add three blank lines to the display

  FOR /L %%i IN (1,1,3) DO ECHO.


  ECHO  W E L C O M E  TO

  ECHO.

  ECHO  R O C K,  P A P E R,  S C I S S O R S !

  ECHO.

  ECHO.

  ECHO.

  ECHO  Rules:

  ECHO.

  ECHO  1. Guess the same thing as the computer to tie.

  ECHO.
```

```
    ECHO  2. Paper covers rock and wins.

    ECHO.

    ECHO  3. Rock breaks scissors and wins.

    ECHO.

    ECHO  4. Scissors cut paper and wins.


    REM Add five blank lines to the display

    FOR /L %%i IN (1,1,5) DO ECHO.


    REM Make the player press a key to continue

    PAUSE


GOTO :EOF


REM This collects the player's choice

:CollectChoice


    REM Define variables needed to store and analyze the player's response

    SET answer="No Answer"

    SET response=N

    SET results=None


    REM Clear the display

    CLS


    REM Add eight blank lines to the display

    FOR /L %%i IN (1,1,8) DO ECHO.


    REM Ask the player to make their choice

    SET /p answer= Type either rock, paper, or scissors:


GOTO :EOF
```

```
REM This procedure randomly determines the computer's choice
:GetComputerChoice


  REM Get a random number
  SET GetRandomNumber=%random%


  REM If the random number is greater than 22,000, the computer picked rock
  If %GetRandomNumber% GTR 22000 (

    SET CardImage=rock

    GOTO :Continue

  )


  REM If the random number is greater than 11,000, the computer picked scissors
  If %GetRandomNumber% GTR 11000 (

    SET CardImage=scissors

    GOTO :Continue

  )


  REM Otherwise, assign paper as the computer's choice
  SET CardImage=paper


  REM This label is used to skip unnecessary conditional tests in this procedure
  :Continue


GOTO :EOF


REM This procedure determines if the player won, lost, or tied
:CompareChoices


  REM Compare choices when the player selected rock
  IF /I %answer% == rock (

    IF %CardImage% == rock (

      SET results="You Tie"
```

```
      SET /a NoTies = NoTies + 1
  )

  IF %CardImage% == scissors (
    SET results="You Win"
    SET /a NoWins = NoWins + 1
  )

  IF %CardImage% == paper (
    SET results="You Lose"
    SET /a NoLosses = NoLosses + 1
  )
)


REM Compare choices when the player selected scissors
IF /I %answer% == scissors (
  IF %CardImage% == rock (
    SET results="You Lose"
    SET /a NoLosses = NoLosses + 1
  )

  IF %CardImage% == scissors (
    SET results="You Tie"
    SET /a NoTies = NoTies + 1
  )

  IF %CardImage% == paper (
    SET results="You Win"
    SET /a NoWins = NoWins + 1
  )
)


REM Compare choices when the player selected paper
IF /I %answer% == paper (
  IF %CardImage% == rock (
    SET results="You Win"
    SET /a NoWins = NoWins + 1
```

```
      )

    IF %CardImage% == scissors (

      SET results="You Lose"

      SET /a NoLosses = NoLosses + 1

    )

    IF %CardImage% == paper (

      SET results="You Tie"

      SET /a NoTies = NoTies + 1

    )

  )


GOTO :EOF


REM This procedure checks for an invalid choice
:CheckForInvalid


IF %results%==None (

  REM Clear the display
  CLS


  REM Keep a count of the total number of invalid player choices
  SET /a NoInvalid = NoInvalid + 1


  REM Add three blank lines to the display
  FOR /L %%i IN (1,1,3) DO ECHO.


  ECHO  Sorry. Your answer was not recognized.
  ECHO.
  ECHO  Use all lower case when you enter your choice.


  REM Add four blank lines to the display
```

```
  FOR /L %%i IN (1,1,4) DO ECHO.


  REM Make the player press a key to continue
  PAUSE


)


GOTO :EOF



REM This procedure displays the results of the game
:DisplayResults


  REM Clear the display
  CLS


  REM Add three blank lines to the display
  FOR /L %%i IN (1,1,3) DO ECHO.


  ECHO          G A M E   R E S U L T S
  ECHO.
  ECHO  -------------------------------------
  ECHO.
  ECHO    You picked:              %answer%
  ECHO.
  ECHO    The computer picked:     %CardImage%
  ECHO.
  ECHO  -------------------------------------
  ECHO.
  ECHO    Results:                 %Results%
```

```
REM Add nine blank lines to the display
FOR /L %%i IN (1,1,9) DO ECHO.


REM Ask the player whether he would like to play another game
SET /p response=Play another round (y/n)?


GOTO :EOF


REM This procedure displays game statistics
:DisplayStats


  REM Clear the display
  CLS


  REM Add three blank lines to the display
  FOR /L %%i IN (1,1,3) DO ECHO.


  ECHO      G A M E   S T A T I S T I C S
  ECHO.
  ECHO  --------------------------------------
  ECHO.
  ECHO      Category              Results
  ECHO      --------------------  -------
  ECHO.
  ECHO      No of Ties            %NoTies%
  ECHO.
  ECHO      No of Wins            %NoWins%
  ECHO.
  ECHO      No of Losses          %NoLosses%
  ECHO.
  ECHO      No of Invalid Hands   %NoInvalid%
  ECHO.
```

```
ECHO  -----------------------------------


REM Add four blank lines to the display
FOR /L %%i IN (1,1,4) DO ECHO.


GOTO :EOF
```

Now that you have completed the Rock, Paper, Scissors game, I think you'll agree with me that using procedures to organize your scripts is definitely the way to go. Not only do procedures make things more manageable by grouping together related collections of statements, but they also facilitate the development of reusable code by allowing the same procedure to be called repeatedly as many times as necessary.

Summary

In this chapter, you learned how to reorganize your Windows shell scripts using subroutines and procedures. This included learning how to create both internal and external procedures as well as how to localize variables within procedures and how to tunnel out data from procedures. You were also introduced to flow-charting as a tool for assisting your development of Windows script files. Finally, you learned how to create the Rock, Paper, Scissors game and to organize the entire game using procedures.

EXERCISES

1. Modify the Rock, Paper, Scissors game's welcome screen so that it includes a menu with access to Help, About, Exit, and Play menu selections.

2. Display an additional line of text at the bottom of the Game Results screen that explains the results of the game. For example, if the player picked Rock and the computer picked Scissors, the message should read something like "Rock crushes scissors!"

3. Track and display additional statistical information at the end of the Rock, Paper, Scissors game. For example, track how long the player played. (Hint: Perform substring operations against the output produced by the TIME, convert everything to seconds, and then subtract the start time from the finish time.) Also, provide the player with some percentages including the percentage of games won, lost, and tied.

4. Create your own unique version of the Rock, Paper, Scissors game using whatever objects you wish. In addition, expand the number of objects supported by the game.

CHAPTER 8

Debugging and Error Handling

The focus of this final chapter is to help you deal with errors that are bound to occur as you develop your scripts. To begin, I'll discuss the different types of errors that you will experience, and then I will give you advice on how to deal with them. You'll learn how to display intermediary results during script execution and how to create an optional debug execution mode.

In addition to all this, you'll learn how to report on errors that your scripts are unable to avoid. This reporting will include the creation of error reports and the generation of custom error messages. I'll also show you how to set up scripts that, when executed as procedures, will return an exit code to their calling script.

Specifically, you will learn

- How to display intermediate results during script execution

- How to create scripts that include an optional script debug mode

- How to create error reports when problems occur within scripts

- How to pass exit code data back to calling scripts from scripts executed as external procedures

Project Preview: The Tic-Tac-Toe Game

The Tic-Tac-Toe game is a computerized implementation of the classic children's game in which two players go head to head in a game of strategy and wits in an effort to line up three squares in a row (horizontally, vertically, or diagonally).

The Tic-Tac-Toe game begins by displaying its welcome screen, which includes a menu of options at the bottom of the screen, as shown in Figure 8.1.

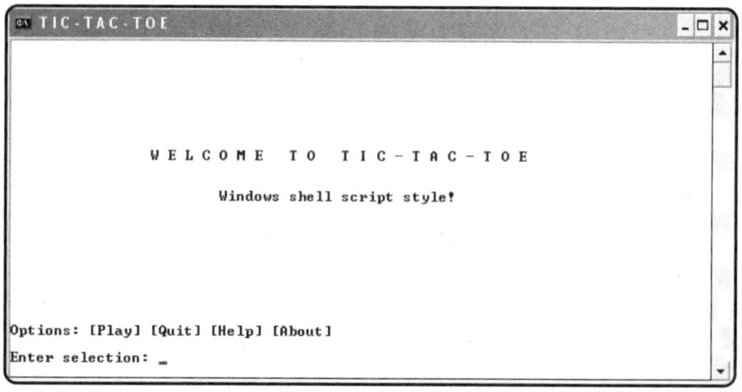

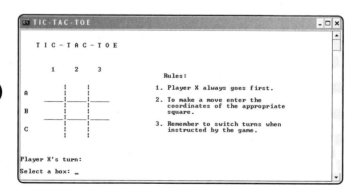

FIGURE 8.1

The Tic-Tac-Toe game's welcome menu presents players with a variety of options.

When the players are ready to begin the game, the Tic-Tac-Toe game board is displayed along with the rules of the game. Player X, always the first player to go, is then prompted to make an initial move, as shown in Figure 8.2.

FIGURE 8.2

The Tic-Tac-Toe game board and rules are displayed throughout the game.

As the game progresses, the Tic-Tac-Toe game board is updated continually to reflect each player's moves, as demonstrated in Figure 8.3.

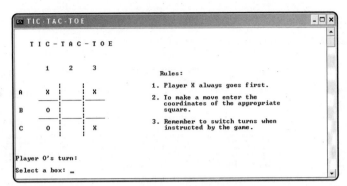

FIGURE 8.3

Player moves are immediately posted on the Tic-Tac-Toe game board.

The game validates each player's move to ensure that it is within the range of coordinates supported by the game (i.e., A1–A3, B1–B3, and C1–C3) and that players do not attempt to select squares that have already been selected. When players do make errors, the screen shown in Figure 8.4 is displayed, and the player who made the error is then given another chance to make their next move.

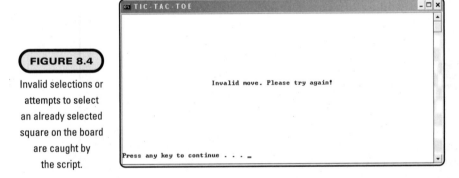

FIGURE 8.4

Invalid selections or attempts to select an already selected square on the board are caught by the script.

The game tracks all game activity and automatically determines when a player wins or when the game ends in a tie, as demonstrated in Figure 8.5.

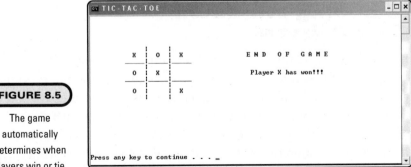

FIGURE 8.5

The game automatically determines when players win or tie.

Like all good computer games, the Tic-Tac-Toe game provides players with access to additional help, as shown in Figure 8.6.

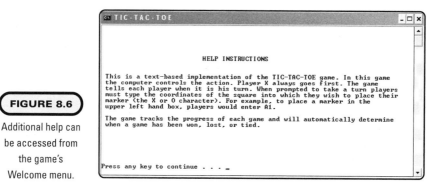

FIGURE 8.6

Additional help can be accessed from the game's Welcome menu.

In addition, the Tic-Tac-Toe game provides access to an About screen where players can find more information about the game and its author, as shown in Figure 8.7.

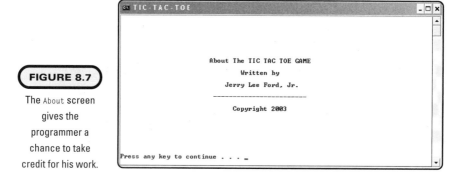

FIGURE 8.7

The About screen gives the programmer a chance to take credit for his work.

I think you will agree that the Tic-Tac-Toe game represents a very good example of how complicated and graphical text-based computer games can be.

Understanding Windows Shell Script Errors

No matter how good a programmer becomes, one thing will always remain true—errors will happen. Errors can be especially frustrating to programmers who are just getting started. One of the goals of this chapter is to help prepare you for dealing with errors when they occur. Another goal is to arm you with advice and tips for avoiding errors in the first place. However, the reality is that some errors simply cannot be avoided; often the best you can hope to do is to set up your scripts to terminate as gracefully as possible, perhaps by logging the error or displaying a user-friendly error message.

Syntax Errors

Windows shell script errors occur at a number of different times and for a number of different reasons. One type of error that you are sure to encounter is a syntax error. These types of errors happen when you mistype statements within your Windows shell scripts. For example, you might mistype the spelling of a command or leave off the closing parenthesis in a multi-line IF statement.

 DEFINITION *Syntax errors* are errors that occur when programmers fail to follow the syntax rules that govern the formatting of commands.

Syntax errors are usually caught by the Windows shell when your script first begins to run and will prevent your script from executing. The Windows shell displays an error message indicating the cause of the first syntax error that it finds within the script. Using the information provided by the error message and a little detective work, you can eliminate most syntax errors during script development and testing.

Run-Time Errors

Another category of error that you will run into is execution, or run-time, errors. Run-time errors occur only when the statements that generate them execute. Therefore, unless you are careful to test the execution of every statement within your script, run-time errors can sneak through. For example, you might have a script that contains a procedure that is not always used. If this procedure contains a statement that would generate a run-time error, you would not know it until some time later.

 DEFINITION An *execution error,* or *run-time error,* is one that happens as a result of the script attempting to perform an illegal action. A good example is when a GOTO or CALL command attempts to reference a label that has not been defined within the Windows shell script.

The good news is that in most cases you can avoid run-time errors by carefully designing and then testing your scripts during development. Unfortunately, you may not be able to entirely prevent run-time errors from occurring. For example, users can be unpredictable. You can never be completely assured that they will supply your scripts with data that make sense, resulting in run-time errors. Other causes of run-time errors include environment problems. For example, if your script is designed to create a report but the user's hard disk has become full, your script will fail with an error.

Logical Errors

Another category of errors that every programmer runs into from time to time is logical errors. Logical errors occur when you tell a script to do one thing when you really meant for it to do something else. As a result, the script does exactly what you told it to do but the output that you expected is wrong.

DEFINITION A *logical error* is one that occurs as a result of a mistake made by the programmer, such as telling a script to add two numbers that should have been subtracted.

Logical errors usually make their presence known in the form of unexpected output. In other words, the script seems to run without any problems, but the end result isn't what you intended. Since logical errors do not announce themselves in the form of error messages, they can be the most difficult type of errors to track down and fix. As a result, most logical errors are fixed only by reviewing all or part of your script line-by-line to figure out where you went wrong. However, I will show you a few tricks in this chapter that will help you track down logical errors.

Fortunately, most logical errors can be prevented by taking the time to plan the design of your scripts properly. For example, a good design might start with a flowchart and a pseudo code outline of the logic involved in critical procedures. But even with the best preliminary designs, logical errors sometimes still manage to creep into scripts. However, by developing your scripts in a modular fashion using subroutines and procedures, and by carefully testing, you can usually catch any logical errors during script development.

Examining Windows Shell Script Error Messages

The Windows shell automatically generates error messages for both syntax and run-time errors. By default all errors messages are displayed in the Windows command console. However, using I/O redirection, as discussed in Chapter 3, "Windows Shell Scripting Basics," you have the option of redirecting errors messages elsewhere.

Common Syntax Errors

Unfortunately, error messages produced by the Windows shell often leave much to be desired. Unlike other scripting languages, which display an error code and description as well as information regarding the line number of the statement that generated the error, the information provided by the Windows shell is extremely meager and is limited to a cryptic message that often provides very little helpful information. For example, consider the following Windows shell script.

```
@ECHO OFF


SET /A X = 5
SET /A Y = 10


IF X GTR Y
  ECHO X is greater than Y
) ELSE (
  ECHO Y is greater than X
)


PAUSE
```

There is an error in this script. If you were to save and run the script, the error message you would see is shown below.

```
The syntax of the command is incorrect.
```

As you can see, the Windows shell has told you that it found an error but has not provided you with any other useful information. If you look closely, you'll see that the error is a missing left parenthesis at the end of the fourth line in the script. Now look at another example of a common Windows shell script error.

```
@ECHO OFF


SET WindowsFiles=%indir%


ECHO %WindowsFiles%


PAUSE
```

In this example, the name of the `windir` environment variable has been misspelled. The Windows shell automatically assigns an empty value to any undefined variable. As a result, the script variable called `WindowsFiles` does not have any data associated with it. At this point, the script is still running happily along. However, when the script's ECHO statement attempts to display the contents assigned to the WindowsFiles variable, the following error message will be displayed:

```
ECHO is off.
```

Again, not much information was provided by this error, although it does suggest that the error was generated by the execution of an ECHO statement. Of course, as you can see, the real error exists in the SET statement. This error is easy enough to track down in a small script like this one. However, as scripts grow in size and complexity, finding these types of errors is not always easy.

The next script demonstrates another common Windows shell scripting error.

```
@ECHO OFF


SET /A X = 5
SET /A Y = 10
SET /A Z = 15


IF Z GTR Y (

  IF Y GTR X (

   IF X GTR 0 (

     ECHO All is well with the world!

   )

  (

 )


PAUSE
```

When executed, the following error message will be displayed. While cryptic, some useful information is provided this time. Specifically, you know that somewhere within the script the Windows shell found something other than the) character that it was expecting.

```
) was unexpected at this time.
```

Since the (and) characters are commonly used to create multi-line IF statements, you might begin by examining the syntax of any recently added IF statement within the script. If you do, you will find that the closing) character associated with the second IF statement was accidentally inverted to a (character.

TRICK Start script development by defining the contents of the Initialization Section. Even though it will not do anything at this point, run the script to make sure that no syntax errors are generated. Then start creating the rest of the script by adding a few lines to the Main Processing Section and rerunning the script again to look for errors. From this point, as you begin to define subroutines and procedures, write and test them one at a time rather than trying to create them all at once. This way, when an error occurs, you will likely find it in the most recently added collection of statements.

A Typical Run-Time Error

Now look at an example of a run-time error. In this example, a small Windows shell script has been written that is supposed to copy all files with a .log file extension found in the computer's C:\Temp folder to a network drive. Access to this drive is supposed to be provided by a mapped drive letter called Z. A script like this one could be run at the end of each working day as a quick way to store copies of log files on a company's network server.

```
@ECHO off


COPY C:\TEMP\*.log Z:\LogFiles
```

Now suppose that something happened one day to the company's network. Maybe the network went down or the computer where the shared network drive resides might have crashed. If you tried to run this script before the network problem was resolved, the following error could occur.

```
The system cannot find the drive specified.
```

In this example, there is nothing wrong with the script. Instead, an uncontrollable environmental problem has inhibited its execution as run-time.

A Typical Logical Error

Next, look at an example of a common logical error. In this example, shown below, I created a script that attempts to multiply the values stored in two numeric variables. However, only one of the variables has been defined. Syntactically, there is nothing wrong with the script, and it will not experience a run-time error because of the lenient manner in which the Windows shell handles variables.

```
@ECHO off

SET /A X = 5

SET Y=C:\Temp

SET Z = X * Y

ECHO Z = %Z%

PAUSE
```

Logically, however, the script falls short and generates the output shown below. To fix this type of error, you must track down the location within your script where the other variable should have been defined and add it.

```
Z =

Press any key to continue . . .
```

Examining Different Ways of Dealing with Errors

There are a number of different ways that you can attempt to cope with errors in your Windows shell scripts. To begin with, you could

- Educate your users so that they'll know what to do in the event that your scripts run into an error.
- Develop a script trace capability that assists you in tracking down and fixing errors.
- Try to anticipate commands that are most likely to result in errors and attempt to programmatically fix or work around problems.
- Record errors that occur in error log files for later review.
- Report errors by displaying them as soon as they occur.

I'll discuss each of these options in detail in the sections that follow.

Educating Your Users

Even the best and most experienced programmers run into errors. That's just part of the reality of modern-day programming and script development. One way you can deal with errors that you did not anticipate or cannot prevent is to educate the people with whom you share your scripts.

By educate, I mean that you should provide them with detailed instructions as to what to do should problems occur. For example, you might

- Ask users to document any error messages that are displayed.
- Ask users to document exactly what steps they had taken that led up to the errors (e.g., what input they had given the script, how and when the script was started, etc.).
- Ask users to report immediately any problems that occur.

By supplying you with this type of information, users might enable you to reproduce and identify the error, so you can try to prevent the error from happening again in the future. Just remember this: Unless you provide them with some instruction, most users will have no idea what to do when a script error occurs. By providing them with instructions up front, you not only minimize any inconvenience and facilitate problem resolution but also encourage user feedback and support, which can be critical in a professional setting.

Tracing Logic Flow within Scripts

Sometimes errors can be difficult to track down, especially if the script is fully written and you have not looked at it in a while. Unfortunately, unlike some advanced programming languages, Windows shell scripting does not provide any sort of built-in debugging or tracing mechanism that allows you to track the operation of your scripts as they execute.

One way to deal with this is to remove the @ECHO off statement from the beginning of your script. This will allow you to observe the execution of each command as it executes. However, this option can flood the Windows command console's display, and it may soon become difficult to follow. Fortunately, other options are available.

One very basic way of implementing tracing within your Windows shell scripts is to embed ECHO statements throughout your scripts. For example, to track script execution, you could place an ECHO statement at the beginning and ending of the script's Initialization and Main Processing Sections as well as in procedures in order to identify which portion of the script is currently executing. These ECHO statements could be as simple as those shown below.

```
ECHO Procedure :DisplayResults not executing

ECHO Procedure :DisplayResults finished executing
```

By dispersing ECHO statements throughout your scripts in this manner, you can trace the execution of each component of your scripts during testing. In addition to tracing script execution, you'll also want to keep track of your variables to make sure they are being assigned data properly. Again, you can do this by using the ECHO statement to display variable values, as demonstrated below.

```
ECHO Variable: TotalCount = %TotalCount%
```

By adding ECHO statements after any statement that sets or modifies variables, you can track their values during the execution of your scripts. Once you have your scripts fully tested and working as you want them to work, you can either delete these extra ECHO statements or, better yet, comment them out using the REM statement, as demonstrated below.

```
REM ECHO Variable: TotalCount = %TotalCount%
```

By commenting out these statements, you can keep them around should you need to use them again later to debug the script again. I have an even better suggestion that you can use to make this tracing and debugging technique even more useful. It involves a little more work up front, but if you are working on a critical script, it is probably worth the extra effort.

You'll still need to embed statements throughout your scripts that display information about which sections are currently executing and what the current values assigned to variables are. What changes is the manner in which you enable and disable debugging statements. Instead of writing a debugging statement as

```
ECHO Variable: TotalCount = %TotalCount%
```

you would write it as

```
%trace% Variable: TotalCount = %TotalCount%
```

Notice that a variable called trace has been substituted for the ECHO or REM commands. When written in this manner, you provide the ability to toggle statements between ECHO and REM mode by placing a statement similar to the following at the beginning of your script:

```
IF /I "%1"=="Debug" (SET trace=ECHO) ELSE (SET trace=REM)
```

As you can see, this statement sets the value of trace equal to ECHO when the script is passed an argument of Debug. Otherwise, it sets the value of trace to REM. The net effect is that if you run the script by simply entering its name at the command prompt and pressing Enter, the value of trace is set equal to REM and all of the extra statements that you embedded in your script are turned into comments. This would be the default execution mode for the script.

Using this example, all it takes to enable debugging is to use the following syntax to pass the word Debug as the first argument to the script when you run it:

ScriptName Debug

 TRICK The tracing and debugging technique presented in this chapter works because the Windows shell always substitutes variable values before executing statements.

Now look at an example of this debugging technique in action. The following script is called TestScript.bat. As you can see, it is rather small and includes a number of debugging statements, the first of which enables or disables tracing mode based on whether the word Debug is passed to it as a script argument.

```
@ECHO off

IF /I "%1"=="Debug" (SET trace=ECHO) ELSE (SET trace=REM)

%trace% TestScript.bat executing in trace mode.

%trace% Beginning copy operations.

COPY *.bak C:\TEMP > C:\Temp\ScriptLog.log 2>&1

IF ERRORLEVEL 1 (
  %trace% No backup files were found.
)

COPY *.rpt C:\TEMP > C:\Temp\ScriptLog.log 2>&1

IF ERRORLEVEL 1 (
  %trace% No report files were found.
)

%trace% All copy operations now complete.

GOTO :EOF
```

When executed in non-debug mode, this script will execute without displaying any text in the Windows command console. However, when executed in debug mode, output similar to the following will be displayed:

```
c:\scripts>TestScript.bat debug

TestScript.bat executing in trace mode.

Beginning copy operations.

No backup files were found.

No report files were found.

All copy operations now complete.


c:\scripts>
```

TRICK   **If you find that data is passing by too quickly on the Windows command console's screen when you're testing scripts in debug mode, you can always slow things down a bit by adding a few well placed** PAUSE **commands to your script.**

As you can see, this is a very good debugging technique, but it does take extra effort on your part to implement it. Its usefulness will depend on a number of factors, including the complexity and importance of the script with which you are working. A small script consisting of a few lines probably won't justify the extra work, whereas a script that you are writing for your employer might very well require the extra effort.

Command Error Checking

Another important debugging technique is to try to anticipate which commands in your scripts are most likely to result in errors and to develop processes that try to deal with errors should they arise. Some options available to you for handling errors include

- Displaying instructions to the user for contacting you to report the error.
- Rewording cryptic error messages so that users can understand them.
- Attempting to take a corrective action such as giving users another try.
- Logging error messages for later review.

To implement error checking, you must become familiar with the IF ERRORLEVEL statement. This statement enables you to test the value of the previously executed command's exit code to determine if it executed successfully or if it completed with an error. The exit code 0 indicates that the previous command was successful. Anything higher generally means an error occurred.

The following is an example of how to use the IF ERRORLEVEL statement to determine if a file copy operation was successful. If the operation fails, an error code of 1 will be returned as the exit code of the COPY command, and the script will display an error message. However, the script will continue to run and try to perform a second copy operation.

```
@ECHO off


CLS


ECHO.
ECHO Beginning copy operations.
ECHO.
PAUSE


COPY *.bak C:\TEMP > C:\Temp\ScriptLog.log 2>&1


IF ERRORLEVEL 1 (
  ECHO.
  ECHO No backup files were found.
  ECHO.
)


COPY *.rpt C:\TEMP > C:\Temp\ScriptLog.log 2>&1


IF ERRORLEVEL 1 (
  ECHO No report files were found.
)


ECHO.
ECHO All copy operations now complete.
```

```
ECHO.
PAUSE


GOTO :EOF
```

In this example, the script was set up to report on errors while continuing to execute. Another way that this script could have been written would have been to stop its execution at the first occurrence of an error. Alternatively, additional logic could have been added to retry the copy operation.

The Windows shell supports different variations of the IF ERRORLEVEL statement. To learn more about how this statement works, refer to Chapter 5, "Applying Conditional Logic."

Logging Error Messages

One way to handle errors is to write them to a log or report file for later review and analysis. This way, by reviewing the log file, you can observe problems that occur over time, including those that the user may not have bothered to report. For example, the following statements demonstrate how to create and append statements to an error log file called ScriptLog.log.

```
@ECHO off


COPY *.bak C:\TEMP


IF ERRORLEVEL 1 (

  IF EXIST C:\TEMP\ScriptLog.log (

    ECHO %date% %time% - Backup files copied to C:\TEMP >> C:\Temp\ScriptLog.log

  ) ELSE (

    ECHO %date% %time% - Backup files copied to C:\TEMP > C:\Temp\ScriptLog.log

  )

)


GOTO :EOF
```

This script begins by attempting to copy any files found in the current working directory to the computer's C:\TEMP folder. It then checks to see if an error occurred. If an error did occur, the IF EXIST statement checks to see if the ScriptLog.log file already exists. If it does not exist, it is created and written to. Otherwise, the data produced by the script is appended to the end of the log file. Note that each log entry includes both a date and time stamp.

Figure 8.8 shows how this error log might look over time.

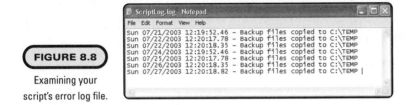

FIGURE 8.8

Examining your script's error log file.

Using the logic in this example, you could easily adapt any of your scripts to record similar entries to the log file, making it a shared error log. For more detailed information on how to generate report and log files, refer to Chapter 3, "Windows Shell Scripting Basics."

Displaying Error Messages

Another way to handle errors is to display them. Better yet, you could suppress cryptic Windows shell error messages and display useful English-like error messages that users can understand. The easiest way to display error information is as text in the Windows command console using the ECHO command. Another option is to take advantage of the NET SEND command to display error messages in graphical pop-up dialogs. Both of these options are explored further in the sections that follow.

Creating User-Friendly Error Messages

As you have seen many times already in this book, the ECHO command provides an easy way to display text within the Windows command console. When used in conjunction with the IF ERRORLEVEL statement as shown below, it provides an effective option for displaying error messages that are easily understood by the average user.

```
@ECHO off


COPY *.bak C:\TEMP > C:\Temp\ScriptLog.log 2>&1


IF ERRORLEVEL 1 (

  ECHO No backup files were found!
```

```
)
```

```
GOTO :EOF
```

 TRICK Note that in the previous example both the standard and error output produced by the COPY command were redirected to an error log file named ScriptLog.log by appending 2>&1 to the end of the COPY statement.

Displaying Errors Using Graphical Pop-Up Dialogs

Depending on the amount of data already displayed in the Windows command console, it may be difficult for errors to stand out. Therefore, users may miss them entirely. In addition, Windows shell scripts run by the Windows scheduler service may not be visible when they run, making it impossible for the user to see error messages. A solution to both of these issues is to use the Windows NET SEND command to display the error message in a graphical pop-up dialog. This way, as long as someone is logged on to the computer when the script is executed, the error message will be seen.

For example, consider the following example, which was adapted from the previous script. Instead of using the ECHO command, this new script uses the NET SEND command to display the message. The first argument passed to the NET SEND command is %computername%, which is an environment variable that contains the name of the local computer. By passing the command this variable, the script tells it to display the message on the local computer (as opposed to sending it to another computer). The rest of the data passed to the NET SEND command makes up the text of the error message.

```
@ECHO off


COPY *.bak C:\TEMP > C:\Temp\ScriptLog.log 2>&1


IF ERRORLEVEL 1 (

  NET SEND %computername% No backup files were found!

)


GOTO :EOF
```

TRAP The `NetSend.bat` script depends on the built-in Messenger service being enabled and running. This service enables Windows operating systems to send and receive network messages. If you are working from a computer on your company's network, you may find that your system administrator has disabled this service, in which case the `NET SEND` command and this script will not be able to work.

Figure 8.9 shows the graphical pop-up dialog that is displayed when this script executes and experiences an error.

FIGURE 8.9

Using the `NET SEND` command to display script output in a graphical pop-up dialog.

Creating Scripts That Return a Custom Exit Code

If you plan on developing scripts that take advantage of external procedures as a means of creating reusable code that can be shared by multiple Windows shell scripts, then you'll appreciate this next topic. As you know, one of the advantages of using procedures is that you can use them to isolate access to procedure variables. However, this also limits the ability of procedures to share variable access with the rest of the script.

Variable tunneling provides a way to pass data back to calling statements or scripts. Another way to return data back from an external procedure is to set it up to pass back an exit code. The calling script can then interrogate this exit code and ascertain what it represents. To accomplish this trick you'll need to use the `EXIT` command. This command terminates the execution of the external procedure (or script) and, alternatively, sends back a customized exit code.

The syntax of the `EXIT` command is outlined below.

```
EXIT [/B] [ExitCode]
```

The `/B` switch is optional. When used, it passes back to the calling script a numeric value specified by the `ExitCode` placeholder. To see how this works, look at the following pair of scripts.

The first script will be called as an external procedure. When executed, it attempts to copy all files with a .bak file extension from the current working directory to C:\Temp. Any output or errors are redirected to C:\Temp\ScriptLog.log. If an error occurs when performing the copy operation, the script's :EXIT procedure is executed. This procedure issues the EXIT command and passes back an exit code of 4 to the calling or parent script.

```
@ECHO off


COPY *.bak C:\TEMP > C:\Temp\ScriptLog.log 2>&1


IF ERRORLEVEL 1 GOTO :EXIT


GOTO :EOF


:EXIT
  EXIT /B 4
```

The following statements make up the calling, or parent, script. As you can see, it calls the external procedures (e.g., TestScript.bat), waits for it to finish executing, and then checks the exit code returned by the external procedure to see if it is equal to 4.

```
@ECHO off


CALL TestScript.bat


IF ERRORLEVEL 4 (
  ECHO No backup files were found
)
```

Other Things to Look Out For

Finally, the sections that follow will review some of the other issues and problems that you might run into as you begin working more and more with the Windows shell and Windows shell scripts. In addition, I'll provide you with suggestions for avoiding, fixing, or working around these issues and problems.

Insufficient Authority

At some point you may find that your scripts fail because you do not have the appropriate set of security permissions or rights to perform a given task. The main thing to remember is that if you do not have the ability to perform a particular task from the Windows desktop, then you won't have the ability to perform it from the Windows shell either.

The bottom line is that unless you have been assigned administrative-level access to the computer, you run the risk of not being able to perform certain tasks. For example, Windows provides key functionality by running internal programs and utilities known as services. While you may be an administrator over your local computer with complete control over your computer's services, you may find that if you create a script that starts and stops services and then take it to another computer, it will not be allowed to do its job. This may be because you lack the appropriate level of security permissions on that computer.

Security issues often arise when you are developing scripts on corporate networks and are subject to the security restrictions imposed by system administrators. Perhaps all you'll need to do in this situation is ask for additional security privileges. Security issues also arise when you attempt to run scripts on a computer other than the one where you develop and test your scripts. Again, you'll probably have to seek out your system administrator's assistance.

In addition to the above security concerns, you may find that your scripts begin failing when other people begin running them. This may happen if they do not have the same level of security access that you do.

Dealing with Scripts That Are Difficult to Read and Understand

As you write your scripts, take care to make sure you always document them using plenty of comments and a script template such as the one presented in this book. Use indentation as a technique for making your code easier to read and understand, and add plenty of blank spaces in between groups of statements to help visually organize things.

In addition to following these tips, make sure that you focus on keeping things as simple as possible. For example, use SET /A X +=1 instead of SET /A X = X + 1. It is shorter and just as easy to understand. Finally, consider adding checks to your scripts that prevent them from being inappropriately executed. For example, I recommend always including the following check as part of your script template.

```
IF NOT "%os%" == "Windows_NT" GOTO :EOF
```

Working with Windows Commands

Windows commands are not case-sensitive, so you won't get into trouble if you mix up their case when you include them in your Windows shell scripts. However, mixing case in this manner can make your scripts difficult to read. So be consistent in whatever case you decide to use. However, you need to remember that while mixing case will not cause script errors, you still need to closely follow the syntax rules specified for each individual command. For example, keep an eye on the order of command switches. While most Windows commands allow you to list command switches in any order you wish, others will not. Also, make sure that you run any command that you plan to use manually from the command prompt first to ensure that you understand how it works before adding it to your script.

Managing Arguments and Variables

The Windows shell imposes many rules upon the use of arguments and variables, which you need to watch out for. Below is a brief overview of some of these rules.

- Arguments and variables that contain spaces must be enclosed within double quotes.
- Blank spaces included just before or after the equal sign in SET statements result in the inclusion of blank spaces in variable names and values (except when assigning data to numeric variables).
- Arguments or variables that may contain spaces should be enclosed inside double quotation marks.
- Use the SET command's /A switch to explicitly define any values that you wish to treat as numeric.
- Make sure you apply the order of precedence implemented by the Windows shell when setting up mathematical expressions.
- By default, the Windows shell returns an empty value when a referenced variable does not exist. Therefore, you also need to make sure that you use the IF DEFINED or IF NOT DEFINED statements in any situation where there is a chance that a critical variable might not already be defined.

TRICK

Whenever possible, reference your environment variables to avoid having to hard code data into your scripts. This will make your scripts easier to support. It also makes them more portable. For example, Microsoft has changed the location of the Windows system root folders. On Windows NT and 2000 it's C:\Winnt but on Windows XP it is C:\Windows. If you ever need to access this folder, you can reference the environment variable %systemroot% to find it without having to be concerned with what operating system your script is running on.

Handling Files and Folders

File and folder administration can be tricky. You never know when someone will come along and rename or delete them. Likewise, a file that you expect to be automatically created by another application or script may not have been created. Perhaps the application was not run or perhaps it experienced an error. In any event, you can guard against these types of situations by using the IF EXIST statement to verify in advance that a file or folder exists before attempting to access, create, modify, or delete it.

Also, when working with files and folders, be sure to enclose any file names or folder names that contain blank spaces inside a matching pair of double quotation marks. Otherwise errors will occur. Also beware that you don't append data to files that you wish to overwrite and don't overwrite files to which you wish to append data. When keying in statements, you must therefore be careful to make sure that you use the › character only once when you begin to write to a file and ensure that all remaining write operations are performed using the ›› characters to append data instead of overwriting it.

Taking Precautions with Loops

A loop is a very powerful scripting tool. It enables you to execute a collection of statements repeatedly and to process enormous amounts of data. However, loops can also create problems when not constructed properly. To begin with, you must always make sure that when you create a loop that you provide a way to break out of it in order to avoid the creation of endless loops.

 DEFINITION An *endless loop* is one that runs forever, preventing your script from ever finishing or completing its task.

For example, you could accidentally create an endless loop by setting up a FOR command that is supposed to count from 1 to 5 using an increment of 1. However, by accidentally typing in an increment of −1, an endless loop is created because no matter how many times the Windows shell adds −1 to the value of the loop's iterator, it will never equal 5. So double-check any code that creates a loop and make sure that it will eventually end.

 TRICK If, despite your best efforts, an endless loop does occur, you can break out of it if it's a script that you started manually. Press CTRL+C and respond with a Y when prompted to terminate the script. However, if the script was started in background mode using the Windows Task Scheduler service, you'll need to terminate it using the Windows Task Manager.

Also, remember that the FOR command's iterator character is case-sensitive. Therefore %%a and %%A are not the same variable.

Keeping Procedures Straight

Procedures are a powerful tool for organizing scripts and creating collections of reusable code. However, they are not without their own set of issues. Don't forget that procedures do not have access to script arguments. If your procedures need to access script arguments, pass the arguments to the procedure as procedure arguments. Alternatively, you can store data in files and then set up your procedure to read and access them that way.

When you use the SETLOCAL and ENDLOCAL commands in conjunction with procedures, you can exercise strict control over procedure variables by localizing their access. However, when you do this you also make it difficult for a procedure to return any results back to its script. However, you do have different ways of enforcing strict control over procedure variables without preventing your procedures from returning any output. One option is to tunnel out a variable using variable tunneling. And, if your procedure has a lot of data that it needs to return, you can always try writing it to a file and then having the script open and read the file.

Back to the Tic-Tac-Toe Game

Now let's begin work on the book's last major chapter project, the Tic-Tac-Toe game. This script will facilitate the execution of a computerized two-player, head-to-head game. The computer will display the game board, collect player input, control player turns, ensure that only valid selections are processed, and ultimately determine who, if anyone, has won the game.

Given the game's size and complexity, you are certain to run into some errors as you develop this game. This will give you the opportunity to put to the test some of the debugging and error resolution techniques that you have learned in this chapter. Along the way, I'll arm you with a few tricks to avoid problems, and I'll point out a few pitfalls that you'll want to avoid.

Designing the Game

The overall construction of the Tic-Tac-Toe game consists of the development of the following sections, which nicely correspond to the three sections that make up this book's standard shell template:

• **The Initialization Section.** This section will set up the script's execution environment.

- **The Main Processing Section**. This section will control the display and processing of the game's main menu and will initiate and ultimately terminate the game's execution.
- **The Procedure Section**. This section will consist of a collection of 10 procedures, each of which will be designed to perform a specific subset of the game's functionality.

Because this script will be rather long, you'll want to focus on using procedures as the primary means of organizing the script. Otherwise, given the complexity of this script, you'll run into trouble early on as the number of variables and tasks that you'll need to work with begin to pile up and all your code begins to become intertwined.

The tasks that need to be performed by these 10 procedures are outlined below. This chapter will develop the procedures in the order suggested below. However, that is not a requirement. You can work on the development of these procedures in almost any order that makes sense to you, although a few of the procedures are closely related and are best developed in sequence.

1. Initialize game board values
2. Display the welcome screen
3. Display the game board
4. Create a `Help` screen
5. Create an `About` screen
6. Create a game controlling procedure
7. Validate player input
8. Associate player choices with game board squares
9. Display game results
10. Check for wins, losses, or ties

Performing Script Initialization Tasks

To begin the Tic-Tac-Toe script, create a new script file, copy in the shell script template, and then add the following statements to the Initialization Section:

```
@ECHO off


COLOR 0E
TITLE = T I C - T A C - T O E
CLS
```

The first statement turns off the automatic display of script statements, and the next three statements set the Windows command console's color scheme to yellow on black, post the name of the game in the console's title bar, and clear the console's display.

Constructing the Script's Main Processing Section

The script's Main Processing Section, shown below, begins with a label called :StartOver. This label will be used later in the script to allow players to restart the game. Next, a series of four variables are defined. Player is used when determining which player's turn it is. By default, Player X always goes first. Winner is used to determine when one of the players has won the game. Initially, it is set equal to None. NoMoves is used to keep count of the total number of moves made by both players. When the total number of moves becomes equal to 9, and no player has managed to line up three Xs or Os, the game board is full and the game is declared a tie.

```
:StartOver


SET Player=X

SET Winner=None

SET /A NoMoves = 0


CALL :InitializeBlanks


CALL :Welcome


IF /I "%reply%" == "" CLS & GOTO :StartOver

IF /I %reply% == Play CLS & CALL :Play

IF /I %reply% == Quit CLS & GOTO :EOF

IF /I %reply% == Help CLS & CALL :Help

IF /I %reply% == About CLS & CALL :About

GOTO :StartOver


GOTO :EOF
```

Next, the :InitializeBlanks procedure is called. This procedure sets variables located in each square of the game board equal to a blank space. This way, when the game board is initially displayed, it will look empty. Next, the :Welcome procedure is called. Its job is to greet the players and prompt them to perform one of the following actions:

- **Play**. Type Play and press Enter to begin the game.
- **Quit**. Type Quit and press Enter to terminate the game.
- **Help**. Type Help and press Enter to view the game's Help screen.
- **About**. Type About and press Enter to view the game's About screen.

A series of IF statements follow next, each of which is designed to analyze the input supplied by the players and determine the correct course of action.

Initializing Game Board Values

As previously stated, the :InitializeBlanks procedure, shown below, sets all of the variables embedded in the game board equal to blank spaces.

```
:InitializeBlanks


  SET A1=

  SET A2=

  SET A3=


  SET B1=

  SET B2=

  SET B3=


  SET C1=

  SET C2=

  SET C3=



GOTO :EOF
```

TRAP Make sure that when you work on this procedure you remember to type a blank space at the end of each SET statement. Without them, the game board, which is displayed by the :DisplayBoard procedure, won't display correctly.

Building the Welcome Screen

The game's welcome screen, shown below, should look familiar to you by now. It uses the FOR and ECHO commands to format and display a greeting message and to display a menu of options. It then collects the player's instruction using a SET statement.

```
:Welcome


  CLS


  FOR /L %%i IN (1,1,8) DO ECHO.


  ECHO                 W E L C O M E   T O   T I C - T A C - T O E
  ECHO.
  ECHO.
  ECHO                       Windows shell script style!


  FOR /L %%i IN (1,1,9) DO ECHO.


  ECHO Options: [Play] [Quit] [Help] [About]
  ECHO.


  SET /p reply=Enter selection:


GOTO :EOF
```

Displaying the Tic-Tac-Toe Game Board

The game needs to display its game board when it first starts and after each player has made a move. This is accomplished by calling on the :DisplayBoard procedure shown below.

```
:DisplayBoard


  CLS


  ECHO.
```

```
ECHO.

ECHO    T I C - T A C - T O E

ECHO.

ECHO.

ECHO.

ECHO          1     2     3

ECHO.                             Rules:

ECHO.

ECHO          ^|     ^|            1. Player X always goes first.

ECHO  A    %A1% ^| %A2% ^| %A3%

ECHO        ____^|____^|____        2. To make a move enter the

ECHO          ^|     ^|               coordinates of the appropriate

ECHO  B    %B1% ^| %B2% ^| %B3%              square.

ECHO        ____^|____^|____

ECHO          ^|     ^|            3. Remember to switch turns when

ECHO  C    %C1% ^| %C2% ^| %C3%              instructed by the game.

ECHO          ^|     ^|

ECHO.

ECHO.

ECHO.

ECHO Player %player%'s turn:

ECHO.
```

```
GOTO :EOF
```

The trick to making the :DisplayBoard procedure work is the embedding of variables within each square of the board. Of course, when embedded in this manner it makes it difficult to line up the game board. Therefore, you will probably have to test this procedure a few times and make small adjustments until you get it right.

TRICK

Make things easy on yourself when working on this procedure by first copying the procedure into its own script. Then hard code variables representing each location on the board and assign these variables an X or an O. In addition, assign a hard-coded value to the player variable. By temporarily turning the procedure into its own mini-script, you can focus on getting it to look and work just the way you want it to (less the temporarily hard-coded variables) before you copy it back into the Tic-Tac-Toe game.

TRICK At this point, all you should have is your template and the first two sections. Next, I recommend that you create the :Play, :Help, :About, :InitializeBlanks, **and** :Welcome **procedures but that you leave them empty. Once you have done this, stop and test the script to make sure it doesn't have any syntax errors. In addition, by testing each of the conditions that are tested for in the Main Processing Section, you can verify the welcome screen's menu operation.**

Providing Help

The game's :HELP procedure, shown below, is designed to provide the players with access to additional instruction should they need it.

```
:HELP

  CLS


  FOR /L %%i IN (1,1,5) DO ECHO.


  ECHO                    HELP INSTRUCTIONS
  ECHO.
  ECHO.
  ECHO  This is a text-based implementation of the TIC-TAC-TOE game. In this game
  ECHO  the computer controls the action. Player X always goes first. The game
  ECHO  tells each player when it is his turn. When prompted to take a turn players
  ECHO  must type the coordinates of the square into which they wish to place their
  ECHO  marker (i.e., the X or O character). For example, to place a marker in the
  ECHO  upper left hand box, players would enter A1.
  ECHO.
  ECHO  The game tracks the progress of each game and will automatically determine
  ECHO  when a game has been won, lost, or tied.


  FOR /L %%i IN (1,1,6) DO ECHO.


  PAUSE


GOTO :EOF
```

Taking Credit for Your Work

The game's :About procedure, shown below, works in the exact same manner as the :HELP procedure.

```
:About

  CLS

  FOR /L %%i IN (1,1,7) DO ECHO.

  ECHO                        About The TIC TAC TOE GAME
  ECHO.
  ECHO                                Written by
  ECHO.
  ECHO                          Jerry Lee Ford, Jr.
  ECHO.
  ECHO                        ------------------------
  ECHO.
  ECHO                              Copyright 2003


  FOR /L %%i IN (1,1,7) DO ECHO.

  PAUSE

GOTO :EOF
```

TRICK

Now that you have filled in the statements that go in the :HELP and :About procedures, I recommend that you stop and test your script to make sure that you have not
accidentally made any typos that result in syntax errors. If you did, it will be a lot
easier to track them down now, before you add any more complexity to the script.

Creating a Procedure to Control Game Activity

OK, now things start to get fun. The :Play procedure, which is outlined in this section, is responsible for controlling game play. However, for the most part its success depends on the procedures that it calls. Because of its complexity, I will break down this procedure into small pieces and cover each piece in sequence.

The :Play procedure begins, as shown below, with three IF statements that determine whether the game has been won. These three statements determine whether Player X or Player O has won the game or if a tie has occurred. If the game has been won or a tie has occurred, then the game is over and the :DisplayGameResults procedure is called, after which the game's Welcome menu is displayed by executing a GOTO statement that switches processing control back to the :StartOver label.

```
:Play

  IF "%Winner%"=="X" (

    CALL :DisplayGameResults

    PAUSE

    GOTO :StartOver

  )


  IF "%Winner%"=="O" (

    CALL :DisplayGameResults

    PAUSE

    GOTO :StartOver

  )


  IF "%Winner%"=="Nobody" (

    CALL :DisplayGameResults

    PAUSE

    GOTO :StartOver

  )
```

If the game has not yet been won or tied, then the :DisplayBoard procedure is called and any already selected squares are shown as being filled in with their respective Xs or Os. The current player (initially Player X) is then prompted to take a turn. The data entered by the player is then validated by the :ValidateResponse procedure to ensure that it's a valid board game square and that the chosen square has not already been taken.

```
CALL :DisplayBoard

SET /P response=Select a box:

CALL :ValidateResponse
```

Next an `If...Else` statement is executed. If the player's move was valid, the value of `NoMoves` is incremented by 1, and the `:FillInSquare` procedure is called. Otherwise, an error message is displayed and the player will be given another chance (because the value of `NoMoves` is not incremented and the game will not switch player turns).

```
IF %ValidMove%==True (

  SET /A NoMoves = NoMoves += 1

  CALL :FillInSquare

) ELSE (

  CLS

  FOR /L %%i IN (1,1,11) DO ECHO.
  ECHO                      Invalid move. Please try again!
  FOR /L %%i IN (1,1,11) DO ECHO.

  PAUSE
)
```

The next `IF` statement in the `:Play` procedure is charged with either declaring the game a tie when all the squares on the game board have been filled and a winner has not been declared at the beginning of the procedure or with calling the `:SeeIfWon` procedure. The job of the `:SeeIfWon` procedure is to examine the game board and see if either player has managed to line up three consecutive squares.

```
IF %NoMoves% == 9 (
  SET Winner=Nobody
) ELSE (
```

```
     CALL :SeeIfWon

   )
```

The procedure's final IF statement switches the value of the player variable from X to O or from O to X at the end of each turn.

```
  IF %ValidMove%==True (

    IF "%player%"=="X" (

      SET Player=O

    ) ELSE (

      SET Player=X

    )

  )
```

Finally, the last statement in the procedure uses the GOTO command to restart the procedure again, as shown below.

```
  GOTO :Play


GOTO :EOF
```

TRICK Because of its complexity and because its success depends on the procedures it calls, I recommend that after keying in the statements that make up this procedure that you stop working on the script and that you develop the rest of the procedures as temporary, stand-alone scripts. You can then use hard-coded variables to independently test each procedure and make sure they work as expected before copying them all back into the Tic-Tac-Toe game. At that point, your script will be fully assembled. Following this approach, and assuming that you properly tested the operation of each remaining procedure before copying it into the Tic-Tac-Toe script, any errors that occur are likely to be found in the :Play procedure.

Making Sure Player Selections Are Valid

The :ValidateResponse procedure begins by setting the default value of the ValidMove variable equal to true. This variable is used in the :Play procedure to determine whether to increase the value of NoMoves and switch between players.

Because of its size, I'll break down this procedure into several pieces and cover each piece in sequence. For starters, the procedure checks to see if the current player pressed the Enter key without first selecting a move. If this is the case, the value of ValidMove is set equal to false.

```
:ValidateResponse

  SET ValidMove=True


  IF /I "%response%" == "" (

    SET ValidMove=False

    GOTO :EOF

  )
```

Next, the procedure examines the player's move to see if it matches a valid board entry, as shown below. If the player did not enter A1, A2, A3, B1, B2, B3, C1, C2 or C3 then the value of ValidMove is set equal to false.

```
  IF /I NOT %response%==A1 (

    IF /I NOT %response%==A2 (

      IF /I NOT %response%==A3 (

        IF /I NOT %response%==B1 (

          IF /I NOT %response%==B2 (

            IF /I NOT %response%==B3 (

              IF /I NOT %response%==C1 (

                IF /I NOT %response%==C2 (

                  IF /I NOT %response%==C3 (

                    SET ValidMove=False

                    GOTO :EOF

                  )

                )

              )

            )

          )

        )

      )

    )

  )
```

The next collection of tests performed by the procedure checks to see whether the square selected by the player has already been taken. The variable embedded within an available square will either be set equal to a blank or will contain either an X or and O if it has been taken previously.

```
IF /I %response%==A1 (

    IF NOT "%A1%"==" " (

      SET ValidMove=False

    )

 )

 IF /I %response%==A2 (

   IF NOT "%A2%"==" " (

     SET ValidMove=False

   )

 )

 IF /I %response%==A3 (

   IF NOT "%A3%"==" " (

     SET ValidMove=False

   )

 )

 IF /I %response%==B1 (

   IF NOT "%B1%"==" " (

     SET ValidMove=False

   )

 )

 IF /I %response%==B2 (

   IF NOT "%B2%"==" " (

     SET ValidMove=False

   )

 )

 IF /I %response%==B3 (

   IF NOT "%B3%"==" " (

     SET ValidMove=False

   )
```

```
  )

  IF /I %response%==C1 (

    IF NOT "%C1%"==" " (

      SET ValidMove=False

    )

  )

  IF /I %response%==C2 (

    IF NOT "%C2%"==" " (

      SET ValidMove=False

    )

  )

  IF /I %response%==C3 (

    IF NOT "%C3%"==" " (

      SET ValidMove=False

    )

  )


GOTO :EOF
```

Associating Player Moves with Game Board Squares

The :FillInSquare procedure, shown below, is straightforward. It sets the variable stored in the selected square equal to the letter associated with the current player (i.e., either X or O as specified by the player variable's current value).

```
:FillInSquare


  IF /I %response%==A1 SET A1=%player%

  IF /I %response%==A2 SET A2=%player%

  IF /I %response%==A3 SET A3=%player%

  IF /I %response%==B1 SET B1=%player%

  IF /I %response%==B2 SET B2=%player%

  IF /I %response%==B3 SET B3=%player%

  IF /I %response%==C1 SET C1=%player%

  IF /I %response%==C2 SET C2=%player%
```

```
IF /I %response%==C3 SET C3=%player%
```

```
Goto :EOF
```

Displaying the Results of the Game

The :DisplayGameResults procedure, shown below, checks the value assigned to the Winner variable to determine whether one of the players has won the game. Otherwise, a tie is declared. The results of the game, as determined by the value of the Winner variable, are then displayed in the messagetext variable, which is embedded in the screen displayed by this procedure.

```
:DisplayGameResults

  CLS

  SET messagetext=Tie - No Winner

  IF "%Winner%"=="X" SET messagetext=Player X has won!!!
  IF "%Winner%"=="O" SET messagetext=Player O has won!!!

  FOR /L %%i IN (1,1,5) DO ECHO.

  ECHO              ^|     ^|
  ECHO        %A1%  ^|  %A2%  ^|  %A3%                E N D   O F   G A M E
  ECHO       ____^|____^|____
  ECHO              ^|     ^|
  ECHO        %B1%  ^|  %B2%  ^|  %B3%                %messagetext%
  ECHO       ____^|____^|____
  ECHO              ^|     ^|
  ECHO        %C1%  ^|  %C2%  ^|  %C3%
  ECHO              ^|     ^|

  FOR /L %%i IN (1,1,9) DO ECHO.

GOTO :EOF
```

Determining When a Game Is Over

The script's final procedure is the `:SeeIfWon` procedure, which is shown below. Each time this procedure is called, it checks to see if the current player (either Player X or Player O) has managed to string together three consecutive squares (vertically, horizontally, or diagonally). It then sets the value assigned to the `Winner` variable to either `X` or `O` if appropriate.

```
:SeeIfWon


 IF /I "%A1%"=="%player%" (

   IF /I "%A2%"=="%player%" (

     IF /I "%A3%"=="%player%" (SET Winner=%player%)

   )

 )

 IF /I "%B1%"=="%player%" (

   IF /I "%B2%"=="%player%" (

     IF /I "%B3%"=="%player%" (SET Winner=%player%)

   )

 )

 IF /I "%C1%"=="%player%" (

   IF /I "%C2%"=="%player%" (

     IF /I "%C3%"=="%player%" (SET Winner=%player%)

   )

 )


 IF /I "%A1%"=="%player%" (

   IF /I "%B2%"=="%player%" (

     IF /I "%C3%"=="%player%" (SET Winner=%player%)

   )

 )

 IF /I "%A3%"=="%player%" (

   IF /I "%B2%"=="%player%" (

     IF /I "%C1%"=="%player%" (SET Winner=%player%)

   )
```

```
      )

    IF /I "%A1%"=="%player%" (

      IF /I "%B1%"=="%player%" (

        IF /I "%C1%"=="%player%" (SET Winner=%player%)

      )

    )

    IF /I "%A2%"=="%player%" (

      IF /I "%B2%"=="%player%" (

        IF /I "%C2%"=="%player%" (SET Winner=%player%)

      )

    )

    IF /I "%A3%"=="%player%" (

      IF /I "%B3%"=="%player%" (

        IF /I "%C3%"=="%player%" (SET Winner=%player%)

      )

    )


GOTO :EOF
```

The Final Result

For your convenience, I have assembled the complete Tic-Tac-Toe game below. As you will see, I have added the standard script template and made liberal use of comments to make the script self-documenting.

```
@ECHO off


REM ***********************************************************************

REM

REM Script Name: TicTacToe.bat

REM Author: Jerry Ford

REM Date: July 22, 2003

REM

REM Description: This is a Windows shell script implementation of the popular
```

```
REM child's game called "Tic-Tac-Toe".
REM
REM *************************************************************************


REM ****** Script Initialization Section ******

REM Set the color scheme to yellow on black
COLOR 0E

REM Display the name of the game in the Windows command console's title bar
TITLE = T I C - T A C - T O E

REM Clear the display
CLS


REM ****** Main Processing Section ******

REM This label is called whenever the game needs to be restarted
:StartOver

REM Global variables used throughout the script
SET Player=X
SET Winner=None
SET /A NoMoves = 0
SET /A NoMoves = 0

REM Reset all the squares on the game board to show blanks
CALL :InitializeBlanks

REM Display the Welcome screen and prompt the players for instructions
```

```
CALL :Welcome


REM Process the player's instruction

IF /I "%reply%" == "" CLS & GOTO :StartOver

IF /I %reply% == Play CLS & CALL :Play

IF /I %reply% == Quit CLS & GOTO :EOF

IF /I %reply% == Help CLS & CALL :Help

IF /I %reply% == About CLS & CALL :About

GOTO :StartOver


GOTO :EOF



REM ****** Main Processing Section ******


REM Reset all squares on the game board to blanks

:InitializeBlanks


  SET A1=

  SET A2=

  SET A3=


  SET B1=

  SET B2=

  SET B3=


  SET C1=

  SET C2=

  SET C3=


GOTO :EOF


REM Display the Welcome screen when called
```

```
:Welcome


  REM Clear the display
  CLS


  REM Add 8 blanks lines to the display
  FOR /L %%i IN (1,1,8) DO ECHO.


  ECHO                 W E L C O M E   T O   T I C - T A C - T O E
  ECHO.
  ECHO.
  ECHO                         Windows shell script style!


  REM Add 9 blanks lines to the display
  FOR /L %%i IN (1,1,9) DO ECHO.


  REM Display a menu of options
  ECHO Options: [Play] [Quit] [Help] [About]
  ECHO.


  REM Prompt the player to make a selection
  SET /p reply=Enter selection:


GOTO :EOF


REM Display the game board
:DisplayBoard


  REM Clear the display
  CLS


  ECHO.
```

```
ECHO.

ECHO      T I C - T A C - T O E

ECHO.

ECHO.

ECHO.

ECHO           1    2    3

ECHO.                                    Rules:

ECHO.

ECHO           ^|     ^|                1. Player X always goes first.

ECHO  A    %A1%  ^|  %A2%  ^|  %A3%

ECHO       ____^|____^|____             2. To make a move enter the

ECHO           ^|     ^|                      coordinates of the appropriate

ECHO  B    %B1%  ^|  %B2%  ^|  %B3%               square.

ECHO       ____^|____^|____

ECHO           ^|     ^|                3. Remember to switch turns when

ECHO  C    %C1%  ^|  %C2%  ^|  %C3%               instructed by the game.

ECHO           ^|     ^|

ECHO.

ECHO.

ECHO.

ECHO Player %player%'s turn:

ECHO.


GOTO :EOF


REM Display the help screen when called
:HELP


REM Clear the display
CLS


REM Add 5 blank lines to the display
```

```
FOR /L %%i IN (1,1,5) DO ECHO.

ECHO                        HELP INSTRUCTIONS
ECHO.
ECHO.
ECHO  This is a text-based implementation of the TIC-TAC-TOE game. In this game
ECHO  the computer controls the action. Player X always goes first. The game
ECHO  tells each player when it is his turn. When prompted to take a turn players
ECHO  must type the coordinates of the square into which they wish to place their
ECHO  marker (the X or O character). For example, to place a marker in the
ECHO  upper left hand box, players would enter A1.
ECHO.
ECHO  The game tracks the progress of each game and will automatically determine
ECHO  when a game has been won, lost, or tied.


REM Add 6 blank lines to the display
FOR /L %%i IN (1,1,6) DO ECHO.


REM Make the player press a key to continue
PAUSE


GOTO :EOF


:About


REM Clear the display
CLS


REM Add 7 blank lines to the display
FOR /L %%i IN (1,1,7) DO ECHO.


ECHO                     About The TIC TAC TOE GAME
```

```
ECHO.

ECHO                                Written by

ECHO.

ECHO                             Jerry Lee Ford, Jr.

ECHO.

ECHO                         ------------------------

ECHO.

ECHO                              Copyright 2003


REM Add 7 blank lines to the display

FOR /L %%i IN (1,1,7) DO ECHO.


REM Make the player press a key to continue

PAUSE


GOTO :EOF


REM This procedure controls the actual play of the game
:Play


  REM If player X has won then find out if a new game should be started

  IF "%Winner%"=="X" (

    CALL :DisplayGameResults

    REM Make the player press a key to continue

    PAUSE

    GOTO :StartOver

  )


  REM If player O has won then find out if a new game should be started

  IF "%Winner%"=="O" (

    CALL :DisplayGameResults

    REM Make the player press a key to continue

    PAUSE
```

```
    GOTO :StartOver

)


REM If the players tied find out if a new game should be started
IF "%Winner%"=="Nobody" (

  CALL :DisplayGameResults

  REM Make the player press a key to continue

  PAUSE

  GOTO :StartOver

)


REM display the game board
CALL :DisplayBoard


REM Collect current player's selection
SET /P response=Select a box:


REM Validate the specified selection
CALL :ValidateResponse


REM If the selection is valid
IF %ValidMove%==True (


  REM Add 1 to the total number of valid selections made in the game
  SET /A NoMoves = NoMoves += 1


  REM Associate the player's selection with the right square
  CALL :FillInSquare


REM If the player's selection is invalid
) ELSE (


    REM Clear the display
```

```
      CLS


      REM Add 11 blank lines to the display
      FOR /L %%i IN (1,1,11) DO ECHO.


      ECHO                       Invalid move. Please try again!


      REM Add 11 blank lines to the display
      FOR /L %%i IN (1,1,11) DO ECHO.


      REM Make the player press a key to continue
      PAUSE
   )


REM If a total of 9 valid selections have been made the board is full
IF %NoMoves% == 9 (

  SET Winner=Nobody

) ELSE (

  CALL :SeeIfWon

)


REM Its now time to switch players
IF %ValidMove%==True (

  IF "%player%"=="X" (

    SET Player=O

  ) ELSE (

    SET Player=X

  )

)


REM Loop back to the beginning and keep playing
```

```
    GOTO :Play


GOTO :EOF


REM Ensure that the selection supplied by the player is valid
:ValidateResponse


    REM By default assume a valid selection was made
    SET ValidMove=True


    REM Hitting enter without entering a selection is invalid
    IF /I "%response%" == "" (
      SET ValidMove=False
      GOTO :EOF
    )


    REM Ensure that a valid square was specified (A1-A3, B1-B3 & C1 - C3)
    IF /I NOT %response%==A1 (
      IF /I NOT %response%==A2 (
        IF /I NOT %response%==A3 (
          IF /I NOT %response%==B1 (
            IF /I NOT %response%==B2 (
              IF /I NOT %response%==B3 (
                IF /I NOT %response%==C1 (
                  IF /I NOT %response%==C2 (
                    IF /I NOT %response%==C3 (
                      SET ValidMove=False
                      GOTO :EOF
                    )
                  )
                )
              )
            )
```

```
            )

          )

        )

      )

    )


    REM Previously selected squares are invalid

    IF /I %response%==A1 (

      IF NOT "%A1%"==" " (

        SET ValidMove=False

      )

    )

    IF /I %response%==A2 (

      IF NOT "%A2%"==" " (

        SET ValidMove=False

      )

    )

    IF /I %response%==A3 (

      IF NOT "%A3%"==" " (

        SET ValidMove=False

      )

    )

    IF /I %response%==B1 (

      IF NOT "%B1%"==" " (

        SET ValidMove=False

      )

    )

    IF /I %response%==B2 (

      IF NOT "%B2%"==" " (

        SET ValidMove=False

      )

    )

    IF /I %response%==B3 (
```

```
  IF NOT "%B3%"==" " (

    SET ValidMove=False

  )

)

IF /I %response%==C1 (

  IF NOT "%C1%"==" " (

    SET ValidMove=False

  )

)

IF /I %response%==C2 (

  IF NOT "%C2%"==" " (

    SET ValidMove=False

  )

)

IF /I %response%==C3 (

  IF NOT "%C3%"==" " (

    SET ValidMove=False

  )

)


GOTO :EOF


REM Associate the player's selection with the appropriate square
:FillInSquare


  IF /I %response%==A1 SET A1=%player%

  IF /I %response%==A2 SET A2=%player%

  IF /I %response%==A3 SET A3=%player%

  IF /I %response%==B1 SET B1=%player%

  IF /I %response%==B2 SET B2=%player%

  IF /I %response%==B3 SET B3=%player%

  IF /I %response%==C1 SET C1=%player%

  IF /I %response%==C2 SET C2=%player%
```

```
    IF /I %response%==C3 SET C3=%player%


Goto :EOF


REM Display the results of the game
:DisplayGameResults


  REM Clear the display
  CLS


  REM Set the default message to indicate a tie
  SET messagetext=Tie - No Winner


  REM If either player won set a variable containing a custom message
  IF "%Winner%"=="X" SET messagetext=Player X has won!!!

  IF "%Winner%"=="O" SET messagetext=Player O has won!!!


  REM Add 5 blank lines to the display
  FOR /L %%i IN (1,1,5) DO ECHO.


  REM Display the final board and display a message indicating game results
  ECHO                ^|     ^|
  ECHO         %A1%  ^|  %A2%  ^|  %A3%              E N D   O F   G A M E
  ECHO        _____^|_____^|_____
  ECHO                ^|     ^|
  ECHO         %B1%  ^|  %B2%  ^|  %B3%                  %messagetext%
  ECHO        _____^|_____^|_____
  ECHO                ^|     ^|
  ECHO         %C1%  ^|  %C2%  ^|  %C3%
  ECHO                ^|     ^|


  REM Add 9 blank lines to the display
```

```
    FOR /L %%i IN (1,1,9) DO ECHO.


GOTO :EOF



REM Check up, down, & diagonally to see if the player has won
:SeeIfWon


  REM Check across
  IF /I "%A1%"=="%player%" (

    IF /I "%A2%"=="%player%" (

      IF /I "%A3%"=="%player%" (SET Winner=%player%)

    )

  )

  IF /I "%B1%"=="%player%" (

    IF /I "%B2%"=="%player%" (

      IF /I "%B3%"=="%player%" (SET Winner=%player%)

    )

  )

  IF /I "%C1%"=="%player%" (

    IF /I "%C2%"=="%player%" (

      IF /I "%C3%"=="%player%" (SET Winner=%player%)

    )

  )


  REM Check diagonally
  IF /I "%A1%"=="%player%" (

    IF /I "%B2%"=="%player%" (

      IF /I "%C3%"=="%player%" (SET Winner=%player%)

    )

  )

  IF /I "%A3%"=="%player%" (
```

```
    IF /I "%B2%"=="%player%" (

      IF /I "%C1%"=="%player%" (SET Winner=%player%)

    )

  )


  REM Check up and down
  IF /I "%A1%"=="%player%" (

    IF /I "%B1%"=="%player%" (

      IF /I "%C1%"=="%player%" (SET Winner=%player%)

    )

  )

  IF /I "%A2%"=="%player%" (

    IF /I "%B2%"=="%player%" (

      IF /I "%C2%"=="%player%" (SET Winner=%player%)

    )

  )

  IF /I "%A3%"=="%player%" (

    IF /I "%B3%"=="%player%" (

      IF /I "%C3%"=="%player%" (SET Winner=%player%)

    )

  )


GOTO :EOF
```

OK, now that you have the complete script, it's time to kick its tires and see how it handles. While you can certainly play the Tic-Tac-Toe game by yourself, it is designed for two. So grab a friend and impress them with your new Windows shell script game.

Summary

In this final chapter, I provided you with lots of different ways of dealing with problems that are bound to arise as you begin developing your own shell scripts. This information included a discussion of syntax, logic, and run-time errors. I then provided you with instruction on how to trace logic flow and display intermediate results within scripts. I also showed you how to write scripts that, when called as external procedures, provide calling scripts a custom exit code that indicates whether any problems occurred during the external procedure's execution.

EXERCISES

1. Modify the Tic-Tac-Toe game so that it visually identifies whose turn it is. For example, use a yellow-on-black color scheme when it is Player X's turn and a green-on-black color scheme when it is Player O's turn.

2. There is a lot of room for improvement in the Tic-Tac-Toe game's lone error message. Modify the game so that instead of simply reporting all player errors as an invalid move, the game tells players exactly what they did wrong. For example, differentiate between invalid sections and attempts to select a square that has already been selected.

3. Modify the Tic-Tac-Toe game so that it tracks wins, losses, and ties over time, and present this information to players at the final conclusion of the game.

(APPENDIX)

Windows Shell Scripting Administrative Scripts

I n addition to serving as a great introductory computing language, Windows shell scripting serves a very practical purpose: assisting the automated administration of computer and network tasks. As such, this book would be remiss if it did not provide you with some practical examples of Windows shell scripts designed to do something other than play games. In this appendix, you will find a collection of seven scripts that demonstrate various tasks that can be automated using Windows shell scripts. Some of the scripts have more practical value than others. However, you can use them as a foundation for developing scripts that suit your specific needs.

Specifically, you will learn

- **How to programmatically connect to network disk drives**

- **How to automate the creation of user and administrator accounts**

- **How to automate the Windows disk defrag process**

- **How to automate the execution of your Windows shell scripts**

- **How to create a network chat script**

- **How to execute and control third-party utilities and programs from within Windows shell scripts**

Working with Network Drives

If your computer is connected to a home network or if your desktop computer at work is connected to a network, you are probably familiar with many of the advantages of computer networks. These advantages include things like group e-mail and instant messaging. They also include the sharing of resources such as disk drives and printers.

Using the NET USE command, you can automate the establishment of connections to network resources. For example, you can create a mapped-network drive connection to shared network drives or folders using the following syntax:

NET USE *DriveLetter*: *ServerName**ShareName*

DriveLetter specifies an available drive letter on the local computer which will be used to represent the network connection. *ServerName* specifies the name of the computer where the shared network folder or drive resides, and *ShareName* is the name assigned to the shared resource.

DEFINITION *DriveLetter* **is an alphabetic representation of a disk drive. Windows computers use letters of the alphabet to represent connections to local and network drives. As such, a maximum of 26 network drive connections can be set up or *mapped* on your computer.**

DEFINITION **The** *ServerName**ShareName* **parameter defined previously is an example of the application of the *Universal Naming Convention,* or UNC. The UNC establishes standards for identifying local and network resources. UNC names begin with two back slashes followed by the name of a network device, another slash, and then the name of the shared resource.**

You can also use the NET USE command to break connections to network resources. To disconnect a connection to a shared network drive, use the following syntax:

NET USE *DriveLetter*: /DELETE

DriveLetter represents the drive letter currently associated with the connection and /DELETE is a switch that tells the NET USE command to terminate the computer's connection.

The following example provides a working demonstration of how to set up and break network connections to shared network drives. In order to adapt and test this example, you'll need access to a local area network that has a shared network folder or drive to which you are authorized to connect.

```
@ECHO off


REM ***************************************************************************
REM
REM Script Name: MapNtwkDrive.bat
REM Author: Jerry Ford
REM Date: August 1, 2003
REM
REM Description: This script demonstrates how to connect to and disconnect
REM from network drives.
REM
REM ***************************************************************************


REM Abort execution if run on a computer running Windows NT, 2000, XP, or 2003.
IF NOT "%os%" == "Windows_NT" (
  ECHO.
  ECHO.
  ECHO Unsupported Operating system
  ECHO.
  ECHO.
  GOTO :EOF
)


REM Define a variable that specifies the drive letter to be used.
SET DriveLetter=X:


REM Define a variable that specifies the location of the network drive.
```

```
SET NetworkDrive=\\SERV0001\C


REM Display the name of the script in the Windows command console's title bar.
TITLE = MapNtwkDrive.bat


REM Set the color scheme to yellow on black.
COLOR 0E


REM ****** Script Initialization Section ******


REM Call the procedure that displays an introduction message.
CALL :DisplayUserMsg


REM Call a procedure that creates the network drive connection.
CALL :EstablishConnection


REM Determine if an error occurred.
IF %ERRORLEVEL%==0 (

  REM If an error did not occur, then prompt the user to verify that the
  REM mapped drive connection was created.
  CALL :VerifyConnection


  REM Call the procedure that disconnects the network drive connection
  CALL :BreakConnection


)
GOTO :EOF



REM ****** Main Processing Section ******


REM Display an introductory message.
```

```
:DisplayUserMsg

  CLS

  ECHO.
  ECHO.
  ECHO DEMO: Connecting to and disconnecting from network drives
  ECHO.
  ECHO.

  PAUSE

GOTO :EOF


REM Set up a connection to the specified network drive.
:EstablishConnection

  CLS

  ECHO.
  ECHO Issuing NET USE Command.
  ECHO.

  REM Use the NET USE command to connect to the specified network drive
  REM and set up a connection using the specified drive letter.
  NET USE %driveletter% %NetworkDrive%

  IF ERRORLEVEL 1 (

    ECHO.
    ECHO.
    ECHO Error occurred setting up network drive connection.
    ECHO.
```

```
      ECHO.

      PAUSE


  )


GOTO :EOF


REM Prompt the user to check to make sure the drive connection was
REM established.
:VerifyConnection


  ECHO.

  ECHO.

  ECHO Please verify that the new network drive connection has been established

  ECHO before you respond by pressing the a key.

  ECHO.

  ECHO.

  ECHO Instructions:

  ECHO ------------

  ECHO.

  ECHO Click on Start and then My Computer. You should not see a drive

  ECHO connection labeled X: listed in the Hard Drives section of the

  ECHO My Computer dialog.

  ECHO.

  ECHO.


  PAUSE


GOTO :EOF


REM Disconnect the connection to the network drive.
```

```
:BreakConnection

  CLS

  REM Use the NET USE command to delete the connection as specified by its
  REM drive letter assignment.
  NET USE %driveletter% /DELETE

  IF ERRORLEVEL 1 (
    ECHO.
    ECHO.
    ECHO Error occurred when disconnecting the network drive connection.
    ECHO.
    ECHO.
  ) ELSE (
    ECHO.
    ECHO.
    ECHO The network drive connection has been disconnected.
    ECHO.
    ECHO.
  )

GOTO :EOF
```

The script begins by verifying that it has been started on a computer running Windows NT, XP, 2000, or 2003. It then defines a variable named *DriveLetter* and assigns it a value of X:. Next a variable named *NetworkDrive* is defined and assigned the UNC address of a shared network folder. The script then posts a text message in the Windows command console's title bar and changes the console's color scheme to yellow on black.

TRAP This example assumes that the X: drive letter is not already in use on the computer where the script will be executed. If X: is already used, change this drive letter assignment to a different letter.

Next, a series of procedure calls is executed. The `:DisplayUserMsg` procedure displays an informational message in the Windows command console and waits for the user to press a key. The `:EstablishConnection` then uses the `NET USE` command to create a network connection with the network folder specified by the *NetworkDrive* variable. This procedure then uses an `IF ERRORLEVEL` statement to determine whether the command was successful, and displays an error message if it was not. Next, the `:VerifyConnection` procedure is executed. This procedure displays a message instructing the user to verify that the network connection has indeed been established and waits for the user to press a key, as shown in Figure A.1.

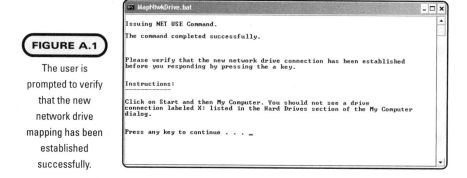

FIGURE A.1

The user is prompted to verify that the new network drive mapping has been established successfully.

Figure A.2 demonstrates how the network drive would appear if the script were run on a computer running Windows XP.

FIGURE A.2

The mapped network drive appears as an icon with a network cable connection shown beneath it.

Finally, the :BreakConnection procedure runs, this time using the NET USE command to disconnect the network connection. Once the last procedure is executed, the script terminates its own execution with the GOTO :EOF statement.

Account Administration

Windows offers a number of commands that support the command line administration of user accounts. These commands include

- NET USER. Creates new user accounts.
- NET GROUP. Adds user accounts to global groups.
- NET LOCALGROUP. Adds user accounts to local groups.
- NET ACCOUNTS. Configures user account password policies.

These commands enable you to configure both local and domain user accounts and groups.

In the next Windows shell script example, I will demonstrate how to automate the creation and administration of user accounts. The name of the script will be AdminCreator.bat. It will be designed to create a new user account whose name will be passed to it as an argument, and the script will then add that user account to the local administrators group. The syntax required to execute this script properly is outline below.

AdminCreator *UserName*

TRICK Windows Resource Kits provide a command line utility called ADDUSERS.EXE that you can also use to create new accounts. This command line utility is designed to facilitate the creation of accounts stored as a list in a comma-delimited text input file.

The script's source code is listed below.

```
@ECHO off


REM *************************************************************************
REM
REM Script Name: AdminCreator.bat
REM Author: Jerry Ford
REM Date: August 1, 2003
REM
```

```
REM Description: This script demonstrates how to create a local user account
REM and how to add it to the local Administrators group.
REM
REM ***************************************************************************


REM ****** Script Initialization Section ******

REM Abort execution if run on a computer running Windows NT, 2000, XP, or 2003.
IF NOT "%os%" == "Windows_NT" (
  ECHO.
  ECHO.
  ECHO Unsupported Operating system
  ECHO.
  ECHO.
  GOTO :EOF
)


REM Abort if a username was not passed to the script as an argument.
IF "%1"=="" (
  ECHO.
  ECHO.
  ECHO Invalid number of arguments received.
  ECHO.
  ECHO Syntax:
  ECHO.
  ECHO AdminCreator UserName
  ECHO.
  ECHO.
  GOTO :EOF
)


REM Display the name of the script in the Windows command console's title bar.
```

```
TITLE "AdminCreator.bat"


REM Set a variable equal to the argument passed to the script.

SET user=%1


REM Clear the display.

CLS



REM ****** Main Processing Section ******


CALL :GetConfirmation


PAUSE


IF /I "%reply%"=="Y" (

  CALL :CreateAccount

  CALL :AddToAdminGroup

) ELSE (

  CALL :ScriptExecutionAborted

)


GOTO :EOF



REM ****** Procedure Section ******


REM Prompt the user for confirmation before continuing.

:GetConfirmation


  ECHO.

  ECHO.

  ECHO Options: [Y/N]
```

```
    ECHO.

    SET /P reply=You have instructed this script to create a new admin account for %user%. Continue?

GOTO :EOF

REM Create the new user account and check for an error.
:CreateAccount

  NET USER %user% * /ADD

  IF ERRORLEVEL 1 (

    CLS

    ECHO.
    ECHO.
    ECHO Error occurred creating new account for %user%.
    ECHO.
    ECHO.

    PAUSE

    GOTO :EOF

  )

GOTO :EOF

REM Add the new account to the local Administrators group & check for an error.
:AddToAdminGroup

  NET LOCALGROUP Administrators /ADD %user%
```

```
IF ERRORLEVEL 1 (

  CLS

  ECHO.

  ECHO.

  ECHO Error occurred adding %user% to the local Administrators group.

  ECHO.

  ECHO.


  PAUSE


  GOTO :EOF


  )


GOTO :EOF


REM Display the following message if the user chose to abort script execution.

:ScriptExecutionAborted


  ECHO.

  ECHO.

  ECHO Script execution aborted. New account for %user% not created.

  ECHO.

  ECHO.


GOTO :EOF
```

The script begins by first validating that it is executing on a supported Windows operating system. It then checks to make sure that an argument, representing a new user account name, has been passed to the script. If the argument is missing, an error message is displayed; otherwise, the script continues executing.

Next, the script posts a message in the Windows command console's title bar and sets a variable named user equal to the argument passed to the script. The console's screen is then cleared and a series of procedures are executed before the script terminates its own execution.

The first procedure called is :GetConfirmation. It uses the SET command to require that the user respond with a y or Y to confirm that the script should continue executing. Once confirmation is received, the :CreateAccount and :AddToAdminGroup procedures are executed. If confirmation is not received, the :ScriptExecutionAborted runs instead.

The :CreateAccount procedure uses the NET USER command to create the new user account as shown below.

```
NET USER %user% * /ADD
```

An IF ERRORLEVEL statement is then executed to verify that the command processed successfully. If it did, the script keeps executing; otherwise, its execution is terminated. The :AddToAdminGroup procedure uses the NET LOCALGROUP command, as shown below, to add the new user account to the computer's local administrators group.

```
NET LOCALGROUP Administrators /ADD %user%
```

Another IF ERRORLEVEL statement is then executed to verify that this command processed successfully. If it did not, an error message is displayed. When executed, the :ScriptExecutionAborted procedure displays a message indicating that the script's execution was aborted and that the new account was not established.

The following output shows the results the script would display if it were executed and passed an account name of Alex0001.

```
C:\Scripts>admincreator Alex0001



Options: [Y/N]


You have instructed this script to create a new admin account for

Alex0001. Continue?


Options: [Y/N]


You have instructed this script to create a new admin account for

Alex0001. Continue? N
```

```
Press any key to continue . . .


Script execution aborted. New account for Alex0001 not created.


C:\Scripts>


Options: [Y/N]


You have instructed this script to create a new admin account for

Alex0001. Continue? Y

Press any key to continue . . .

Type a password for the user:

Retype the password to confirm:

The command completed successfully.


The command completed successfully.


C:\Scripts>
```

Figure A.3 shows that the new account was created and that it has been added to the local administrators group.

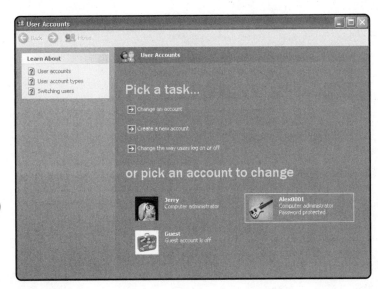

FIGURE A.3

A new user account is created and added to the local administrators group.

Disk Defragmentation

In the next example, I will demonstrate how to execute the DEFRAG.EXE command line utility to run a process that defragments the computer's local hard disk drive. This script will also generate a summary text report of its activities.

DEFINITION Over time, the organization of files stored on hard disk drives becomes fragmented. This results in slow performance and extra wear and tear on the drive. When a drive is *defragmented*, its files are reorganized and stored more efficiently.

```
@ECHO off


REM ****************************************************************************

REM

REM Script Name: Defrager.bat

REM Author: Jerry Ford

REM Date: July 31, 2003

REM

REM Description: This scripts demonstrates how to run the defrag utility from

REM within a Windows shell script.

REM

REM ****************************************************************************


REM ****** Script Initialization Section ******


REM Abort execution if OS is not Windows NT, 2000, XP, or 2003

IF NOT "%os%" == "Windows_NT" (

  ECHO.

  ECHO.

  ECHO Unsupported Operating system

  ECHO.

  ECHO.

  GOTO :EOF
```

```
)


   SET DefragRpt=C:\Temp\Defrag.txt



   REM ****** Main Processing Section ******


   CALL :DeleteExistingRpt


   CALL :CreateNewDefragRpt


   CALL :PerformDefrag


   GOTO :EOF


   REM ****** Procedure Section ******


   :DeleteExistingRpt


      REM If a defrag.txt report exists, delete it.
      IF EXIST %DefragRpt% DEL %DefragRpt%


   GOTO :EOF


   :CreateNewDefragRpt


      REM Create a new defrag.txt report.
      ECHO. > %DefragRpt%
      ECHO DEFRAG.EXE Execution Report >> %DefragRpt%
      ECHO. >> %DefragRpt%
      ECHO %date% %time% Defragging C: >> %DefragRpt%
```

```
    ECHO. >> %DefragRpt%


GOTO :EOF


:PerformDefrag


  REM The defrag command cleans up disk fragmentation.
  ECHO System is now being defragmented. Please wait...
  DEFRAG C: /F >> %DefragRpt%


  IF ERRORLEVEL 1 (
    ECHO %date% %time% Error: %ERRORLEVEL% occurred. >> %DefragRpt%
  ) ELSE (
    ECHO %date% %time% DEFRAG.EXE has completed its execution. >> %DefragRpt%
  )


GOTO :EOF
```

The script is designed to run as a background process so that it can be executed by the Windows scheduler service, which I will show you how to use a little later in this appendix. Therefore it does not bother to post messages in the Windows command console's title bar or alter its color scheme. Of course, you can run the script manually if you wish.

The script begins by ensuring that it has not been started on an unsupported operating system. It then defines a variable called DefragRpt that specifies the location where a report file will be written and makes a series of procedure calls before terminating its execution. The first procedure called is the :DeleteExistingRpt procedure. This procedure uses an IF EXIST statement to determine if a report file has been created previously on the computer and deletes it if it has. Next, the :CreateNewDefragRpt procedure runs. Its job is to format the beginning portion of the report file. Finally, the :PerformDefrag procedure executes. It issues the DEFRAG.EXE command, specifying the drive to be defragmented using the /F switch. This switch tells the command to run without first prompting for confirmation.

Output produced by the command is redirected to the script's report file. When the command finishes executing, an IF ERRORLEVEL statement is executed to determine whether to write a success or failure message to the report file. Figure A.4 shows an example report produced by the script.

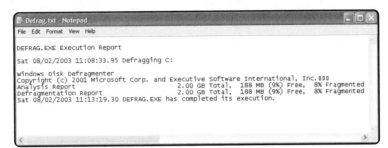

FIGURE A.4

Examining the report created by the defrager script.

Scheduling Script Execution

One of the major benefits of Windows shell scripting is that it facilitates the automated execution of tasks. This enables you to use the Windows operating system's built-in Task Scheduler service to run the script anytime you wish. For example, the `Defrager.bat` script developed earlier in this appendix is a good candidate to set up as a scheduled task. The `DEFRAG.EXE` command used within that script takes a while to run and consumes a lot of system resources, making your computer run slow. By running this script as a scheduled task, you can defrag your hard disk while you sleep or at any other time that suits you.

Windows provides two different ways to work with the Windows Scheduler service. The first option is to use the Windows AT command. The AT command is a text-based interface with which you can view, add, and delete scheduled tasks. The second option is to use the Windows Task Scheduler Wizard, which walks you through the steps required to set up new scheduled tasks manually. Both of these options are discussed in detail in the sections that follow.

The AT Command

The Windows AT command allows you to set up the scheduled execution of your Windows shell scripts. Using the AT command without any additional arguments, you can display a listing of currently scheduled tasks as demonstrated below.

```
C:\>AT

Status ID   Day               Time        Command Line
-------------------------------------------------------------------

        0   Each S            5:00 AM     Defrager.bat

        1   Tomorrow          11:00 AM    DiskClean.bat
```

Here, two scripts have been set up to execute as scheduled tasks. The first script is called Defrager.bat and is set up to run every Saturday at 5 A.M. The second script is named DiskClean.bat and is set up to run at 11 A.M. on the next day.

HINT Only administrators can configure scheduled tasks on Windows NT, XP, 2000, and 2003.

The following command demonstrates how to use the AT command to set up the scheduled execution of a new task for a script called TestScript.bat.

```
AT 22:00 /EVERY:M,T,W,Th,F,S,Su CMD /C TestScript.bat
```

In this example, the Windows shell script that will run as a scheduled task will be executed every day of the week at 10 P.M. You can also use the AT command to delete scheduled tasks by passing it the ID assigned to the task, as demonstrated below.

```
AT 1 /DELETE
```

Here I told the AT command to remove the DiskClean.bat script from the execution schedule.

TRICK If you want to delete all of the currently scheduled tasks, you can save time by executing the AT command as follows:

```
AT /DELETE
```

Just be sure that this is what you really want to do.

The AT command can also be used to set up the execution of scripts on other network computers. To accomplish this, you must use the UNC format of the target computer's computer name, as demonstrated below.

```
AT \\ServerName 22:00 /EVERY:M,T,W,Th,F,S,Su CMD /C Defrager.bat
```

There are more uses of the AT command than I have room to cover in this appendix. To learn more about this command, type AT HELP in the Windows command prompt or search for information about the command in the Windows help system.

TRAP When run by the Windows Scheduler Service, your scripts will not have access to the same set of resources that are available when you execute them manually. For example, any mapped drives you may have set up are not available to the script. In these situations, you must equip your scripts with the ability to set up connections to whatever resources they may require.

The following script demonstrates how you can use the AT command within Windows shell scripts. In this example, I have created a scheduling script that sets up scheduled tasks for five other Windows shell scripts. A script like this would be useful in situations where you are responsible for setting up the same set of scheduled tasks on a large number of computers, such as might be the case if you worked on a company's desktop support team.

```
@ECHO off


REM ************************************************************************

REM

REM Script Name: MastSched.bat

REM Author: Jerry Ford

REM Date: August 1, 2003

REM

REM Description: This script demonstrates how to schedule scripts using the

REM Windows scheduler service and the AT command.

REM

REM ************************************************************************


REM ****** Script Initialization Section ******


REM Abort execution if OS is not Windows NT, 2000, XP, or 2003

IF NOT "%os%" == "Windows_NT" (

  ECHO.

  ECHO.

  ECHO Unsupported Operating system

  ECHO.

  ECHO.

  GOTO :EOF

)


REM Define a variable that specifies the location of this script log file.
```

```
SET ReportFile=C:\Scripts\ATReport.txt



REM ****** Main Processing Section ******

REM Call a procedure that logs this script's execution.
CALL :SetUpSchedLog

REM Call the procedure that sets up scheduled tasks.
CALL :SetUpSchedule


GOTO :EOF



REM ****** Procedure Section ******

REM This procedure writes a date and time entry to a report file.
:SetUpSchedLog

  ECHO %date% %time% MastSched.bat - Now executing. > %ReportFile%


GOTO :EOF


REM This procedure sets up the scheduled execution of other Windows shell
REM scripts using the AT command.
:SetUpSchedule

  AT 20:00 /EVERY:T CMD /C DiskClean.bat >> %ReportFile%
  AT 21:00 /EVERY:M,W,F CMD /C MapNtwkDrive.bat >> %ReportFile%
  AT 21:00 /EVERY:M,W,F CMD /C Archiver.bat >> %ReportFile%
  AT 22:00 /EVERY:M,W,F CMD /C BreakDriveMap.bat >> %ReportFile%
  AT 22:00 /EVERY:Th CMD /C Defrager.bat >> %ReportFile%


GOTO :EOF
```

The script begins by ensuring that is has not been started on an unsupported Windows operating system. It then defines a variable named `Reportfile` and assigns it the location of a file where the script is to maintain a log file. The script then executes two procedures before terminating its own execution.

The first procedure called by the script is `:SetUpSchedLog`. This procedure redirects the output of an `ECHO` statement to the specified log file in order to record the date and time each time the script ran. Next, the `:SetUpSchedule` procedure is executed. This procedure executes a series of five `AT` commands, as shown below.

```
AT 20:00 /EVERY:T CMD /C DiskClean.bat >> %ReportFile%

AT 21:00 /EVERY:M,W,F CMD /C MapNtwkDrive.bat >> %ReportFile%

AT 21:00 /EVERY:M,W,F CMD /C Archiver.bat >> %ReportFile%

AT 22:00 /EVERY:M,W,F CMD /C BreakDriveMap.bat >> %ReportFile%

AT 22:00 /EVERY:Th CMD /C Defrager.bat >> %ReportFile%
```

Each of these scripts is set up to run at different times and different days of the week. The procedure also redirects any output produced by the execution of each of these `AT` commands to the script's log file.

Figure A.5 shows the scheduled tasks as they will appear when viewed from the Windows Scheduled Tasks folder.

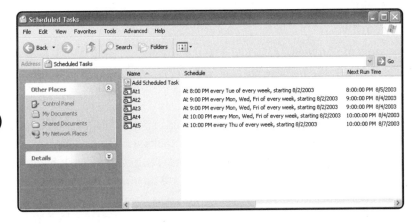

FIGURE A.5

Examining the scheduled tasks configured by the Windows shell script.

Figure A.6 shows how the script's log file will look when the script runs successfully.

TRAP

Scripts set up by the `AT` command to run under the control of the Windows scheduler service but are not associated with specific user accounts may fail if the script attempts to access secured resources. If this is the case, use the Windows Task Scheduler Wizard to configure the automated execution of your scripts. The wizard provides the ability to run scripts using the security access provided by specified user accounts.

FIGURE A.6

Reviewing the text audit report created by the Windows shell script.

```
ATReport.txt - Notepad
File  Edit  Format  View  Help
Sat 08/02/2003 11:16:49.13 MastSched.bat - Now executing.
Added a new job with job ID = 1
Added a new job with job ID = 2
Added a new job with job ID = 3
Added a new job with job ID = 4
Added a new job with job ID = 5
```

The Scheduled Task Wizard

As an alternative to using the AT command to add, view, and delete scheduled tasks, you can also use the Windows Scheduled Task Wizard.

> **HINT** On Windows NT, XP, 2000, and 2003, only administrators are permitted to create and manage scheduled tasks.

The Windows Scheduled Task Wizard walks you through the steps required to set up an automated execution schedule for your scripts using any of the following schedules:

- Daily
- Weekly
- Monthly
- One time only
- At startup
- At login

By default, scheduled tasks run by using a special built-in Windows account called LocalSystem. Unfortunately, this account lacks sufficient security permissions to run many tasks. One advantage the Windows Scheduled Task Wizard has over the AT command is the ability to easily associate user accounts and their associated passwords with specific tasks. This allows tasks that require specific levels of access to execute using the security access of the specified user account.

> **TRAP** If you elect to associate a user account and its password with a scheduled task, the started task will stop executing if the user account's password expires. In addition, the task will stop running if the user account's password is changed and you forget to return and update the password in the scheduled task. One way around this problem is to create a new user account whose sole purpose is to run scheduled tasks. You can then set up the account so that its password will not expire and will never change.

Starting the Task Scheduler Service

To run scheduled tasks on your computer, you must ensure that the Windows scheduled task services is running. The following procedure outlines the steps involved in performing this procedure:

1. Click on Start, Control Panel, and then Administrative Tools.
2. Open the Services console by double-clicking on the Services icon.
3. Find the Task Scheduler service and double-click on it.
4. Ensure that the Startup Type drop-down list is set to Automatic.
5. Click on Start if the service is not already started.
6. Click on OK.

Running the Scheduled Task Wizard

One of the nice things about using the Scheduled Task Wizard instead of the AT command is that you no longer have to worry about the AT command's syntax. All you have to do is follow the wizard's instruction and it will take care of the rest for you. The following procedure outlines the steps involved in starting the Scheduled Task Wizard and using it to set up new scheduled tasks.

1. Click on `Start, Control Panel` and then `Scheduled Tasks`. The Scheduled Tasks folder appears.
2. Double-click on the `Add Scheduled Task` icon, and then click on `Next` when the Scheduled Task Wizard appears.
3. The wizard displays a list of applications, as demonstrated in Figure A.7. Type the name and path of your script or click on `Browse` to locate it. Click on `Next`.

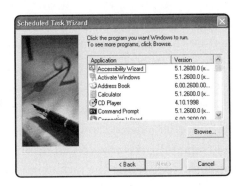

Specifying the name and location of your Windows shell script.

4. Enter a task name and then select an entry from the list of available scheduling options, as shown in Figure A.8.

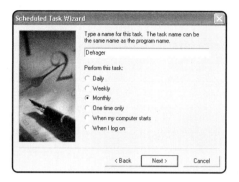

FIGURE A.8

Selecting the
execution frequency
for your Windows
shell script.

5. If you select the Daily schedule, the wizard will display the following list of
options, allowing you to further refine the task execution schedule.

  - **Start time**. Specifies the time that the task is to begin running.
  - **Perform this task**. Configures the task to run daily, on weekdays, or every
  __ days.
  - **Start date**. Specifies the date on which the task should first be run.

  Fill in the required information, click on Next, and then skip to step 11.

6. If you select the Weekly schedule, the wizard will display the following list of
options, allowing you to further refine the task execution schedule.

  - **Start time**. Specifies the time that the task is to begin running.
  - **Every __ weeks**. Configures the task to execute on a set period of weeks.
  - **Select the day(s) of the week below**. Specifies the one or more days of the
  week on which the task should be executed.

  Fill in the required information, click on Next, and then skip to step 11.

7. If you select the Monthly schedule, the wizard will display the following list
of options, as shown in Figure A.9, allowing you to further refine the task
execution schedule.

  - **Start time**. Specifies the time that the task is to begin running.
  - **Day**. Specifies the day of the month that the task is to run.
  - **The _ _**. Specifies the day of the month on which to run the task.
  - **Of the month(s)**. Specifies the month(s) on which to run the task.

  Fill in the required information, click on Next, and then skip to step 11.

8. If you select the One time only schedule, the wizard will display the following
list of options, allowing you to further refine the task execution schedule.

  - **Start time**. Specifies the time that the task is to begin running.
  - **Start date**. Specifies the date on which the task is to start running.

  Fill in the required information, click on Next, and then skip to step 11.

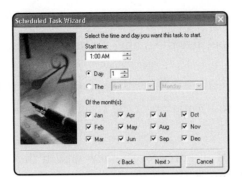

FIGURE A.9

Providing detailed information regarding the script's execution schedule.

9. If you select the `When my computer starts` schedule, the wizard will display the following list of options, as shown in Figure A.10, allowing you to further refine the task execution schedule.

- **Enter the user name.** Specifies the name of a user account to associate with the task.
- **Enter the password.** Specifies the account's associated password.
- **Confirm password.** A confirmation of the specified account's password.

Fill in the required information, click on `Next`, and then skip to step 12.

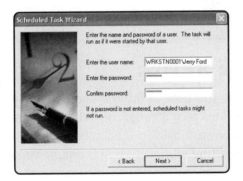

FIGURE A.10

Associating a user account and its password with your Windows shell script.

10. If you select the `When I log on` schedule, the wizard will display the following list of options, allowing you to further refine the task execution schedule.

- **Enter the user name.** Specifies the name of a user account to associate with the task.
- **Enter the password.** Specifies the account's associated password.
- **Confirm password.** A confirmation of the specified account's password.

Fill in the required information, click on Next, and then proceed to step 12.

11. The wizard then displays the following list of options:

- **Enter the user name.** Specifies the name of a user account to associate with the task.

- **Enter the password.** Specifies the account's associated password.

- **Confirm password.** A confirmation of the specified account's password.

12. Click on `Finish`.

Once finished, the wizard adds an entry for the new task in the Scheduled Tasks folder, as demonstrated in Figure A.11.

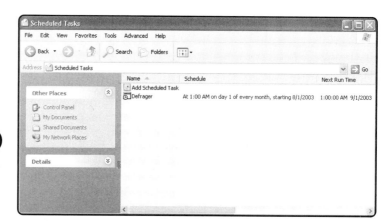

FIGURE A.11

Examining the task created by the Scheduled Task Wizard.

Creating a Chat Script

In the next example, I'll show you how to build a chat-like script. I say chat-like because this script only emulates a chat program. Whereas a true chat program establishes and maintains a communication session between two computers, this script simply facilitates the sending of messages to the same person over and over again. In fact, the script may be more likened to instant messaging. However, because of its interface, it looks and feels more like a chat program.

TRAP In order for this script to work, the computer that runs it must also be running the Windows Messenger service. Otherwise the `NET SEND` won't be able to send and receive any messages.

```
@ECHO off


REM ************************************************************************
```

```
REM

REM Script Name: NetSend.bat

REM Author: Jerry Ford

REM Date: July 25, 2003

REM

REM Description: This script is designed to emulate network chat

REM communication between two network users.

REM

REM ***************************************************************************


REM ****** Script Initialization Section ******


REM Display the name of the script in the Windows command console's title bar.

TITLE = NetSend Messenger


REM Set the color scheme to yellow on black.

COLOR 0E



REM ****** Main Processing Section ******


REM Call the procedure that displays the script's welcome screen.

CALL :WelcomeScreen


REM This label provides a callable marker for restarting the script.

:TryAgain


REM Call the procedure that prompts the user to enter the name of the

REM destination computer.

CALL :CollectUserName


REM If the user hits Enter without specifying a computer name, start over.
```

```
IF /I "%answer%" == "" CLS & GOTO :TryAgain


REM Terminate script execution if the user typed Quit.
IF /I %answer% == Quit CLS & GOTO :EOF


REM Call the procedure that collects and sends messages.
CALL :StartChatting


GOTO :EOF



REM ****** Procedure Section ******

REM This procedure displays the script's welcome screen.
:WelcomeScreen


  CLS


  ECHO.
  ECHO  N e t S e n d   I n s t a n t   N e t w o r k   M e s s a g e
  ECHO.
  ECHO  D e l i v e r y   C l i e n t   Version 1.0
  ECHO.
  ECHO  Operation:
  ECHO.
  ECHO  1. When prompted, enter the network username of the person with whom
  ECHO     you wish to chat and press the Enter key.
  ECHO.
  ECHO  2. Messages from that person will appear in graphical popup dialogs
  ECHO     on your computer screen.
  ECHO.
  ECHO  3. To send messages, type your text messages when prompted and press
  ECHO     the Enter key.
```

```
ECHO.

ECHO  4. To send messages to a different network user, type Switch and press

ECHO     the Enter key. Type a new network username when prompted and press

ECHO.    the Enter Key.

ECHO.

ECHO  5. When done chatting, type Quit and press the Enter key.


FOR /L %%i IN (1,1,2) DO ECHO.


  PAUSE


GOTO :EOF


REM This procedure collects the name of the destination computer.
:CollectUserName


  CLS


  FOR /L %%i IN (1,1,23) DO ECHO.


  SET /P answer=Enter the target computer's name:


GOTO :EOF


REM This procedure collects the message to be sent and sends it.
:StartChatting


  CLS


  FOR /L %%i IN (1,1,4) DO ECHO.


  ECHO You are currently in chat mode with:  %answer%.

  ECHO.
```

```
ECHO.

ECHO Type a message and press the Enter key to send it or type Quit to

ECHO exit NetSend.bat.


FOR /L %%i IN (1,1,6) DO ECHO.


SET /p MsgText=Message:


REM If the user hit Enter without typing any text, prompt for input again

IF /I "%MsgText%" == "" GOTO :StartChatting


REM If the user entered Switch, then start over allowing the user to

REM specify a different destination computer.

IF /I "%MsgText%" == "Switch" GOTO TryAgain


REM If the user entered Quit, terminate the script's execution.

IF /I "%MsgText%" == "Quit" GOTO :EOF


REM Send the message to the appropriate computer.

NET SEND %answer% "%MsgText%"


REM Prompt the user to enter a new message.

GOTO :StartChatting



GOTO :EOF
```

This script begins by posting a message to the Windows command console's title bar. It then changes the console's color scheme to yellow on black. Next, the :WelcomeScreen procedure is called. This procedure displays the welcome screen shown Figure A.12 and waits for the user to press a key before continuing.

Next the script calls the :CollectUserName procedure. This procedure uses a SET statement to prompt the user to enter the name of a networked computer to which messages will be sent (to mimic a chat session). Two IF statements then process the user's response, which is assigned to a variable named answer. If the user didn't type an entry, then a GOTO statement is used to transfer processing control to the

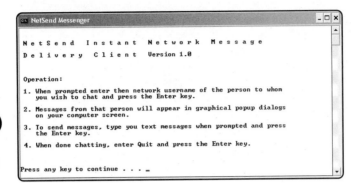

FIGURE A.12

Using the NET SEND command to create a chat script.

:TryAgain label, which is located at the beginning of the script. If the user typed Quit, the script clears the display screen and terminates its own execution.

Next, the :StartChatting procedure is called. This procedure uses a SET statement to collect input from the user and stores it in a variable called MsgText, as demonstrated in Figure A.13.

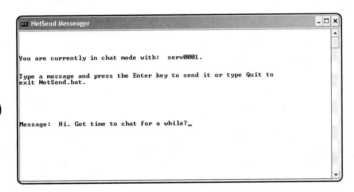

FIGURE A.13

Entering the text message to be sent to the other computer.

The procedure then executes a series of three IF statements to determine what to do next. If the value of MsgText is empty, then the user did not enter a test message, so the procedure gives the user another chance to enter new text by using the GOTO command to run itself again. If the user entered the word switch, a GOTO command is used to switch processing control to the statement following the :TryAgain label located at the beginning of the script. This way the user can enter a different computer name in order to start a chat session with somebody else, or, if the user typed an invalid computer name, they can start over and enter the correct computer name.

Users can also enter Quit instead of a message to terminate the script's execution from this screen. Finally, if the user did not press the Enter key, type Switch, or type Quit, their text message is sent to the other network computer using the NET SEND command, after which another GOTO command restarts the :StartChatting procedure to allow a new chat message to be sent. Figure A.14 demonstrates how the text message will appear on the recipient's computer.

FIGURE A.14

Viewing the text
message as it will
appear on the
destination computer.

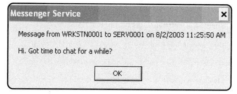

Of course, for the NetSend.bat script to work effectively, copies of it must be distributed to both individuals who wish to chat with one another over the network.

Adding a Graphical Interface

As you saw in the previous chat example, you can take advantage of the Windows NET SEND command to display information to users in graphical pop-up dialogs. This provides an effective alternative for presenting users with information. But what about collecting user information graphically? Well, that can be done as well. To do so, you will need to download any of a number of freely distributed utility programs from the Internet. One such utility is called MESSAGEBOX.EXE, which you can download by visiting http://optimumx.com/ and clicking on the Downloads link. Another similar utility is called MSGBOX.EXE, which you can download from http://claudiosoft.online.fr/msgbox.html.

You can write Windows shell scripts that can execute either of these utility programs and pass messages to be displayed. You can also specify what buttons you want displayed (OK, OK/Cancel, Yes/No, etc). The MSGBOX.EXE utility downloads as a Zip file. One way to use it is to unzip its contents into the folder where your Windows shell scripts are stored. To learn its syntax, open a Windows command console and change the current working directory to the folder where you unzipped the utility and then type MSGBOX as demonstrated below.

```
C:\>MSGBOX


Claudiosoft MessageBox 1.2


This program is FREEWARE for private use.

(C) Claudiosoft 2001


Usage : MsgBox Message Title Flag | YESNO | OKCANCEL | YESNOCANCEL
```

```
Example : MsgBox 'Do you want to continue?' 'Title' YESNO

MsgBox returns :

7 if the answer is NO,

6 if the answer is YES,

2 if the answer is CANCEL,

1 if the answer is OK.
```

The MESSAGEBOX.EXE utility's syntax is even easier to access. Simply locate and double-click MESSAGEBOX.EXE, and you'll see the pop-up dialog shown in Figure A.15.

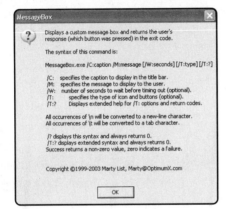

Viewing the
MESSAGEBOX.EXE
command line
utility's syntax.

As an example of how to work with these types of external command line utilities, look at the following Windows shell script. It uses the MSGBOX command line utility to generate a graphical pop-up dialog that displays a message with YES/NO buttons asking the players if they would like to play another game.

```
@ECHO off


REM ***********************************************************************

REM

REM Script Name: Popup.bat

REM Author: Jerry Ford

REM Date: August 1, 2003

REM

REM Description: This script demonstrates how to use Claudiosoft's MSGBOX.EXE

REM program to interact with users via popup dialogs.

REM
```

```
REM ***********************************************************************

REM ****** Script Initialization Section ******

REM Abort execution if run on a computer not running
REM Windows NT, 2000, XP, or 2003.
IF NOT "%os%" == "Windows_NT" (
  ECHO.
  ECHO.
  ECHO Unsupported operating system
  ECHO.
  ECHO.
  GOTO :EOF
)


REM Define a variable that specifies the location of the MSGBOX.EXE program.
SET msgbox=C:\Scripts\MSGBOX.EXE



REM ****** Main Processing Section ******

REM Call a procedure that demonstrates how to use MSGBOX.EXE.
CALL :DisplayResults

REM If MSGBOX.EXE returned an exit code of 7, the user clicked on NO.
IF ERRORLEVEL 7 GOTO :Exit

REM If MSGBOX.EXE returned an exit code of 6, the user clicked on YES.
IF ERRORLEVEL 6 GOTO :PlayAgain



REM ****** Procedure Section ******
```

```
REM This procedure demonstrates how to display a message in a popup

REM dialog that includes YES and NO buttons.

:DisplayResults


  %msgbox% "You win! \n\nWant to play again?" "MSGBOX.EXE Demo" YESNO


GOTO :EOF




REM This procedure demonstrates how to display a message in a popup

REM dialog that includes the OK button.

:Exit


  %msgbox% "Thanks for playing! \n\nPlease come back soon!" "MSGBOX.EXE Demo"


GOTO :EOF


REM This procedures shows how the script waits on the user to

REM respond to the previous popup dialogs before continuing.

:PlayAgain


  ECHO.

  ECHO.

  ECHO This is where you would execute the GOTO command to restart the game.

  ECHO.

  ECHO.


GOTO :EOF
```

The script begins by ensuring that it has not been inadvertently started on an unsupported Windows operating system. Next it defines a variable named msgbox that stores the location of the MSGBOX.EXE command line utility. The script then calls the :DisplayResults procedure. This procedure uses the MSGBOX.EXE command line utility to display the graphical pop-up dialog shown in Figure A.16.

FIGURE A.16

Collecting user input using a pop-up dialog.

Note that the MSGBOX.EXE utility translates the occurrence of \n characters into line feed and character return operations. This gives you some control over the manner in which text is displayed within the pop-up dialog.

Next, a pair of IF ERRORLEVEL statements interrogate the exit code returned by the MSGBOX.EXE utility to determine which button the player clicked. An exit code of 7 indicates that the player clicked on the NO button, and an exit code of 6 indicates that the player clicked on the YES button. If the NO button was clicked, the :Exit procedure is called. This procedure uses the MSGBOX.EXE utility to display a message in another pop-up dialog as shown in Figure A.17. If the player clicked on the YES button, the :PlayAgain procedures is called instead.

FIGURE A.17

Displaying text messages using a pop-up dialog.

Working with Third-Party Applications

You can create Windows shell scripts that interact with and control many Windows applications developed by software developers other than Microsoft. You can do this because many software developers include built-in command line support for their applications, allowing you to control the application from the Windows command line.

The amount of functionality of an application's command line interface will vary. Some software developers provide no command line functionality, others provide basic application functionality, while some others attempt to make available every feature and function that is built into their GUI interface.

An excellent example of a third-party application that exposes application functionality via the command line is WinZip. WinZip is a popular file-compression and archive-management program. WinZip is a shareware application that you can download and try before deciding whether you want to purchase it. You can download a copy of the latest version of WinZip from www.winzip.com.

To start WinZip, you double-click on its executable file, named `WINZIP32.EXE`, which by default is installed in `C:\ProgramFiles\WinZip`. However, `WINZIP32.EXE` also provides a command line interface which gives you the ability to create and extract Zip files under the control of Windows shell scripts. The syntax for `WINZIP32.EXE` is outlined below.

```
WINZIP32 [-min] action [options] filename[.zip] files
```

The `-min` parameter enables WinZip to run minimized so that you won't see its GUI when your scripts run it. You must select from one of the following switches to define the `action` parameter:

- **-a**. Create a new Zip file.
- **-f**. Refresh an archive.
- **-u**. Update an existing archive.
- **-m**. Move an archive.

You can include any of the following parameters in place of the `options` placeholder:

- **-r**. Adds files and folders to the Zip file.
- **-p**. Includes information about folder membership for each file.
- **-hs**. Includes any hidden and system files.
- **-s**. Specifies an optional password, which results in a Zip file that is password protected and encrypted. The password is specified using the format of `-sPassword`.

You may also optionally specify any one of the following switches in place of the `options` placeholder:

- **-ex**. Applies WinZip's maximum compression rate.
- **-en**. Applies WinZip's default compression rate.
- **-ef**. Applies a lower than normal compression rate.
- **-es**. Applies the lowest available compression rate.
- **-e0**. Creates an uncompressed Zip file.

Finally, the `WINZIP32.EXE` `files` parameter is used to specify the file or files to be added to the Zip file. For example, the following command demonstrates how to use the `WINZIP32.EXE` command to create a new Zip file called `TestArchive` in the C:\Tmp folder and to add to it all .txt files found in the C:\Reports folder.

```
WINZIP32 -A C:\Tmp\TestArchive.zip C:\Reports\*.txt
```

The following Windows shell script demonstrates how to leverage WinZip's built-in command line support to automate the creation of a new Zip file. In this example, the script will create a Zip file that that stores all of the Windows shell scripts found in the computer's C:\Scripts folder.

```
@ECHO off


REM ************************************************************************
REM
REM Script Name: Zipper.bat
REM Author: Jerry Ford
REM Date: August 1, 2003
REM
REM Description: This script demonstrates how to execute WinZip functionality
REM from within Windows shell scripts.
REM
REM ************************************************************************


REM ****** Script Initialization Section ******

REM Specify the location where WinZip was installed.
SET InstallLocation=D:\Program Files\WinZIP


REM Specify the files to be zipped up.
SET ScriptFileLoc=C:\Scripts\*.bat


REM Specify the name of the Zip file that is to be created
SET ZipFileName=C:\Scripts\Script.ZIP


REM Call the procedure that temporarily adds the WinZip folder to the
REM search path.
CALL :UpdatePath


REM Display a message allowing the user an opportunity to halt script
REM execution.
```

```
CALL :DisplayWarning


REM Call the procedure that creates the new Zip file.
CALL :CreateArchive


GOTO :EOF


REM This procedures adds the WinZip folder to the end of the search path.
:UpdatePath


  SET path=%path%;%InstallLocation%


GOTO :EOF


REM This procedure displays a message that gives the user a chance to halt
REM script execution.
:DisplayWarning


  ECHO.
  ECHO.
  ECHO This script creates a new Zip file containing copies of all the
  ECHO .bat script files located in %ScriptFileLoc%.
  ECHO.
  PAUSE


GOTO :EOF


REM This procedure creates the new Zip file.
:CreateArchive


  CLS


  REM Execute the WINZIP32.EXE command, run it in minimized mode, and
```

```
REM pass it the name of the Zip file to create and the name and
REM location of the files to be added to the archive.
WINZIP32 -MIN -A %ZipFileName% %ScriptFileLoc%

REM Check for any errors and display the WINZIP32 command exit code if
REM appropriate.
IF ERRORLEVEL 1 (
  CLS
  ECHO.
  ECHO.
  ECHO An exit code of %ERRORLEVEL% was reported. As a result, the Zip file
  ECHO was not created.
  ECHO.
  ECHO.
) ELSE (
  ECHO.
  ECHO.
  ECHO A Zip file containing all the scripts located in %ZipFileName% has been
  ECHO created in %ZipFileName%.
  ECHO.
  ECHO.
)
PAUSE


GOTO :EOF
```

The script begins by setting up three variables. The first variable is called
InstallLocation. It is assigned a string representing the location of the folder where
WinZip has been installed on the computer. The second variable is named
ScriptFileLoc. It is assigned a string representing the folder where the scripts to be
added to the Zip file are located. The third variable is named ZipFileName. It is assigned a string representing the complete file and path name of the Zip file that
the script is to create.

The script then makes three procedure calls before terminating its own execution. The first procedure called is :UpdatePath. This procedure appends the location of the WinZip folder to the end of the search path. This way, the Windows shell will be able to locate the WINZIP32.EXE command. Next, the :DisplayWarning procedure is called. This procedure displays a warning message that explains to the user what the script is about to do. The script then waits until the user presses a key, at which time the :CreateArchive procedure is finally called. This procedure executes the WINZIP32.EXE command in minimized mode, telling it to create a new Zip file specified by ZipFilename and to add all the files specified by ScriptFileLoc to it. The procedure then uses an IF ERRORLEVEL statement to check the value of the exit code returned by the WINZIP32.EXE command to determine if an error occurred.

Once executed, the script creates a new Zip file containing all the .bat files that were located in the C:\Scripts folder. Figure A.18 demonstrates how the Zip file will look when later opened from the Windows desktop.

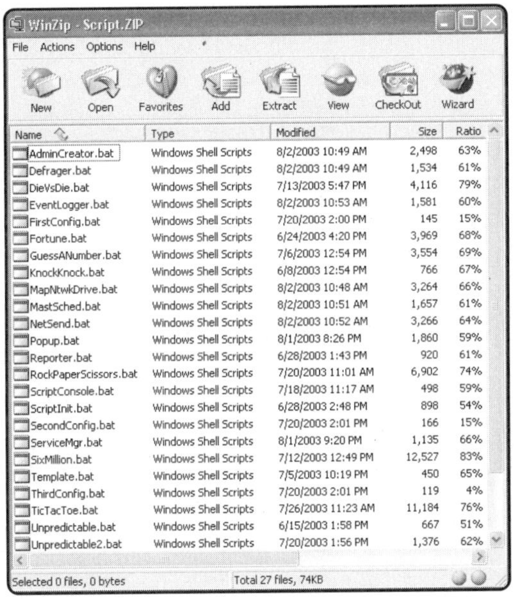

FIGURE A.18

Examining the contents of the Zip file created by the Windows shell script.

What's on the CD-ROM?

To become an expert Windows shell script programmer, you must spend plenty of time writing new scripts. When first starting out, it helps a lot to have a collection of sample scripts from which to begin working. If you created and tested the sample scripts in this book as you read along, you should now have that foundation. However, just in case there were a couple of scripts that you did not get the chance to complete, I have provided copies of each script on the book's CD-ROM. This appendix provides a brief reference to each of the scripts that you will find.

In addition to the book's scripts, you will find shareware copies of two excellent text editors. I will provide you with a high-level overview of the capabilities and benefits of each editor.

Windows Shell Scripting Examples

Table B.1 provides a quick overview of all the sample scripts found in this book that you will also find on the accompanying CD-ROM.

TABLE B.1 SAMPLE SCRIPTS ON THE CD-ROM

Book Reference	Script	Description
Chapter 1	Knock-Knock Joke	Demonstrates how to create a script that tells the player a joke interactively
Chapter 2	Unpredictable Command Prompt	Demonstrates different techniques for having fun while manipulating the Windows command prompt
Chapter 3	Fortune Teller Game	Demonstrates how to create an automated fortune teller that answers the player's every question
Chapter 4	"The Story of Buzz the Wonder Dog"	Demonstrates how to use variable substitution to create a customized story based on player input
Chapter 5	Guess a Number Game	Demonstrates how to use conditional logic to create a game in which the player is prompted to guess a randomly selected number in the least possible number of guesses
Chapter 6	Six-Million-Dollar Quiz	Demonstrates how to create and administer a quiz and how to write a report card file
Chapter 7	Rock, Paper, Scissors	Demonstrates how to recreate the popular children's game, "Rock, Paper, Scissors"

TABLE B.1   SAMPLE SCRIPTS ON THE CD-ROM (CONTINUED)

Book Reference	Script	Description
Chapter 8	Tic-Tac-Toe Game	Demonstrates how to recreate the popular game of Tic-Tac-Toe
Appendix A	Script Scheduler	Demonstrates how to use the AT command programmatically to automate the execution of other scripts
Appendix A	Network Drive Connector	Demonstrates how to map a connection to a network drive programmatically
Appendix A	Network Drive Breaker	Demonstrates how to disconnect a network drive connection programmatically
Appendix A	Windows Service Manager	Demonstrates how to stop and start Windows services programmatically
Appendix A	User Account Manager	Demonstrates how to create new user accounts programmatically
Appendix A	Network Messenger	Demonstrates how to send a network message to another logged-on user
Appendix A	Printer Queue Manager	Demonstrates how to automate the administration of print jobs
Appendix A	Local Network Share Manager	Demonstrates how to automate the administration of shared drives and folders

Shell Scripting Editors

This book's CD-ROM also contains two excellent editors. One is free and the other is distributed as shareware, allowing you to work with it for 30 days before you have to either purchase it or quit using it. Unless you already have a script editor that you really like working with, or you are just stuck on using Windows Notepad, I recommend that you take a few minutes to give each of these editors a test drive.

Unlike Notepad, both of these editors allow you to open or create and work with multiple files at the same time. This is an especially handy feature when you find yourself cutting and pasting lines of code from one script to another.

JGsoft EditPad Lite

The JGsoft EditPad Lite text editor is designed to replace Windows Notepad. Unlike NotePad, EditPad Lite allows you to open an unlimited number of files for editing at the same time. Each open file is displayed with a tab, making it easy to switch between files, as shown in Figure B.1.

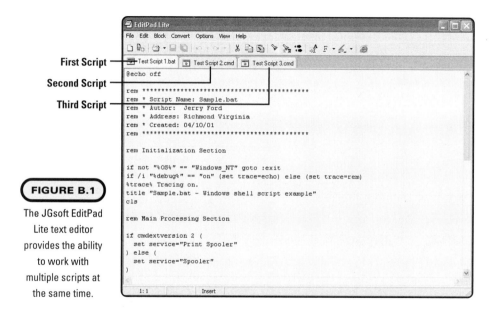

FIGURE B.1

The JGsoft EditPad Lite text editor provides the ability to work with multiple scripts at the same time.

EditPad Lite is distributed as freeware, which means that it is free for non-commercial use. Its major features include

- Advanced search and replace over all open files
- Unlimited redo and undo
- Line and column numbering
- Indent and outdent options
- Optional word wrapping
- The ability to configure dozens of preferences that affect the editor's operation
- Open any of the last 16 files using the Reopen menu
- Perform lowercase, uppercase, and invert case operations
- A print preview capability

HINT   To learn more about the JGsoft EditPad Lite text editor, visit www.editpadlite.com/
editpadlite.html.

JGsoft EditPad Pro

JGsoft's EditPad Pro is a full-featured text editor that provides all the features found
in EditPad Lite plus many more. You can download a copy of EditPad Pro from
www.editpadpro.com/editpadpro.html, as shown in Figure B.2.

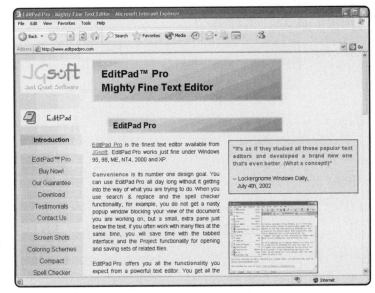

FIGURE B.2

Visiting the EditPad
Pro Web site.

One of EditPad Pro's best features is its ability to define a syntax color-coding scheme
for specific types of files like Windows shell script files. Once configured, the syntax color-coding feature makes Windows shell scripts easier to work with by high-
lighting keywords in scripts using different colors. For example, all comments may
be displayed as red text, making them easier to find and modify. EditPad Pro comes
with a number of predefined syntax color-coding schemes that support many different file types. While it does not provide a default color-coding scheme for Windows shell scripts, you can visit JGsoft's Web site at www.editpadpro.com/cgi-bin/
cscslist.pl (as shown in Figure B.3) and download various predefined color schemes
for a host of different files types, including Windows shell scripts.

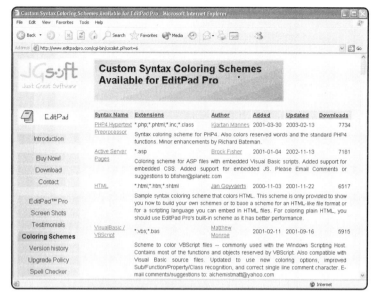

By applying the appropriate syntax color-coding scheme you can turn EditPad Pro into a Windows shell script editor.

EditPad Pro assists you in downloading and installing syntax color-coding schemes on its Preferences dialog, as shown in Figure B.4. Here a scheme named MS-BATCH Files (a term that is synonymous with Windows shell scripts) has been downloaded and then selected from the Syntax Coloring drop-down list. The syntax color scheme is then associated with all files that have a .bat or .cmd file extension.

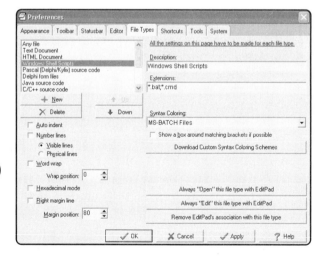

Configuring EditPad Pro to support Windows shell scripts.

Once one of the many available Windows shell script compatible color-coding schemes is downloaded and installed, EditPad Pro can be used as a fully featured Windows shell script editor, complete with syntax color coding (as shown in Figure B.5).

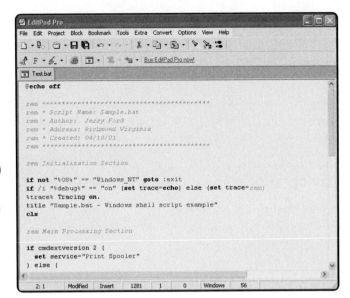

A syntax color-coding scheme uses font color, bold text, and italics to help make scripts easier to read and work with.

Other major features provided by EditPad Pro not found in EditPad Lite include

- Customizable syntax color-coding schemes
- The ability to perform file comparisons
- Spell checking
- The ability to organize and manage multiple scripts as a project
- The ability to bookmark specific lines within a file for later reference
- Support for up to 16 clipboards, allowing the simultaneous storage and retrieval of multiple strings

For more information on the features provided by EditPad Lite and EditPad Pro, check out JGsoft's Web site.

APPENDIX C

What Next?

I nstead of seeing this book as the end of your Windows shell scripting education, you should think of it as the beginning. To become an accomplished Windows shell script programmer, you will need to spend time developing and honing your programming skills by writing and testing new scripts. You also need to continue to read and learn more about Windows shell scripting. To help get you started, I have put together a list of books and Web sites where you can go to learn more.

Recommended Reading

Following is a collection of books that will help you further develop your Windows shell script programming skills.

Microsoft Windows XP Professional Resource Kit Documentation

by Microsoft Corporation

ISBN: 0735614857, Microsoft Press, 2001

This book provides a collection of command line utilities for Windows XP. The utility programs provided by this resource kit are essential tools for any system administrator. Complete documentation for all these utilities is also provided.

Windows Shell Scripting and WSH Administrator's Guide

by Jerry Lee Ford, Jr.

ISBN: 1931841268, Premier Press, 2001

The first half of this book provides additional coverage of Windows shell scripting. This book will also give you a solid introduction to Microsoft's other scripting technology, the Windows Script Host, or WSH. This book serves as a great guide for current or future system administrators, programmers, and power users, or for beginner programmers who are ready to take that next step.

Windows 2000 Commands Pocket Reference

by Aeleen Frisch

ISBN: 0596001487, O'Reilly & Associates, 2001

This little guide provides documentation of the command line commands for Windows 2000. The guide includes a review of Windows shell scripting statements, making it a good resource for any Windows shell script programmer. Additionally, this guide reviews the syntax of the command line utilities provided by the Windows 2000 Resource Kit.

Windows NT Shell Scripting

by Tim Hill

ISBN: 1578700477, Que, 1998

Although this book does not cover recent enhancements to Windows shell scripting available in Windows 2000 and XP, it still provides a solid review of Windows shell scripting.

Locating Internet Resources

Books are not the only source of information available to you for Windows shell scripting. Perhaps the best source of free information is the Internet, where you can find additional documentation and tons of free sample scripts. Following is a list of Web sites where you can go to learn more.

www.labmice.net/scripting

The Scripting and Batch Programming Resources Web site (Figure C.1), provides access to information on Windows shell scripting as well as other programming languages. Here you will find a Windows command reference, a reference for Windows Resource Kit commands and links to articles that provide all kinds of information related to Windows shell scripting.

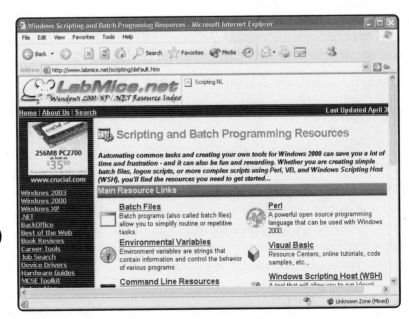

FIGURE C.1

Scripting resources at www.labmice .net/scripting/ default.htm.

www.robvanderwoude.com

Another excellent resource is Rob van der Woude's Scripting Pages Web site (Figure C.2). Here you will find plenty of Windows shell scripting examples. However, the site states that its main objective is to help teach you how to create scripts. So you can expect to find plenty of information on how scripting works. In addition, you will find information about a number of other scripting languages.

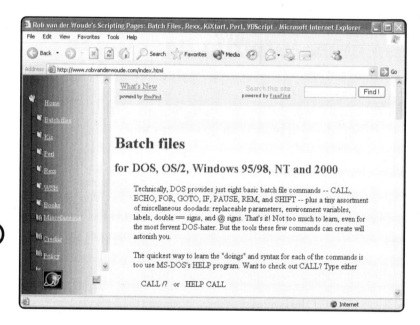

FIGURE C.2

The Batch Files page at www. robvanderwoude .com.

www.onesmartclick.com/programming/batch-files.html

Another excellent site is www.OneSmartClick.com (Figure C.3). This site is loaded with links to articles where you will find all kinds of information related to Windows shell scripting.

www.windowsshellscripting.com

This final recommended site (Figure C.4) is good for finding more information about Windows shell scripting. You will find tutorials covering Windows shell scripting as well as sample scripts that you can download. In addition, this site features an online discussion forum where you can post questions and receive answers from other Windows shell script programmers.

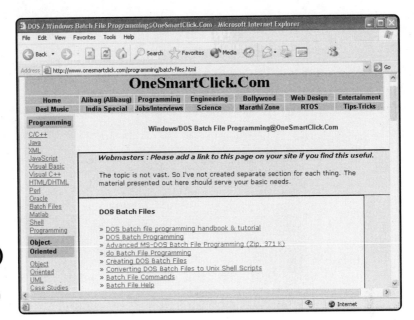

FIGURE C.3

OneSmartClick
.com is loaded with
information links.

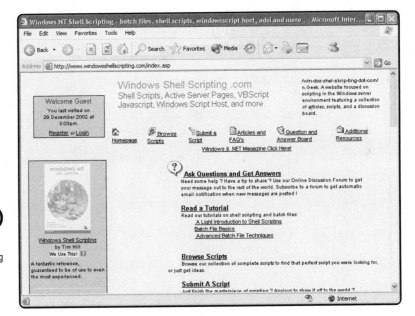

FIGURE C.4

www.
windowsshellscripting
.com offers
downloads and a
discussion forum.

Glossary

@. A Windows shell script command that suppresses the display of any statement from the Windows command console.

@ECHO off. A Windows shell script statement that suppresses the display of all statements within a script.

.bat. The file extension assigned to batch files, also known as Windows shell script files.

.cmd. The file extension assigned to command files, also known as Windows shell script files.

:EOF. A built-in Windows shell script function that simulates the end-of-file marker, providing the ability to terminate procedures and scripts.

Application Event Log. A log file maintained by Windows NT, XP, 2000, and 2003 operating systems where application error messages are written.

Argument. An individual piece of data passed to a command, procedure, or script at execution time.

Arithmetic Operators. Characters that you use to specify the type of mathematical operation to perform within a script (+, -, *, /, and %).

Assignment Operators. Characters that you use when assigning values to numeric variables using expressions (+=, -=, *=, /=, and %=).

ASSOC. A Windows command that displays or modifies file name extension associations.

AT. A Windows command that provides the ability to view, create, and modify scheduled tasks.

Batch Files. Files with a .bat file extension that contain Windows shell scripts.

CALL. A Windows shell command used to execute internal or external procedures in which the calling script pauses and waits for the called script to finish executing before resuming its own execution.

CD (CHDIR). A Windows command used to change the current directory.

CHOICE.EXE. A Windows Resource Kit command that provides the ability to interactively prompt the user for text input.

CLS. A Windows command that clears the Windows command console screen, leaving only the command prompt visible.

COLOR. A Windows command that sets foreground and background colors in the Windows command console.

Command Extensions. Modifications made to Windows shell commands since the initial release of the Windows shell.

Command History. A list of previously executed commands that can be recalled and executed by pressing F7 when using the Windows command console.

Command Prompt. Enables the Windows command console to accept text input which is then passed to the operating system for processing.

Comments. Statements embedded within scripts that document the script without affecting its execution. (See REM.)

Comparison Operators. Characters that you use to specify the type of comparison that you wish to perform when formulating IF statements (==, EQU, LSS, GTR, LEQ, GEQ and NEQ).

Compound Commands. The execution of two or more commands using a collection of reserved characters (&, &&, ||, ()) that specify how and when commands that follow the first command are to be executed.

Computername. An environment variable that stores the name assigned to the local computer.

COMSPEC. An environment variable that identifies the location of the Windows shell (e.g., CMD.EXE).

COPY. A Windows command that copies one or more files from one location to another.

CMD. A Windows command that is used to open a new Windows shell session within the current Windows command console.

CMDEXTVERSION. An environment variable that stores a string identifying the Windows shell version number.

date. A variable that provides access to the current system date.

DATE. A Windows command that displays or modifies the system date.

Debug. A term used to refer to the processes involved in locating and fixing errors within scripts and programs.

Defrag. A Windows command-line utility program that defragments files stored on hard drives to reorganize disk space and improve disk performance by creating larger contiguous sections of free space.

Defragmenter. A graphical Windows utility that defragments files stored on hard drives to reorganize disk space and improve disk performance by creating larger contiguous sections of free space.

DEL. A Windows command that removes or deletes one or more files.

Delimiter. A marker (e.g., a space, comma, tab character, etc.) that identifies the boundaries between individual pieces of data passed to commands, procedures, or scripts.

DIR. A Windows command that displays the files and folders located in the specified folder or directory.

Directory. A term that is synonymous with the terms folder and subfolder.

Dynamic Environment Variables. Environment variables generated by the operating system that change over time.

ECHO. A Windows shell command that displays text and blank lines within the Windows command console.

Endless Loop. A loop that never finishes processing and prevents a script from completing its task.

ENDLOCAL. A Windows shell command that terminates variable localization by restoring variables to their values as they existed before the preceding SETLOCAL command was executed. (See SETLOCAL.)

Environment Variable. A variable defined and managed by the operating system.

ERASE. A Windows command that removes or deletes one or more specified files.

Error. A problem that occurs during the execution of a script.

ERRORLEVEL. A dynamically generated variable that contains a numeric value representing the exit code created by the previously executed command.

Execution Environment. The environment in which a script runs. For Windows shell scripts, this is the Windows shell.

EXIT. A Windows command that terminates script execution and closes the Windows command console. This command is also capable of returning an exit code back to a calling command or script.

Exit Code. A numeric value returned by commands that indicates whether they ran successfully or experienced an error. Also known as a Return Code.

Expression. A script statement that evaluates the value of variables.

External Command. A non-Windows shell script command stored as an executable file on the computer's hard drive. (See Internal Command.)

External Procedure. A Windows shell script that is called by another script. (See Internal Procedure.)

Flowchart. A graphic outline that provides a high-level overview of the components of a script and shows their relationship to one another.

FOR. A Windows shell command that executes one or more commands repetitively to facilitate the processing of files, folders, command output, and scripts.

FTYPE. A Windows command that displays and modifies file types that are associated with file name extensions.

Global Variables. Variables that can be accessed from any location within a script.

GOTO. A Windows shell command that alters processing flow within a script by transferring control to a line containing a specified label.

GUI (Graphical User Interface). The point-and-click graphical interface used to control Windows operating systems and their applications.

HELP. A Windows command that provides command prompt access to additional information regarding Windows commands.

IF. A Windows shell command that performs conditional processing and alters the execution flow within the script based on tested results.

IF CMDEXTVERSION. A form of the IF statement that retrieves a numeric value indicating the current version of the Windows shell.

IF DEFINED. A form of the IF statement that provides the ability to determine whether a variable already exists.

IF...ELSE. A form of the IF statement that provides the ability to execute either of two sets of commands based on the outcome of a conditional test

IF ERRORLEVEL. A form of the IF statement that provides the ability to check the exit code of the previously executed command.

IF EXIST. A form of the IF statement that provides the ability to determine whether a file or folder exists.

IF NOT. A form of the IF statement that provides the ability to perform a conditional test and take an action based on a negative result.

Integrated Development Environment. An application that is used to facilitate the development and debugging of other scripts or programs.

Internal Command. A command built into the Windows shell. (See External Command.)

Internal Procedure. A procedure defined within the script that, when called, executes and then returns control back to the statement that follows the statement that called it. (See External Procedure.)

Iterate. The act of executing one or more commands repeatedly.

JScript. A Microsoft scripting language based on Netscape's JavaScript programming language.

Label. A marker placed inside Windows shell scripts to set up loops, subroutines, and procedures.

Local Variables. Variables created within a procedure that cannot be accessed outside of the procedure.

LOGEVENT.EXE. A Windows Resource Kit command line utility that can be used to write messages to the Windows application event log.

Logical Error. An error created when the programmer tells the script to do something other than what it was actually intended to do, such as adding two numbers that really should have been subtracted.

Loop. A collection of statements that are executed repeatedly.

MD (MKDIR). A Windows command that creates a new subdirectory or subfolder.

Modifiers. Parameters that can be used to change the behavior of a command's switches.

MOVE. A Windows command that moves one or more files from one location to another.

Multi-line IF Statement. A form of the IF statement that allows programmers to embed more than one statement inside IF statements.

Mutually Exclusive. A term that refers to situations in which only one of a collection of options can be selected.

Nested IF Statement. One or more IF statements within another IF statement.

NET CONTINUE. A Windows command that reactivates a suspended service.

NET GROUP. A Windows command that modifies membership of global groups.

NET LOCALGROUP. A Windows command that modifies membership of local groups.

NET PAUSE. A Windows command that suspends the execution of a service.

NET START. A Windows command used to start services.

NET SEND. A Windows command used to send text messages to other network users or computers that will be displayed in the form of a graphical pop-up dialog.

NET STOP. A Windows command that terminates the execution of a service.

NET USE. A Windows command that provides the ability to establish connections to network drivers, folders, and printers.

NET USER. A Windows command that provides the ability to programmatically create new user accounts.

Order of Precedence. A term that refers to the order in which the Windows shell performs different types of mathematical operations when evaluating expressions.

OS. An environment variable that identifies the currently running Windows operating system.

Parameter. One or more arguments to be passed to commands, procedures, or scripts for processing.

Parsing. The act of extracting a portion of a string.

path. An environment variable that specifies which folders are to be searched when looking for a command in which the user has not specified the location of the command.

PATH. A Windows command that provides the ability to modify the path variable for the duration of the execution of a Windows shell session.

pathext. An environment variable that identifies a list of file extensions representing executable programs.

PAUSE. A Windows shell command that halts script execution until the user presses a key.

Perl (Practical Extraction and Reporting Language). A scripting language originally made popular by its use on UNIX operating systems.

Pipe. The redirection of one command's output to another command. This output is then processed by the second command as input.

Pixel. The smallest area on the display screen that a computer can display or print.

POPD. Changes the current folder to the folder stored by a corresponding PUSHD command. (See PUSHD.)

Procedure. A collection of statements that can be executed as a unit. Procedures are used to switch processing control from one portion of a script to another section and then back again when the procedure finishes executing.

Procedure Variable. A variable that has been localized within a procedure, prohibiting other parts of the script from accessing the variable. (See Script Variable.)

PROMPT. A Windows command that is used to modify the format of the Windows command prompt.

Pseudo Code. A rough, English-like outline of the logic used in all or part of a script.

PUSHD. Changes the current working directory to the specified folder and stores the previous folder for later reference by the POPD command. (See POPD.)

Python. A scripting language with a UNIX heritage that is named after the comedic troupe Monty Python.

random. An environment variable that returns a randomly generated number between 1 and 32,767.

RD (RMDIR). A Windows command that removes or deletes a specified folder.

Recursive. The process a script goes through when it reinitiates its own execution or the execution of a specific collection of statements.

Redirection. The altering of a command's input or output from its default source.

REG. A Windows Resource Kit command line utility that provides the ability to access and change information stored in the Windows registry.

Registry. A specialized database used by Windows computers to store information about users, hardware, software, and operating system configuration settings.

REM. A Windows shell command that provides the ability to add comments to a script.

REN (RENAME). A Windows command that renames a file or folder.

Return Code. A numeric value returned by commands and external procedures indicating whether they ran successfully or terminated with an error. Also known as an Exit Code.

ıred Extended Extractor language). A scripting language developed
ecution on mainframe computers and later ported over to Windows.

ır. A type of error that occurs when a script attempts to perform
ın, such as referencing a non-existing disk drive. (Also known as an
or.)

ısk Folder. A folder in which Windows operating systems store and
:duled tasks.

`ask Wizard. A graphical interface that assists in the creation of
.asks.

xecutable text file made up of one of more scripting language statements.

tor. A specialized text editor that facilitates the development of scripts
ıng features such as statement color coding and line numbering.

ŕiable. A variable created during the execution of a Windows shell script
be accessed from any location within the script. (See Procedure Variable.)

indows shell command that provides the ability to collect and assign val-
ariables.

ʟ. A Windows shell command that records the current values assigned to
nment variables in the Windows shell, allowing them to later be restored
: ENDLOCAL command. (See ENDLOCAL.)

A Windows shell command that alters the position of script parameters in
ŕ to allow Windows shell scripts to access more than nine script input pa-
ɘters.

ŕtcut. A graphical link to an application or resource (often placed on the
ndows desktop).

ıT. A Windows shell command that sorts data provided to it as input and sends
.e result to standard output.

ɫandard Error. The default location where the Windows shell sends all error
nessages. (By default, this is the Windows command console.)

Standard Input. The location where the Windows shell looks for command
input. (By default, this is the computer's keyboard.)

Standard Output. The default location where the Windows shell sends all
output. (By default, this is the Windows command console.)

START. A Windows shell command that starts a new Windows shell session by opening a new Windows command console.

Statement. A line of code in a script or program.

String Substitution. The search for and replacement of a portion of text within a string.

Subdirectory. Another term that refers to folders and subfolders.

Subroutine. A collection of statements that scripts jump to and continue processing. Unlike procedures, subroutines do not return processing control back to the statement that follows the statement that executed the subroutine.

Substring. A portion of text extracted from a text string.

Switch. An optional control that modifies the way in which a command is processed.

Syntax. A set of rules that outline the format in which commands must be formulated for execution.

Syntax Error. A type of error that occurs when programmers fail to follow the syntax rules that govern the formatting of commands.

systemroot. An environment variable that specifies the location of the Windows system root folders.

TEMP. An environment variable that identifies the name of a folder that can be used by applications for temporary storage.

time. An environment variable that stores a string representing the current system time.

TIME. A Windows shell command that displays and modifies the system time.

TITLE. A Windows shell command that modifies the text displayed in the Windows command console's title bar.

Token. A representation of a piece of data located in a text string.

TMP. An environment variable that identifies the name of a folder that can be used by applications for temporary storage.

Tracing. The process of tracking either script execution flow or variable values during the execution of a script.

TYPE. A Windows command that displays the contents of files by sending their output to standard output.

username. An environment variable that stores the username of the currently logged on user.

Variable. A reference to a location in the computer's memory where the script stores a value.

Variable Tunneling. A technique used to pass procedure variables and their values out of procedures where variable localization has been implemented.

VBScript. A WSH supported scripting language that consists of a subset of the Visual Basic programming language.

VER. A Windows shell command that displays the Windows version number.

Wild Card. A special character (either * or ?) that can be used to create matches among files based on a pattern.

WINDIR. An environment variable that identifies the folder where Windows system files are stored.

Windows Command Console. A window through which a new Windows shell session can be accessed via the command prompt.

Windows Registry. A special built-in database that is a part of all Windows operating systems, starting with Windows 95, where configuration information is stored regarding system, application, hardware, and users settings.

Windows Shell. A text-based interface to the Windows operating system that provides access to text-based commands and utilities.

Windows Shell Scripting. A built-in scripting language available on Windows NT, XP, 2000, and 2003 that features a complete set of programming statements, thus allowing for the development of scripts that include support for conditional logic, iterative logic, and the storage and retrieval of data via computer memory.

Working Directory. A reference to the Windows folder on which the Windows command console is currently focused.

WSH (Windows Script Host). An alternative scripting environment available on all Windows operating systems starting with Windows 95.

WSH Object Model. A collection of objects provided by the Windows Script Host that provides access to system resources such as printers and drives.

Index

G

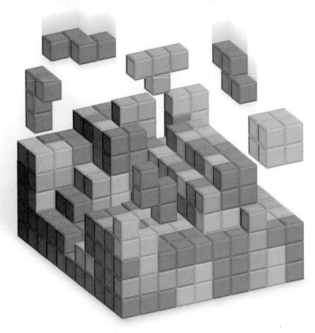

License Agreement/Notice of Limited Warranty